Mastering Quality Engineering for SAP S/4HANA

Build Resilient, Enterprise Grade Software Testing Strategies that Drive Continuous Quality Throughout SAP S/4HANA Transformations

Jeevan Koneti

www.orangeava.com

First Published: December 2025

Published By: Orange Education Pvt Ltd, AVA®

Address: 9, Daryaganj, Delhi, 110002, India

275 New North Road Islington Suite 1314 London,
N1 7AA, United Kingdom

ISBN (PBK): 978-93-49888-88-3

ISBN (E-BOOK): 978-93-49888-42-5

Scan the QR code to explore our entire catalogue

www.orangeava.com

Dedicated To

My Beloved Family,

My Mother,

My Wife, and Our Two Daughters.

About the Author

Jeevan Koneti is a seasoned technology leader with over 18 years of experience in designing intelligent software test automation solutions. He currently works as a principal architect at UiPath. He specializes in architecting and delivering enterprise QA solutions that drive large-scale business transformations across SAP S/4HANA, Oracle, Salesforce, Mainframe, Mobile, and other leading platforms.

Jeevan has successfully designed and led more than 300 SAP testing and automation programs for Fortune 2000 companies. He holds professional certifications as an enterprise architect, SAP consultant, process designer, and an automation practitioner.

Beyond his professional roles, Jeevan is an active contributor to the global SAP testing community through events, insightful articles, and open-source projects. He possesses deep expertise in the end-to-end ecosystem of testing delivery. He has also played a pivotal role in building strategic alliances with ISVs and GSIs, including Microsoft, SAP, Deloitte, Accenture, Infosys, Wipro, EY, Tech Mahindra, KPMG, and several others.

About the Technical Reviewers

Devendra Rao has 17 years of experience in Enterprise Test Automation and Quality Assurance across industries including Retail, Oil and Gas, Banking, Utilities, and Financial Services. As an Automation Architect, has designed solutions for platforms such as SAP, Ariba, and Salesforce using Worksoft Certify, TOSCA, and open-source solutions.

With a background in business process management, TCOE setup, IT planning, and cost optimization, he combines technical depth with strategic insight. An MBA graduate with certifications in PRINCE2, Six Sigma Green Belt, and cloud technologies, he specializes in evaluating complex automation frameworks, ensuring that they deliver business value.

Pomil Proch is a seasoned management consultant with above 11 years of experience helping organizations unlock value at the intersection of business and technology. His work across IT services, product companies, and startups offers a 360° perspective on how enterprises can harness technology to drive transformation, boost efficiency, and achieve measurable outcomes.

Armed with a B.Tech. in Computer Science from NIT Surathkal and an MBA from IIM Mumbai, Pomil blends deep technical expertise with strategic business insight. His career spans software development, consultative sales, presales, product management, SaaS consulting, due diligence, and RFP/RFI leadership—enabling him to connect technology capabilities with real business impact.

As the leader for product growth in UiPath's emerging APAC portfolio—covering Process Mining, Task Mining, Test Suite, and AI-driven Document Processing—he focuses on enterprise adoption, value frameworks, and automation strategy. His earlier roles at Wipro, SHL, and Cognizant encompassed digital transformation, AI/ML product strategy, and large-deal solutioning.

Acknowledgments

I want to express my heartfelt gratitude to a few special people whose unwavering support made this book possible. First and foremost, I thank my family, whose continuous encouragement carried me through every step of this journey. Without their love and support, this book would not have been completed.

I am deeply grateful to my friends, *Devendra Rao* and *Pomil Bachan Proch* for their invaluable help in reviewing the manuscript, and shaping it into a meaningful resource for readers.

My sincere thanks also goes to my colleagues from past and present projects as well as customers, who generously shared their experiences, challenges, and best practices. Their insights enriched this work, and kept it grounded in real-world SAP testing scenarios.

I also extend my sincere thanks to the entire editorial team at Orange Education Pvt. Ltd., whose steady support and encouragement were a strong pillar throughout this journey.

I am especially thankful to the global QA community, and those dedicated professionals who continue to keep the light of quality burning bright, despite demanding circumstances and limited project budgets. Their resilience and commitment inspire us all!

Finally, I thank SAP for providing a dynamic platform that continually evolves, demanding great effort to stay always updated. This ongoing innovation inspires the work shared within this book.

Dedicated to

My Parents,

For Giving Me the Strength and Clarity to Pursue Everything I Dream of

My Wife,

For Her Patience, Love, and Support

About the Author

Sreejith Salgunan is a Lead Frontend Engineer specializing in React, TypeScript, Jest, React Testing Library, and large-scale UI architecture. His career has been defined by solving real engineering problems inside high-pressure enterprise environments, especially platforms that demand reliability, security, and precision testing.

Sreejith has worked extensively on micro-frontend architectures, Module Federation, CI/CD pipelines, developer-experience tooling, and enterprise UI systems. With deep expertise in Jest, React Testing Library, MSW, and modern testing philosophies, he has spent years simplifying complex testing problems into practical, actionable patterns. His guidance has helped multiple teams raise coverage dramatically, while reducing flaky tests and increasing developer confidence.

The insights in this book come from years spent debugging failing test suites, rewriting flaky tests, refining architecture, reviewing high-stakes pull requests, and coaching teams on how to test software the right way.

Thus, this book reflects his commitment to helping front-end developers write resilient, future-proof tests, and establish a strong, scalable testing culture.

About the Technical Reviewer

Anjani Kumar Varma is an Associate at Cognizant Technology Solutions, where he has spent nearly four years architecting and developing high-performance React-based applications. Currently, he partners with a leading retail client to deliver scalable, maintainable digital experiences for millions of users.

Anjani's technical expertise spans the React ecosystem, including Redux, React Testing Library (RTL), Jest, and Module Federation, alongside Adobe Experience Manager. He has a proven track record of optimizing application performance through lazy loading, tree-shaking, and the remediation of memory leaks. As a key member of the core governance team, Anjani ensures code quality across multiple repositories. He has championed several process improvements, such as implementing pre-commit hooks to enforce optional chaining and utilizing Webpack configurations to automate the removal of console logs in production builds.

Beyond core development, Anjani is instrumental in driving business intelligence. By implementing Adobe tagging and Quantum metrics, he has significantly enhanced the client's ability to capture user behavior data. His work focuses on building reliable, analytics-ready applications that translate complex technical data into invaluable business insights.

Acknowledgments

I am deeply grateful to the engineering teams, architects, and colleagues I have worked with across multiple enterprise projects. The real-world challenges we solved — from testing complex UIs, debugging production issues, improving CI pipelines, and stabilizing large codebases — directly shaped the content of this book.

A special thanks to the open-source community behind **Jest**, **React Testing Library**, **MSW**, and the entire React ecosystem. Their continuous innovation is what enables better testing practices for developers like us.

My gratitude goes to everyone who reviewed my ideas, questioned my assumptions, or challenged me to think deeper. Every conversation contributed to improving the clarity and practicality of this book.

Finally, I thank every reader taking this journey. Hence, whether you are starting with testing or refining your expertise, I hope this book becomes a long-term reference that strengthens your engineering mindset.

Preface

Testing is no longer a "nice to have" in modern React development – it is the backbone of reliability, confidence, and long-term maintainability. As React applications grow in complexity with asynchronous flows, dynamic UI rendering, micro-frontends, stateful components, custom hooks, third-party integrations, and continuous deployments, solid testing becomes the only sustainable way to prevent regressions and ship safely.

This book is written to give you mastery of testing in React using Jest and React Testing Library, grounded in how applications are built today – not outdated patterns or implementation-heavy approaches.

The book contains 13 chapters in which you will learn:

Chapter 1. Introduction to Testing: This explains the role of testing in software quality, reliability, scalability, debugging, and CI/CD. You will clearly understand the difference between unit tests, functional tests, and where each fits in the engineering lifecycle.

Chapter 2. Jest Fundamentals: This chapter and chapter 4 gives you everything from installing Jest to advanced techniques such as mocking functions, modules, libraries, parameterized testing, test lifecycle, custom matchers, setup/teardown, and snapshot handling. You will learn how Jest executes tests, how to run specific suites, control execution, build readable test architecture, and avoid common pitfalls.

Chapter 3. Introduction to React and React Testing Library: This chapter introduces React Testing Library (RTL), focusing on behavior, user experience, ARIA roles, and queries based on how users find elements – not implementation details. You will also learn rendering events, async testing, and RTL's cleanup as well as query strategies.

Chapter 4. Advanced Testing Techniques: Learn how to write robust tests using snapshots, parameterized tests, and custom matchers, while fully controlling dependencies through advanced Jest mocking and third-party library handling.

Chapter 5, Testing React Hooks and Asynchronous Operations, and **Chapter 6, Redux Thunk and Context,** cover the hardest parts of real React testing such as:

- **Testing useState, useEffect, and custom hooks**
- **Async operations including Axios**
- **Redux slices, reducers, and thunk-based async logic**
- **Context providers and deeply nested state flows**

These are areas where most developers fail — and this book makes them simple.

Chapter 7. Jest Best Practices and Capabilities: This chapter distills the strongest principles from Jest and RTL avoiding implementation detail traps, stable async testing, correct mocking strategies, proper use of only, skip each, and patterns for team-wide consistency.

Chapter 8. Testing Real-World React Applications: This chapter takes everything learned, and applies it to real-world scenarios such as authentication, routing, protected pages, dynamic data, API mocks, integration tests, and performance pitfalls.

Chapter 9. Jest Coverage and CI/CD Integration teaches you how to interpret coverage reports, set thresholds, automate tests in CI pipelines, run Jest in different environments, and connect testing to real deployment workflows.

Chapter 10. Practical Exercises and Challenges: This chapter gives you practical exercises, quizzes, scenario-based challenges, and GitHub-hosted solutions so that you can test your skills, and build real confidence.

Chapter 11. Future-proof Testing with RTL: It shows why the community moved from Enzyme to React Testing Library, how React 18+ changes testing patterns, and how to adapt your testing strategy as React evolves.

Chapter 12. Mastering Mock Service Worker in Jest: Patterns, Best Practices, and Pitfalls introduces MSW v2 and Vitest that are modern tools for mocking APIs and running tests faster, giving you an edge with the next-gen testing setups.

Chapter 13. Conclusion and Next Steps: This chapter summarizes the complete journey, and prepares you to apply these testing principles in your production applications and engineering teams. It is designed to make you faster, more confident, and more reliable as a React developer.

Thus, if you master the mindset and techniques inside, testing will stop being a task – it will become your strongest engineering skill!

Get a Free eBook

We hope you are enjoying your recently purchased book! Your feedback is incredibly valuable to us, and to all other readers looking for great books.

If you found this book helpful or enjoyable, we would truly appreciate it, if you could take a moment to leave a short review with a 5 star rating on Amazon. It helps us grow, and lets other readers discover our books.

As a thank you, we would love to send you a free digital copy of this book, and a **30%** discount code on your next cart value on our official websites:

www.orangeava.com

www.orangeava.in (For Indian Subcontinent)

☑ **Here's how:**

Leave a review for the book on Amazon.

Take a screenshot of your review, and send an email to **info@orangeava.com** (it can be just the confirmation screen).

Once, we receive your screenshot, we will send you the digital file, within 24 hours.

Thank you so much for your support — it means a lot to us!

Downloading the code bundles and colored images

Please follow the links or scan the QR codes to download the
Code Bundles and Images of the book:

https://github.com/ava-orange-education/Ultimate-React-Testing-with-Jest

The code bundles and images of the book are also hosted on
https://rebrand.ly/78a1de

In case there's an update to the code, it will be updated on the existing GitHub repository.

Errata

We take immense pride in our work at **Orange Education Pvt Ltd,** and follow best practices to ensure the accuracy of our content to provide an indulging reading experience to our subscribers. Our readers are our mirrors, and we use their inputs to reflect and improve upon human errors, if any, that may have occurred during the publishing processes involved. To let us maintain the quality and help us reach out to any readers who might be having difficulties due to any unforeseen errors, please write to us at :

errata@orangeava.com

Your support, suggestions, and feedback are highly appreciated.

DID YOU KNOW

Did you know that Orange Education Pvt Ltd offers eBook versions of every book published, with PDF and ePub files available? You can upgrade to the eBook version at **www.orangeava.com** and as a print book customer, you are entitled to a discount on the eBook copy. Get in touch with us at: **info@orangeava.com** for more details.

At **www.orangeava.com**, you can also read a collection of free technical articles, sign up for a range of free newsletters, and receive exclusive discounts and offers on Print Books and eBooks.

PIRACY

If you come across any illegal copies of our works in any form on the internet, we would be grateful if you would provide us with the location address or website name. Please contact us at **info@orangeava.com** with a link to the material.

ARE YOU INTERESTED IN AUTHORING WITH US?

If there is a topic that you have expertise in, and you are interested in either writing or contributing to a book, please write to us at **business@orangeava.com**. We are on a journey to help developers and tech professionals to gain insights on the present technological advancements and innovations happening across the globe and build a community that believes Knowledge is best acquired by sharing and learning with others. Please reach out to us to learn what our audience demands and how you can be part of this educational reform. We also welcome ideas from tech experts and help them build learning and development content for their domains.

REVIEWS

Please leave a review. Once you have read and used this book, why not leave a review on the site that you purchased it from? Potential readers can then see and use your unbiased opinion to make purchase decisions. We at Orange Education would love to know what you think about our products, and our authors can learn from your feedback. Thank you!

For more information about Orange Education, please visit **www.orangeava.com**.

Table of Contents

CHAPTER 1

Introduction to Testing

Introduction

Modern frontend development has evolved significantly. Frameworks like React have introduced asynchronous rendering, complex state transitions, and dynamic UI flows in testing. Tools such as Jest or React Testing Library are commonly used today. However, before learning about them, it is essential to understand **why testing matters**, **what it is**, and **how different types of tests strengthen software quality**.

This chapter focuses purely on **testing fundamentals**, using simple JavaScript examples without any external frameworks. You will understand the purpose of testing, the types of tests, and the value testing brings to teams and large-scale applications.

Structure

This chapter covers the following topics:

- Importance of Testing in Software Development
- Benefits of Well-Organized and Maintainable Code
- Introduction to Unit Tests and Functional Tests
- Value of Testing Skills for Employers

Importance of Testing in Software Development

Testing is the difference between a codebase that grows and the one that collapses under its own weight. Modern frontend apps deal with the following:

- Concurrent Rendering
- Complex Forms
- Network Failures
- Race Conditions
- Global State (RTK)
- Hundreds of Edge Cases

Testing ensures the system behaves as intended, regardless of how the UI grows.

It is not just about finding bugs—it is about building confidence in every change you ship. As applications grow, even small updates can introduce unexpected issues if they are not validated early. A strong testing strategy ensures stability, reliability, and quality throughout the development lifecycle.

Reducing Bugs and Defects

- Early tests catch issues before they reach users.
- Regression tests guarantee that new changes do not break existing features.
- Your app stays stable as the codebase expands .

Ensuring Software Reliability

- A reliable app behaves the same under different conditions.
- Tests validate predictable outcomes even during unexpected scenarios.
- Well-tested software earns user trust and product credibility.

Enhancing Code Quality

- Writing testable code results in cleaner architecture.
- Tests act as living documentation of how the system works.
- Developers gain confidence to refactor without fear of breaking things.

Facilitating CI/CD

- Automated builds
- Automated deployments
- Zero-fear code merges

Modern software ships continuously. Without tests, CI/CD is reckless. With tests, CI/CD becomes your biggest productivity weapon.

Benefits of Well-Organized and Maintainable Code

Clean code makes testing easier, and effective testing reinforces clean code by encouraging small, predictable functions. This practice helps developers catch bugs early, refactor safely, and build reliable features in real-world applications such as business logic, form validation, calculations, and API data processing.

Readability and Code Understanding

- A well-structured codebase is simple to test.
- Predictable folder and component structures reduce confusion.
- New developers can be onboarded quickly without endless hand-holding.

Ease of Collaboration

- When code is consistent, reviews are faster.
- Parallel development becomes smooth.
- Merge conflicts reduce drastically.

Scalability and Future Development

- Clean architecture supports new features without rewrites.
- Tests make refactoring safe.
- Technical debt stays under control.

Debugging and Troubleshooting Efficiency

- A clean, predictable code structure makes it easy for users to locate the source of a given problem. You spend less time guessing and more time fixing.
- Well-organized code works naturally with automated tests. When a test fails, the failure directly indicates the exact function or module that is responsible, thus reducing debugging time dramatically.
- In a structured codebase, the impact of a change is obvious. You know what affects what, which reduces the risk of breaking unrelated functionality when modifying or fixing code.

Introduction to Unit Tests and Functional Tests

Modern testing is a nuanced process, where each layer serves a different purpose. These tests fall in three major categories that are mentioned as follows:

- Unit Tests
- Functional (Integration) Tests
- End-to-End Tests

Unit Tests—Small, Fast, Isolated

Unit tests validate small and isolated pieces of your application. These include functions, hooks, Redux reducers, or utility modules.

A good unit test is:

- Isolated
- Deterministic
- Blazing Fast
- Self-Validating

The following example demonstrates a simple function and a basic test that verifies its output. It shows the core idea of unit testing by checking a small piece of logic in isolation.

```
//calculator.js
 function add(a, b) {
   return a + b;
 }
```

Now, let us write a basic test:

```
//calculatorTest.js
 function testAddFunction() {
   let result = add(1, 2);
   let expected = 3;

   if (result !== expected) {
     console.error(`Test failed: Expected ${expected}, but got
${result}`);
   } else {
     console.log('Test passed!');
   }
```

```
}

testAddFunction();
```

This simple test demonstrates the basic idea: call the function, compare the result, and log pass/fail. Here, no external tools are required.

Characteristics of Effective Unit Tests

Effective unit tests are essential for maintaining high-quality software. They act as the first line of defense against bugs and ensure that individual components work as expected.

- **Isolation:** Test only the logic in front of you. You must mock everything that is external (such as APIs, timers, modules).
- **Simplicity:** Each test checks a single behavior. No multi-step workflows are employed here.
- **Repeatability:** You must ensure that the same input must always yield the same output.
- **Fast Execution:** Fast tests lead to fast feedback, which results in fast development.
- **Self-Checking:** Assertions determine whether a software passes or fails.

Functional Tests—Definition and Purpose

Functional tests answers if the system produces the correct outcome when these steps follow a certain order.

They simulate:

- Workflows
- Sequences
- Multi-Step Operations
- Cross-Module Interactions
- Realistic Behavior

Here is a code illustrating a simple function workflow test:

```
function add(a, b) { return a + b; }
function subtract(a, b) { return a - b; }

function testWorkflow() {
  let value = add(5, 3);      // 8
  value = subtract(value, 2); // 6
```

```
  if (value === 6) {
    console.log("Workflow test passed");
  } else {
    console.error("Workflow test failed");
  }
}

testWorkflow();
```

This example code simulates a multi-step operation, which a user might perform in a real-life scenario. Functional tests validate how multiple units behave together, focusing on flows rather than isolated logic.

Functional Tests vs Unit Tests and Use Cases

Aspect	Unit Tests	Functional Tests
Scope	One function	Multiple functions/modules
Focus	Correctness of isolated logic	Correctness of flow/sequence
Speed	Very fast	Slower
Failure Means	A specific function is wrong	A workflow or interaction is broken
Complexity	Low	Higher

Table 1.1: *Functional vs Unit tests*

Use Cases for Unit Tests and Functional Tests

Understanding when and why to use each type of test helps teams write fewer tests with higher value—catching bugs early, validating real user flows, and maintaining long-term code quality without slowing development.

Unit Tests

- Pure Functions (such as math, formatting, or transformations)
- Business Rules and Domain Logic
- Edge Cases (such as divide-by-zero, invalid values, or boundary conditions)
- Logic That is Stable and Predictable Over Time

Functional Tests

- Multi-Step Workflows
- State Progression Through Multiple Operations
- Input Flowing across Several Functions
- Interaction between Multiple Modules or Layers

Value of Testing Skills for Employers

Modern engineering teams expect developers who understand testing because it directly results in the following:

Improved Software Quality

- Bugs are caught early, before reaching the production stage.
- Releases become more stable and predictable.

Time and Cost Savings

- Fixing issues during development is far cheaper than addressing them after the software is deployed.
- Fewer regressions mean fewer emergency patches.

Enhanced Team Collaboration

- Clear expectations reduce friction in code reviews.
- Teams work more confidently when behavior is well-defined.

Adaptability to Industry Best Practices

- Testing aligns developers with modern engineering workflows.
- Encourages clean architecture and safe refactoring.
- Ensures long-term maintainability of large projects.

Conclusion

Testing is not optional. It is the backbone of professional software engineering.

In this chapter, you have learned: why testing matters, how tests enforce reliability, how testability improves code quality, what is the difference between unit and functional tests, and where does each test type fit in real-world development.

With these fundamentals strongly embedded in your understanding, you can now move onto the next chapters, where we will transform these ideas into automated tests using Jest and React Testing Library.

Chapter 2
Jest Fundamentals

Introduction

This chapter provides a complete foundation for using **Jest**, which is a fast, reliable JavaScript testing framework.

You will learn about: How to set up Jest in a project, How tests are structured, Common matchers, Test lifecycle methods, CLI usage, Configuration, Coverage, Custom matchers, and Best practices for writing maintainable tests.

The goal of this chapter is to provide you a strong base before moving onto advanced topics like React component testing and integration tests.

Structure

This chapter covers the following topics:

- Jest Setup
- Jest Basics and Test Execution
- Jest Syntax Overview and Matchers
- Jest Coverage in Code Quality Assessment

Jest Setup

Before writing your first test, you will need to configure Jest in order to work seamlessly with your project's environment and dependencies.

Installation and Project Configuration

To get started with Jest for testing applications, we will go through each step in detail, beginning with setting up the environment and moving on to initializing a JavaScript project.

Setting up the Environment

To run Jest and manage project dependencies, your system must have Node.js and a package manager installed. These tools provide the foundation required to install libraries, run scripts, and execute tests locally.

Node.js: Node.js is a runtime environment that lets you run JavaScript on the server side.

`npm` and `yarn`: `npm` (Node Package Manager) and yarn are package managers that help install and manage dependencies in your projects.

Here are the steps to install Node.js and `npm/yarn`:

Downloading Node.js: Visit the official Node.js website and download the installer for your operating system.

Figure 2.1: *Downloading Node.js*

Download Link: https://nodejs.org/en

Installing Node.js: Run the downloaded installer and follow the prompts to install Node.js and npm.

Verifying Installation: After installation, open the command line or the terminal and type `node -v` and `npm -v`. This will display the installed versions of `Node.js` and `npm`, thus confirming their successful installation.

```
node -v => v20.11.0
npm -v   =>  10.2.4
```

Installing yarn (Optional): If using yarn, install it by typing `npm install --global yarn` in the terminal. Verify its installation by typing `yarn -v`.

```
Yarn -v  => v4.0
```

Tips

- Choose the LTS (Long Term Support) version of Node.js for stability, especially if you are operating a production environment.
- `npm vs. yarn`: While both are popular, yarn is known for faster performance and more secure package installs. npm is directly bundled with Node.js, which makes it the default choice for many. Stick with npm if you are new to Node.js as it simplifies the learning curve.
- **Windows Users**: The installer may ask you to install necessary tools and Chocolatey (which is a package manager for Windows). It is a good idea to allow these installations for a smoother experience.
- If the versions do not show up, restart your command line tool or your system to refresh the environment variables.
- If you encounter permission issues while installing yarn globally, try running your command line tool as an administrator or use a version manager for Node.js, such as `nvm` (Node Version Manager).
- Keep Node.js and npm/yarn updated to benefit from performance improvements, new features, and security patches.

Integrating Jest to the Project

Set up Jest to seamlessly integrate with your project for efficient and reliable testing.

Creating and Setting Up a New Project:

- Make a new folder for projects on your system.
- Open terminal and create/navigate to a new folder(Jest) via the `cd` command.

Initializing the Project with `npm`: Use `npm init` to start a new Node.js project. This command will walk you through creating a **`package.json`** file which is central to Node.js ecosystems. It contains metadata about the project and manages project dependencies.

```
mkdir jest-fundamentals
cd jest-fundamentals
npm init -y
```

Filling Out Project Details

- **Package Name (`jestsetup`)**: This is the name of the project and is also the name that is used when it is published to **`npm`** (Node Package Manager).
- **Version (1.0.0)**: This is the initial version of the project. Semantic versioning is typically used to manage further project versions.
- **Description**: This refers to a short description of the project. Here, it is about setting up and installing Jest.
- **Entry Point (`index.js`)**: This is the main file of the project. Node.js will execute this file first.
- **Test Command (test)**: It is the command used to run tests. When you type npm test in the terminal, npm will run the test.
- **Keywords**: These help in categorizing the project on npm and can improve discoverability.
- **Author (`sreejith`)**: This refers to the name of the author of the project.
- **License (ISC)**: This refers to the license under which the project is distributed. ISC is a permissive free software license.

After confirming the details, npm will create the **`package.json`** file in the project directory with the provided details.

Creating the `index.js` File

You can create a new file named index.js in the project directory if it does not exist already.

Writing the Greet Function: In **`index.js`**, define a function named greet. This function should take one parameter, typically a name. Inside the function, return a greeting string that includes the name. This is shown in the code as follows:

```
function greet(name) {
  return `Hello, ${name}!`;
}
console.log(greet('jest'));
```

Exporting the Function

To use this function in other files, export it using:

```
module.exports = greet;
```

Run the Function

Run this function directly in terminal by calling:

```
node index.js
```

This will generate the following output:

```
Hello, jest!
```

Tips

- Familiarize yourself with basic terminal commands like **cd** (change directory) for easier navigation.
- Experiment with different inputs to see how your function behaves.
- Before writing automated tests, try running your function manually to ensure that it is behaving as expected.
- Make sure that your Jest version is compatible with your Node.js version.

Setting Up Jest

Configure Jest with the necessary settings to run tests smoothly in your project environment.

Installing Jest

To install Jest in the JavaScript project, follow these steps:

1. **Open Terminal or Command Prompt:** Install Jest via npm or Yarn, from the root directory of the JavaScript project.

   For npm, type the following command:

   ```
   npm install --save-dev jest
   ```

   For Yarn, use this command instead:

   ```
   yarn add --dev jest
   ```

   This will install Jest as a development dependency in your project, which will allow you to write and run tests using Jest's framework.

2. **Running Tests with Jest:** To run your tests using Jest, we have two straightforward options mentioned as follows:

Using `npm test`

- This is a common and simple way to run tests.
- In your project, you will typically have a script in your **`package.json`** file that is set up to use Jest. When you run npm test in your command line, it triggers this script, which in turn runs Jest and executes your tests.

```
"scripts": {
 "test" : "jest"
},
```

Directly Using `jest`:

- If you prefer it, you can run Jest directly by typing jest in your command line.
- This method works well if you have Jest installed globally or if you want to use Jest-specific command-line options.
- It is a direct approach, especially useful for more customized test runs.

If you are using Yarn, enter:

`yarn test`

Tips

- Both **`npm test`** and **`jest`** run your tests. Choosing one of these options depends on your project setup and personal preference.
- Stick to either npm or Yarn throughout your project to avoid conflicts and maintain consistency.
- Avoid global installation whenever possible. While installing Jest globally is convenient, it might result in version mismatches in projects. Using local installation ensures that you are using the correct version of Jest for each project.
- To ensure that npm test runs Jest, double-check the scripts section in your **`package.json`** file. It should have an entry like **`"test": "jest"`**.

Configuring Jest

Jest is designed to be effective and user-friendly out of the box, yet it also offers extensive configuration options for those situations where more specific or advanced customization is needed. You can create a **`jest.config.js`** file in your project for custom Jest configuration. It is not automatically generated; you will need to create it manually or initialize it via command line. Here is how to do it:

Manual Creation

1. Create a new file in your project's root directory and name it **`jest.config.js`**.
2. Open this file and write your Jest configurations using JavaScript. Here, you can set your preferences for how Jest will behave when the tests are being run.

Using Jest Command Line Interface (CLI)

- If you have Jest installed globally on your computer, you can set up your configuration file more easily using a command.
- In your command line or terminal, type **`jest --init`** and press Enter.
- Jest will then ask you a series of questions about how you want to run your tests. These questions will address questions like where your test files are located, whether you want to generate coverage reports, and what environment your tests should run in (like **`Node.js`** or a browser environment).
- As you answer these questions, Jest will create a **`jest.config.js`** file for you, which will be configured with the settings based on your answers. This makes it easier to create a configuration that matches the specific needs of your project.

After creating **`jest.config.js`**, you can define various configuration options like test environment, global setup and teardown scripts, coverage reports, and so on. This file will offer flexibility to customize the behavior of Jest as per your project's needs.

Some Commonly Used Configurations

- **Customizing Test Environments:** Imagine a magical toy box (that is, Jest) that can change into different playrooms. Sometimes it is a room with lots of computers (like **`'node'`**) and other times it has a big TV screen (like **`'jsdom'`** for browsers).

  You can set the environment to **`Node.js`**. via:

  `testEnvironment: "node"`

  You can set the environment to Browser:

  `testEnvironment: "jsdom"`

- **Setting Up Globals:** For instance, a secret word (like "**`MY_GLOBAL_VAR`**") can make special toys appear in any room.

You can define a global variable accessible in all tests, as shown in the following example:

```
globals: {  MY_GLOBAL_VAR: 'some value'}
```

- **Specifying Test Paths:** This is like a treasure map ("`testMatch`") that shows you where to find hidden games in the toy box. It tells Jest to look for tests in specific directory patterns, as shown here:

```
testMatch: ['**/__tests__/**/*.js']
```

- **Configuring Test Behavior:** If a game is too hard, the toy box stops and tries another game (like "`bail`"). It also has a timer that does not let you play too long on one game ("`testTimeout`").

  Stops at the first test failure and sets a timeout for tests. This is illustrated as follows:

```
bail: true,
testTimeout: 5000
```

- **Mocking and Setup/Teardown:** Before playing a new game, the toy box sets up special things that are required for the specific game ("`setupFilesAfterEnv`").

  It specifies scripts for setting up the testing environment after the Jest environment is set up. Note: In Jest, `rootDir` is a token that represents the root directory of your project, which is located typically where your `package.json` resides. This is demonstrated as follows:

```
setupFilesAfterEnv: ['<rootDir>/setupTests.js']
```

- **Code Transformation:** It can also turn drawings into real toys ("`transform`" with Babel). It transpiles JSX and JS files using Babel and is shown as follows:

```
transform: {
  '^.+\\.jsx?$': 'babel-jest'
}
```

- **Coverage Reporting:** This keeps count of all the games you have played ("collectCoverage"), so that you know which ones you have not tried yet!

  It enables coverage collection and specifies the files to include. This is shown in the example below:

```
collectCoverage: true,
collectCoverageFrom: ['src/**/*.js']
```

Tips

- If you are testing React components, `jsdom` will often be the preferred environment as it simulates the DOM.

- Coverage reports are great for identifying untested parts of your codebase, but do not chase 100% coverage at the expense of test quality.
- Regularly review your Jest configuration as your project evolves. Do not hesitate to refactor your setup to keep it efficient and relevant to current needs.

Jest Basics and Test Execution

You must be aware about the fundamentals of Jest and how to write, run, and interpret your tests.

Writing Your First Jest Test

In this section, you will create your first Jest test and learn how test files are structured, named, and organized within a project.

- **Creating Test Files:** Create a new file in the project directory. The file name should reflect the functionality that would be tested. For example, if testing a function in index.js, the name test file should be **`index.test.js` or `index.spec.js`.**
- **Jest's Naming Conventions:** Jest automatically detects files with .test.js or .spec.js suffixes. It also looks for tests within any folders named **`__tests__`.**
- **Placing Test Files:** Place the test files next to the code that would be tested under the same directory or in a `separate __tests__ folder.`
- **Create a Test File:** Create a file named **`index.test.js`** next to the index.js file (where the greet function is defined),. This file will contain test cases.

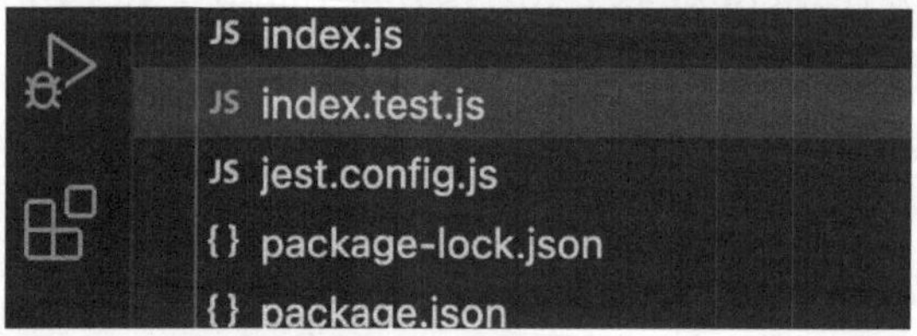

Figure 2.2: *Test file*

- **Import the Function to Test:** Import the greet function from index.js at the top of index.test.js,. This will display the call to greet in the test cases.

```
const greet = require('./index');
```

- **Writing a Test Case:** Use Jest's test function to define a test case. Describe what the test is for and provide a callback function that contains the test logic.

Inside the test, use Jest's expect and **toBe** functions to assert the expected behavior. For example, if you call **greet('Alice')**, you expect the result to be **'Hello, Alice!'**.

```
test('greets a user by name', () => {
 expect(greet('Alice')).toBe('Hello, Alice!');
});
```

The expect function is Jest's way of asserting that something is true about a piece of code. Here, **expect(greet('Alice'))** calls the greet function and checks its output. The **toBe** function is a matcher that tests for equality with the provided argument. So, **toBe('Hello, Alice!')** asserts that the output of **greet('Alice')** should exactly match the string **'Hello, Alice!'**.

In the upcoming sections, we will delve deeper into how these functions work, exploring various matchers and testing techniques in Jest.

- **Running Tests:** Run the tests using the command **npm test/ jest** or **yarn test**. Jest will automatically find and run tests in any files ending in **.test.js** or **.spec.js.**

This setup checks whether the greet function behaves as expected when the test runs, thus validating your function's correctness with following output:

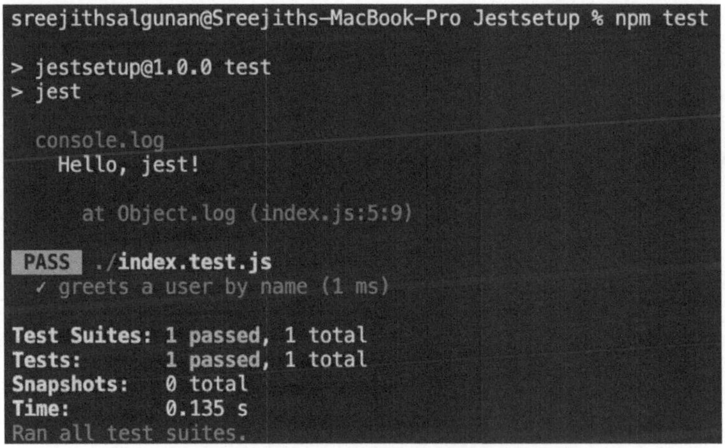

***Figure 2.3**: Test output*

Test Execution Lifecycle

The Test Execution Lifecycle in Jest involves several stages such as:

Global Setup: Runs once before all tests; is ideal for global tasks like database setup

```
// globalSetup.js
module.exports = async () => {
  // Code to set up a global resource, like a database
};
```

In **jest.config.js: globalSetup: ‘<rootDir>/globalSetup.js’**

File-Level Setup and Teardown: **beforeAll** and **afterAll** run once before and after all tests in a file.

```
beforeAll(() => {
  // Code to run once before all tests in this file
});

afterAll(() => {
  // Code to run once after all tests in this file
});
```

Test-Level Setup and Teardown: **beforeEach** and **afterEach** run before and after each test in a file.

```
beforeEach(() => {
  // Code to run before each test in this file
});

afterEach(() => {
  // Code to run after each test in this file
});
```

Practical Use Cases Explained for (beforeAll, afterAll, beforeEach, afterEach)

```
const calculator = require(‘./calculator’);

// Global Setup
beforeAll(() => {
 console.log(‘Global setup for Calculator tests’);
});

// Global Teardown
afterAll(() => {
 console.log(‘Global teardown for Calculator tests’);
});

// Test Setup
beforeEach(() => {
 calculator.resetOperationCount(); // Reset operation count before each
test
```

```
 console.log('before each test');
});

// Test Teardown
afterEach(() => {
 // Potentially log the operation count after each test
 console.log('after each test');
});

test('add function calculates correctly', () => {
 expect(calculator.add(2, 3)).toBe(5);
});

test('operation count increments correctly', () => {
 calculator.add(2, 3);
 calculator.add(4, 5);
 expect(calculator.getOperationCount()).toBe(2);
});
```

Output in console:

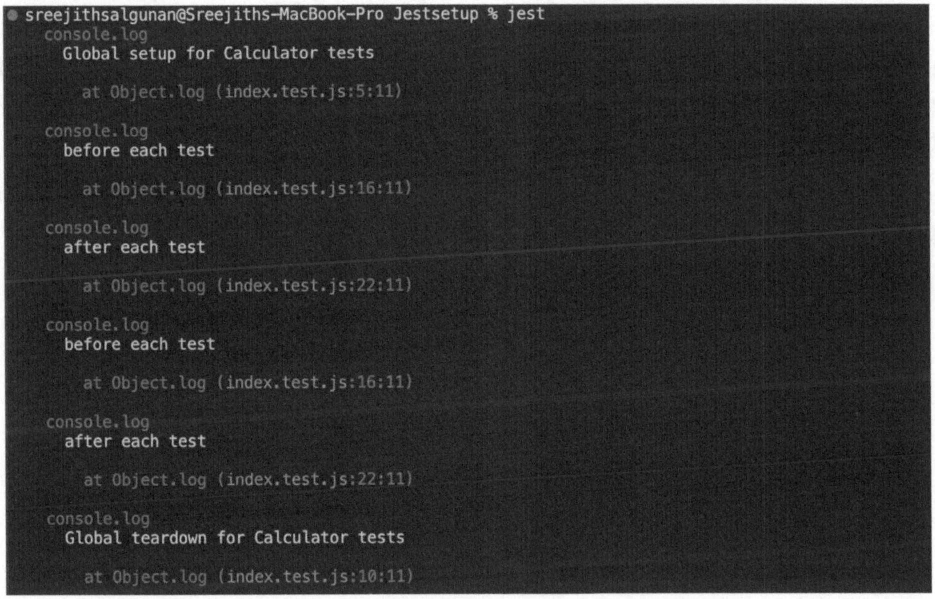

Figure 2.4: *Output*

Test Execution: Tests defined by test or it are executed.

```
 test('example test', () => {
  // Test code
});
```

Global Teardown: Runs once after all tests, for global cleanup tasks

Each stage ensures tests run in a controlled environment, which is important for consistent and reliable results.

```
// globalTeardown.js
module.exports = async () => {
  // Code to clean up global resources
};
```

In **`jest.config.js: globalTeardown: '<rootDir>/globalTeardown.js'`**

Imagine you are playing with toy blocks. Before you start, you get all your favorite blocks out (which is like the "**`Global Setup`**"). Then, for each game you play, you might build a base first (like "**`beforeAll`**") and clean it up after playing (like "**`afterAll`**"). When playing, you might get new blocks (that's "**`beforeEach`**") to create a new structure and put them back after each creation (like "**`afterEach`**"). The building part is like running the tests. When you are done playing, you put all the toys away (like the "*Global Teardown*"). This is how Jest tests work as well.

Command-Line Options for Jest

Jest command line options provide a range of functionalities to customize how tests are run and reported. The Jest CLI offers numerous options for fine-tuning test execution.

Think of Jest's command-line options as a set of special tools or "**`shortcuts`**" that help you manage and control your testing process more efficiently.

- **`--init`:** Generates a basic configuration file. Based on your project, Jest will ask you a few questions that will help to generate a **`jest.config.js`** file with a short description for each option. *This is like asking a game to set up a new playground for you.*

  `npx jest --init`

- **`--onlyChanged`:** The game only shows levels that are new or changed since you last played. This runs tests related to changed files in a Git repository.

  `npm test -- --onlyChanged`

  The **`-o`** option in Jest, also known as **`--onlyChanged`**, is designed to run tests that are affected by the recent changes in your code. It is particularly useful in a version-controlled environment like Git. This option relies on a static structure of code dependencies, which means that it works best when your code imports are fixed and not dynamically generated. This feature streamlines testing by focusing only on parts of the codebase that are modified, which saves time and resources during development.

- **--json**: *It is like asking the game to write down your scores in a special secret code.*

  `npm test -- --json`

  This outputs test results in JSON format.

- **--watch**: *The game keeps an eye on your toys, and if you change a toy, it starts a new game.*

  `npm test -- --watch -- path/to/my-test-file.test.js`

  It also watches specified files for changes and reruns tests accordingly.

- **--watchAll**: *The game always starts new ones whenever anything changes.*

  `npm test -- --watchAll`

  It watches all files for changes and reruns all tests when any change is detected.

- **--silent**: *Playing the game without any sound, so it is really quiet.*

  `npm test -- --silent`

  These magic commands make playing the game (or running tests) more fun and fit just how you like it!

  This command suppresses the console output from tests.

- **--coverage**: *This is like all the points you score in every game.*

  `npm test -- --coverage`

  This is used for collecting code coverage. This command will execute your tests and produce code coverage reports in a **coverage/** directory by default. Inside the **coverage/** directory, you will find HTML and text-based reports that show the parts of your code that are covered/not covered by the tests.

  `npm test -- --coverage --coverageDirectory=path/to/custom/directory`

  This will place the coverage reports in the specified directory.

  You can also set coverage thresholds to fail the test run if the coverage falls below a certain percentage. To do this, you can add a **coverageThreshold** configuration in your Jest configuration file (usually **jest.config.js**), like:

```
module.exports = {
  // other Jest configuration options
  coverageThreshold: {
    global: {
      statements: 90,
```

```
        branches: 80,
        functions: 90,
        lines: 90,
      },
    },
  };
```

- `--config`: This is like telling the game where your secret map is hidden.

  `npm test -- --config path/to/your-custom-config.js`

  This option allows specifying a configuration file path.

- `--no-cache`: This button cleans up old game data so you can start fresh.

  `npm test -- --no-cache`

  However, you must disable the cache. This exercise is useful for troubleshooting caching-related issues. When you use this option, Jest will not use cached test results or cached module dependencies during the current test run. This can be useful in situations where you suspect that cached data might be causing issues or when you want to ensure that all tests are executed from scratch

- `--verbose`: *It is like asking the game to tell you every tiny detail about your adventure.*

  It provides more detailed information about each test run.

  `npm test -- --verbose`

  When you run Jest with `--verbose`, you will typically see the following information:

  - **Detailed Test Output:** Jest will display detailed information about each test, including the test name, test status (pass or fail), and additional details about the test execution.
  - **Console Logs:** Any `console.log()` or other console output from your test code will be displayed in the console, which will help you debug and understand what is happening during test execution.
  - **Coverage Information:** If you are generating code coverage reports with Jest, the `--verbose` option can provide more detailed coverage information and reports.

- `--changedSince`: This is like playing only the levels that are new or you have not played since the last time you changed your toys.

  This runs tests related to changes from a specific branch or commit hash.

  `npm test -- --changedSince=main`

- **`--updateSnapshot`:** Imagine you have a toy that you take a picture of. Sometimes the toy changes a little, and you need to take a new picture to show how it looks now. This command tells your computer to take new pictures of your toys (tests) and replace the old ones if they have changed.

  ```
  npm test -- --updateSnapshot
  ```

  This is used for updating Jest snapshots.

- **`--testEnvironment --verbose`**: Think of your computer like a playground where you play with your toys (tests). Sometimes, you want to change how the playground works, like making it a snowy place or a sunny one. This command lets you change the playground, and "**`verbose`**" means your computer talks a lot and tells you everything that is happening while you play.

  ```
  npm test -- --testEnvironment=jsdom -verbose
  ```

  This is used for customizing the test environment and output.

- **`--bail`:** Imagine you are playing a game, and if you make a mistake, you lose a point. But if you make too many mistakes, you want to stop playing because it is no fun anymore. This command tells your computer to stop playing the game (stop running tests) if you make too many mistakes (tests fail).

  ```
  npm test -- --bail=3
  ```

  This is used to stop tests after a certain number of failures.

These options provide great flexibility in managing and executing tests to suit various development workflows.

Running Specific Test and Specific Test Suites

You must execute only the tests or test suites you need to save time and focus on relevant checks.

Running Specific Tests

Using **`testNamePattern`**

- **What It Is**: The **`testNamePattern`** is a way to run tests whose names match a specific pattern. This is particularly useful when you have a large number of tests and you want to run only a subset that shares a common naming convention.

- **How to Use:**
  - **Command Line**: You use this pattern directly in the command line when executing Jest.

    `npm test -- -t "your test name"`
  - **Pattern Matching**: The pattern you provide is case-insensitive and matches any part of the test name. It means that if you have a test named "should test feature A", you can run it using **`npm test -- -t 'feature A'`**, **`npm test -- -t 'should test'`**, and so on.
  - **Regular Expressions**: The pattern can be a regular expression. For example, **`npm test -- -t 'feature (A|B)'`** would run tests named "**`feature A`**" and "**`feature B`**".
  - **Use Cases**: These are ideal for the times when you remember part of the test name or when your tests are systematically named following a pattern.

Using `.only`

- **What It Is**: The **`.only`** method is a way to mark a specific test or test suite to run while skipping all others in the test files. It is a part of Jest's API.
- **How to Use**: In Test Files: You append **`.only`** to either test or its function, which are aliases in Jest.
- **Example**: **`test.only('should do something', () => {...})`**
- **Isolation**: This will cause Jest to run only this particular test, while skipping all other tests in all test files.
- **Multiple `.only`**: If there are multiple tests with **`.only`**, Jest will run all of them and skip the rest.
- **Use Cases**: Extremely useful during development or debugging when you are focused on a specific test. It is a temporary change, and you should remove .only before committing code to avoid disabling other tests accidentally.

Specifying File Names Directly

- Run tests from specific files by directly specifying file names or paths.

  Example: `jest path/to/yourTestFile.test.js`

Using `test.only` or `test.skip`

- Isolate a test with **`test.only`** or skip it with **`test.skip`**.

  Example: **`test.only('should do something', () => {...})`**

Environment Variables for Test Logic

- Control test execution with environment variables.

  Example: Use environment variables to conditionally run tests based on certain criteria.

Tagging Tests (Custom Approach)

- Implement a custom tagging system in tests and use scripts to filter and run tests based on these tags.

  Example: Use comments or naming conventions for tagging and a script to parse and execute these tests.

Tips

- **Avoid Committing `.only`**: Always remember to remove `.only` before committing your code. Accidentally committing it can lead to incomplete test runs in continuous integration environments.
- **Combine with Other Jest Features**: These methods can be combined with other Jest features like describe blocks or `beforeEach` for more complex test setups.
- **Watch Mode**: When used in combination with Jest's watch mode `(npm test -- --watch)`, these methods become more powerful as Jest will only rerun the specified tests as you make changes to your code, speeding up your test-driven development (TDD) process.
- **Automated Check for `.only`**: Consider setting up a pre-commit or pre-push hook in your version control system to check for .only in test files. This can prevent accidentally skipping tests in shared repositories or CI environments.

Running Specific Test Suites

Run targeted test suites to quickly validate specific parts of your codebase.

Using `testPathPattern`

- **What It Is**: `testPathPattern` is a feature in Jest that allows you to specify a pattern to match test file paths. This enables the execution of tests that are within files whose paths match the provided pattern.
- **How to Use**:
  - **Command Line Usage**: This pattern is used directly in the command line when running Jest.
  - **Example Command**: `npm test -- testFolder/__tests__/*.test.js`

- **Pattern Matching**: The pattern is a regular expression that matches against the entire path of the test files. It is not limited to just file names; you can include directory names in the pattern as well.
- **Flexibility**: This feature is particularly useful when your tests are organized in a directory structure and you want to run all tests in a specific folder or matching a certain naming convention.
- **Common Use Cases**: Running all tests in a specific component directory, or running all tests that are labeled as integration tests, assuming they follow a naming pattern like `*.integration.test.js`.

Using `describe.only` or `describe.skip` Method

- **What It Is**: `describe.only` is a Jest API method that allows you to run only the tests within a specific describe block, skipping all other tests.
- You can also skip it with `describe.skip.`
- **How to Use**:
  - In Test Files: You use `describe.only` in your test files to mark a group of tests (test suite) that you want to run exclusively.
  - For example, look at the code here:

```
describe.only('My Test Suite', () => {
      test('should do something', ()=>{...});
      test('should do something else', ()=>{...});
});
```

  - **Isolation**: Jest will run only the tests inside the `describe.only` block and will skip all other tests in all test files.
  - **Multiple Suites**: If you have multiple `describe.only` blocks across your tests, Jest will run all the tests in all those blocks and skip the rest.
  - **Use Cases**: Ideal for focusing on a specific group of related tests, such as when working on a particular feature or component.

Using `--findRelatedTests`

- Run tests related to specific files.

  Example: `npm test -- --findRelatedTests path/to/sourceFile.js`

Using `--changedSince`

- Run tests related to changes since a specific branch.

  Example: `npm test -- --changedSince=master`

Jest Configurations

- Define patterns for test files in a Jest configuration file.

  Example: Use `testMatch` or `testRegex` in `jest.config.js`.

Running Tests by Coverage

- Run tests that cover a modified set of files.

  Example: `npm test -- --coverage --onlyChanged`

Custom Test Runners

- Use or develop custom test runners for specific execution requirements.

  Example: Implementing a test runner that runs tests based on custom-defined logic.

Tips

- **Watch Mode**: Both `testPathPattern` and `describe.only` are highly effective when used in Jest's watch mode `(npm test -- --watch)`, as they allow you to continuously run a subset of tests as you develop.
- **Avoiding Accidental Skips**: Like with .only on individual tests, it is important to remove `describe.only` before committing your code. This ensures that your continuous integration (CI) system runs the full test suite.
- **Combining Methods**: You can combine `testPathPattern` with `describe.only` for more refined control. For example, you might use a path pattern to run tests in a specific directory and then use `describe.only` to further isolate a subset of those tests.
- **Test Organization**: To make the most of these features, it is helpful to have a well-organized test suite, where tests are grouped logically and file names and paths are named consistently.

Using these methods, we can manage large test suites in Jest, which allows for targeted testing and helps us create efficient development workflows. This targeted approach is particularly beneficial in large projects where full test suites can take a lot of time to run.

Jest Syntax Overview and Matchers

Writing tests using intuitive syntax and powerful matchers for clear, reliable assertions.

Understanding Jest Syntax

Simplifying Jest's Building Blocks

describe: Think of describe as a way to group similar tests. It is like putting all tests for a specific feature in one box.

```
describe('Feature A Tests', () => {
    // Tests for Feature A go here
});
```

it/test: Both it and test are interchangeable and used for writing individual tests. It is like saying, "*It should do this*" or "*Test that this happens.*"

```
it('should do something', () => {
    // Tests code here
});
```

expect: expect is how you make an assertion. Imagine that you are a detective looking for clues; expect is your way of saying, "*I expect to find this clue here.*"

expect(someValue).toBe(expectedValue);

Example: **calculator.test.js**

```
describe('Calculator', () => {
 describe('Add function', () => {
    it('should return the sum of two positive numbers', () => {
      expect(calculator.add(1, 2)).toBe(3);
    });

    it('should return the sum of two negative numbers', () => {
      expect(calculator.add(-1, -2)).toBe(-3);
    });

    it('should return the sum of a positive and a negative numbers',
() => {
      expect(calculator.add(-1, 2)).toBe(1);
    });
  });
});
```

beforeEach and afterEach: Functions that run before/after each test in a describe block. Useful for setting up and tearing down conditions common to all tests.

beforeAll and afterAll: Functions that run once before/after all the tests in a describe block.

Matchers

These are methods that let you test values in different ways.

Common Matchers for Assertions

Matchers are methods that let you test values in your code. They are used in test cases to assert whether a particular outcome is as expected.

Think of matchers as a way to ask questions about your code and get back "*yes*" or "*no*" answers. For example, if you want to check whether a function returns a specific value, you use a matcher to compare the actual result of the function with the expected result.

Here is a simple analogy: Imagine you baked a cake and you want to ensure it is chocolate-flavored. You taste it and then confirm, "*Yes, this is chocolate.*" In this scenario, your taste test is like a matcher in Jest; it checks if the actual flavor (result) matches your expectation (chocolate).

In Jest, you typically use matchers in combination with the expect function. You call expect with the value you want to test, followed by a matcher method that defines how you want to test that value. For example:

`expect(myFunction()).toBe(5);`

`toBe(value)`

- Checks if a value is exactly the same as the expected value. It is similar to using === in JavaScript.
- For example, **`expect(can.ounces).toBe(12);`** checks if **`can.ounces`** is exactly 12.

`toEqual(value)`

- Checks for value equality. This is useful for comparing objects or arrays where you want to check if the values are the same, not necessarily the same reference.
- For example, **`expect(can).toEqual({ name: 'pamplemousse', ounces: 12 });`**

`toHaveBeenCalled()`

- It verifies that a mock function has been called at least once.
- For example, **`expect(drink).toHaveBeenCalled();`**

`toHaveBeenCalledTimes(number)`

- It checks that a mock function has been called a specific number of times.

- For example, `expect(drink).toHaveBeenCalledTimes(2);`

`toHaveBeenCalledWith(arg1, arg2, ...)`

- It ensures that a mock function was called with specific arguments.
- For example, `expect(f).toHaveBeenCalledWith(beverage);`

`toHaveBeenLastCalledWith(arg1, arg2, ...)`

- It tests that a mock function was last called with specific arguments.
- For example, `expect(drink).toHaveBeenLastCalledWith('mango');`

`toHaveBeenNthCalledWith(nthCall, arg1, arg2, ...)`

- It checks that a mock function was called with specific arguments on its nth call.
- For example, `expect(drink).toHaveBeenNthCalledWith(1, 'lemon');`

`toHaveReturned()`

- It confirms that a mock function has returned at least once.
- For example, `expect(drink).toHaveReturned();`

`toHaveReturnedTimes(number)`

- It ensures that a mock function returned successfully a specific number of times.
- For example, `expect(drink).toHaveReturnedTimes(2);`

`toHaveReturnedWith(value)`

- It checks that a mock function returned a specific value.
- For example, `expect(drink).toHaveReturnedWith('La Croix');`

`toHaveLength(number)`

- It verifies that an object has a .length property and it is set to a certain numeric value.
- For example, `expect([1, 2, 3]).toHaveLength(3);`

`toHaveProperty(keyPath, value?)`

- It ensures that an object has a specified property, optionally checking the value of that property.
- For example, `expect(houseForSale).toHaveProperty('kitchen.area', 20);`

`toBeCloseTo(number, numDigits?)`

- It compares floating-point numbers for approximate equality.

- For example, **`expect(0.2 + 0.1).toBeCloseTo(0.3, 5);`**

`toBeDefined()`

- Checks that a variable is not undefined.
- For example, **`expect(fetchNewFlavorIdea()).toBeDefined();`**

`toBeFalsy()`

- Tests that a value is falsy (evaluates to false in a boolean context).
- For example, **`expect(getErrors()).toBeFalsy();`**

`toBeGreaterThan(number), toBeLessThan(number)`

- For numerical comparisons (greater than or less than).
- For example, **`expect(ouncesPerCan()).toBeGreaterThan(10);`**

`toMatch(regexp | string)`

- It checks that a string matches a regular expression or string.
- For example, **`expect(essayOnTheBestFlavor()).toMatch(/grapefruit/);`**

`toMatchObject(object)`

- It ensures that an object matches a subset of the properties of another object.
- For example, **`expect(houseForSale).toMatchObject(desiredHouse);`**

`toThrow(error?)`

- It tests that a function throws an error when called.
- For example, **`expect(() => drinkFlavor('octopus')).toThrow();`**

These matchers are essential tools in Jest for asserting various conditions in your tests, which makes them powerful and versatile for different testing scenarios.

Tips

- **Choose the Right Matcher**: Jest offers a wide range of matchers for different use cases. Make sure to choose the one that best suits your testing needs. For example, use **`toBe`** for primitive types and **`toEqual`** for objects and arrays.
- **Readability Matters**: Choose matchers that make your tests easy to read and understand. The test suite should clearly communicate your intentions. For instance, **`toBeNull()`** is more expressive and easier to understand than **`toBe(null)`**.

- **Use Precise Matchers**: Prefer more specific matchers over general ones. For example, if you are checking for a boolean value, `toBeTruthy()` or `toBeFalsy()` is more specific than `toEqual(true)` or `toEqual(false)`.
- **Floating Point Numbers**: When dealing with floating-point arithmetic, use `toBeCloseTo` instead of `toBe` or `toEqual` to avoid issues with precision.
- **Error Handling**: To test if a function throws an error, use the `toThrow` matcher. This is more effective than trying to catch the error in the test manually.
- **Mock Functions**: For mock functions, utilize matchers like `toHaveBeenCalled`, `toHaveBeenCalledTimes`, and `toHaveBeenCalledWith` to test various aspects of the mock function's behavior.
- **Asymmetric Matchers**: Take advantage of Jest's asymmetric matchers (like `expect.anything()` or `expect.any(Constructor)`) when you want to assert only part of an object or array.
- **Combining Matchers**: Sometimes you might need to combine matchers for more complex assertions. This can be done using .not or by chaining matchers.
- **Custom Matchers**: For unique test scenarios, you can create custom matchers in Jest. This is useful when the existing matchers do not meet your requirements.
- **Regular Expressions**: Use the `toMatch` matcher for testing strings against regular expressions, which can be very powerful for pattern matching within strings.
- **Avoid Over-testing**: While it is good to be thorough, avoid writing tests that are too specific and break with any minor change in the implementation. Aim for a balance between thoroughness and maintainability.
- **Stay Updated**: Jest occasionally adds new matchers. Keeping up with the latest changes in Jest documentation can help you take advantage of new and improved matchers.

Custom Matchers and Assertions

While the built-in matchers cover a wide range of use cases, there might be situations where you need something more specific to your application's logic. This is where custom matchers come into play. Custom matchers allow you to extend Jest with your own comparison logic, while providing a way to add reusable assertive methods tailored to your needs.

Using `expect.extend`:

- Jest provides **`expect.extend`** to add your custom matchers. This method takes an object where keys are the names of your custom matchers and values are the matcher functions.

Matcher Function Structure:

- Each custom matcher function receives two arguments. The first is the value being tested, and the second is the expected value.
- The function must return an object containing two properties: pass (a boolean indicating if the test passed) and message (a function that returns a string message for when the test fails).

Suppose you want a matcher to test whether a number is even, you will use the following code:

```
expect.extend({
  toBeEven(received){
    const pass = received % 2 === 0;
    if (pass) {
 return {
   message: () => `expected ${received} to be even`,
   pass: true,
 };
      } else {
         return {
            message: () => `expected ${received} not to be even`,
            pass: false,
         };
       }
   }
});
// Usage
test('2 is even', () => {
  expect(2).toBeEven();
});
```

Tips

- **Clear Naming:** Name your matcher clearly and intuitively. The name should reflect what the matcher is checking.
- **Comprehensive Message:** Provide a clear and informative message for both passing and failing scenarios. This helps to debug when a test fails.

- **Reusability**: Design your custom matchers to be generic and reusable across different parts of your tests.
- **Keep It Simple**: Start with simple logic. Avoid overcomplicating custom matchers as they can become hard to maintain.
- **Testing Custom Matchers**: Write tests for your custom matchers to ensure they work correctly and remain reliable as you make changes to your codebase.
- **Documentation**: Document your custom matchers, especially if they are used by other team members. Clear documentation ensures that everyone understands how and when to use them.

Custom matchers can significantly enhance your testing capabilities in Jest by allowing you to assert conditions that are unique to your application in a clean and reusable way.

Jest Coverage in Code Quality Assessment

Ensuring robust applications by measuring test completeness and maintaining high code quality standards.

Code Coverage

Code coverage is a metric used in software testing to describe the degree to which the source code of a program is executed when a particular test suite runs. It provides an indication of how well your tests exercise or "`cover`" your code. High coverage indicates that most of your code is tested by automated tests, which can lead to higher software quality and reliability.

Configuring Jest for Code Coverage

Setting Configuration in `jest.config.js`: If you have a `jest.config.js` file in your project, it is often the preferred place to put your Jest configurations. This is especially true for larger projects or configurations that are complex. The equivalent configuration in jest.config.js would be:

```
module.exports = {
  collectCoverage: true,
  coverageReporters: ['text', 'lcov'],
  collectCoverageFrom: [
    '**/*.{js,jsx}',
```

```
    '!**/node_modules/**',
    '!**/vendor/**'
  ]
};
```

Setting Configuration in `package.json`: Alternatively, if you do not have a jest. config.js file or prefer to keep your configuration centralized, you can include the Jest configuration directly in your **`package.json`** file. This is a common approach for smaller projects or when there are fewer configurations.

```
"jest": {
   "collectCoverage": true,
   "coverageReporters": ["text", "lcov"],
   "collectCoverageFrom": ["**/*.{js,jsx}", "!**/node_modules/**", "!**/
vendor/**"]
 }
```

This configuration tells Jest to collect coverage data and generate reports in both text and **`lcov`** (which can be visualized in coverage tools) formats. It also specifies which files should be included in the coverage.

Choosing the Right Approach

- **Separate Configuration File (`jest.config.js`):** Ideal for larger projects or when you have extensive configurations. It helps keep your configurations organized and your **`package.json`** cleaner.
- **Directly in `package.json`:** Suitable for smaller projects or when you have a minimal Jest configuration. This approach keeps all configurations in one place and avoids additional files in the project.

Both methods are perfectly valid and Jest will automatically detect and use the configuration from either source. The choice mainly depends on how you wish to organize your project.

Run Jest with Coverage: Use the following npm script to generate a coverage report:

```
"scripts": {
   "test": "jest --coverage"
 }
```

Then execute the script using:

```
npm test
```

Interpreting Code Coverage Reports

Interpreting Code Coverage Reports in Jest helps you understand which parts of your codebase are tested, identify gaps, and ensure overall test quality.

Types of Code Coverage

- **Statement Coverage**: Checks if each statement in the code has been executed
- **Branch Coverage**: Ensures that every branch (like in if-else statements) has been executed
- **Function Coverage**: Verifies that each function in the codebase is called
- Line Coverage: Measures whether each line of code is executed at least once

Importance of Code Coverage

- **Identifies Untested Code**: Helps find parts of the code that are not tested, which might contain hidden bugs
- **Improves Code Quality**: Leads to more thorough testing, thereby enhancing code reliability
- **Facilitates Maintenance**: Well-tested code is usually easier to maintain and refactor.

Understanding Percentages:

- A higher percentage typically indicates more thorough testing.
- 100% coverage is often not necessary or practical; focus on critical parts of the code.

After running the tests with coverage, Jest will create a coverage directory in your project root. This directory contains files that report the coverage statistics. You can review these to understand the coverage of your tests, by opening it in a browser.

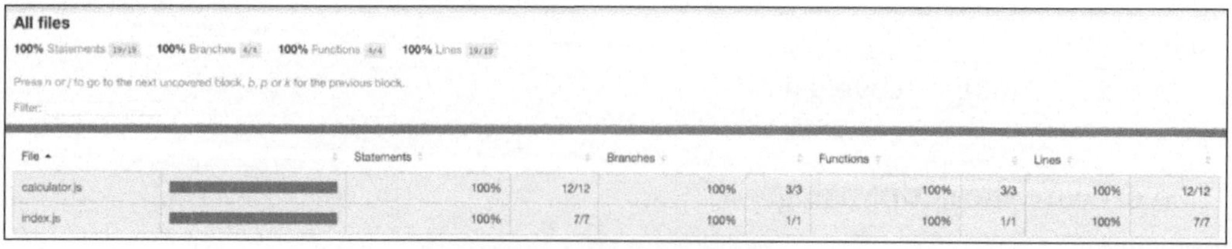

Figure 2.5: *Code Coverage*

Setting Coverage Thresholds

It is a way to enforce a minimum level of code coverage. If the tests do not meet these thresholds, Jest will fail the test run. This practice ensures that a certain quality standard for testing is maintained. Here is how you can set coverage thresholds:

Coverage Thresholds

- **Thresholds**: Specific percentages that your code coverage metrics must meet or exceed.
- **Metrics**: Usually include statement coverage, line coverage, function coverage, and branch coverage.

Configuring Coverage Thresholds in Jest: You can set coverage thresholds in your Jest configuration. This can be done in the `jest.config.js` file or inside the jest field in `package.json`.

```
module.exports = {
  collectCoverage: true,
  coverageThreshold: {
    global: {
      branches: 80,
      functions: 85,
      lines: 90,
      statements: 90
    }
  }
};
```

This configuration sets global thresholds for different coverage metrics. If any of these percentages are not met when running tests, Jest will exit with an error.

Understanding Threshold Values

- **Branches**: The percentage of `if/else` branches that must be tested
- **Functions**: The percentage of functions or methods that must be called during testing
- **Lines**: The percentage of code lines that must be executed
- **Statements**: The percentage of executable statements that must be executed

Setting Per-File Thresholds: Besides global thresholds, you can also set thresholds for individual files or directories, which is particularly useful for critical parts of your codebase.

```
coverageThreshold: {
 global: {
   // Global thresholds
 },
 "./path/to/specific/file.js": {
   lines: 95,
   statements: 95
 }
}
```

Best Practices for Coverage Thresholds:

- **Start with Reasonable Thresholds**: Begin with achievable thresholds and gradually increase them as your test coverage improves.
- **Do Not Overemphasize**: While important, do not rely solely on thresholds. The quality of tests matters more than meeting arbitrary percentages.
- **Use as a Guideline**: Treat thresholds as a guide to maintain and improve test coverage, not as an absolute measure of code quality.
- **Consider the Project Context**: Set thresholds according to the complexity and criticality of your project. Critical projects might require higher thresholds.

Running Tests with Threshold Checks: Execute your tests as usual. If the coverage falls below the specified thresholds, Jest will provide an error message and exit with a non-zero status:

```
npm test
```

Setting and gradually increasing coverage thresholds is a great way to incrementally improve the test coverage of your project. Remember, the goal is to ensure meaningful tests that genuinely contribute to the stability and reliability of your code.

Tips

- **Do Not Aim for 100% Blindly**: While high code coverage is good, it does not always equate to effective testing. Focus on meaningful tests rather than artificially inflating coverage metrics.
- **Prioritize Critical Paths**: Ensure key functionalities and critical code paths have thorough coverage.
- **Coverage Types:** Familiarize yourself with the different types of coverage (statement, branch, function, line) and understand what each signifies in the context of your project.

- **Gaps in Coverage**: Use the report to identify areas with low coverage. These might be opportunities to add more comprehensive tests.
- **Quality Over Quantity**: It is better to have fewer, high-quality tests that cover key functionalities than many superficial tests that don't provide value.
- **Team Understanding**: Ensure that all team members understand the importance of test coverage and how to interpret coverage reports.

Best Practices for Quality

Jest involves strategic planning of the testing approach, writing effective tests, and understanding the metrics. Here are some key practices to consider:

Write Comprehensive and Meaningful Tests

- **Behavioral Testing**: Focus on the behavior of the code rather than its implementation details. This makes tests more resilient to code changes.
- **Test Edge Cases**: Ensure tests cover various edge cases, error conditions, and unusual inputs to validate the robustness of the code.

Utilize Jest's Full Feature Set

- **Mocking and Spies**: Use Jest's mocking features to isolate units of code and test them in isolation. Spies can be used to verify that functions are called with the correct arguments.
- **Asynchronous Code Testing**: Effectively test asynchronous code by using Jest's support for promises and async/await.

Understand and Act on Coverage Reports

- **Aim for High Coverage but Not Blindly**: While high test coverage is a good indicator, it does not always guarantee code quality. Aim for meaningful tests rather than hitting arbitrary coverage numbers.
- **Review Coverage Reports**: Regularly review coverage reports to identify untested code areas. Use these insights to write tests that improve coverage in meaningful ways.

Regular Refactoring of Tests

- **Keep Tests Clean and Maintainable**: Regularly refactor test suites and test cases to keep them efficient, readable, and maintainable.
- **Update Tests Alongside Code**: When modifying code, ensure that corresponding tests are updated to reflect those changes.

Ensure Test Independence

- **Avoid Test Interdependence**: Design tests to run independently of each other to avoid cascading failures and ensure reliability.

Balance Different Types of Testing

- **Follow the Testing Pyramid**: Balance unit tests with integration tests and a few end-to-end tests. This approach provides quick feedback and broad coverage.

Integrate Testing into the Development Workflow

- **Continuous Integration**: Incorporate Jest tests into your continuous integration (CI) process to automatically run tests for new commits and pull requests.

Code Reviews and Collaboration

- **Review Tests in Code Reviews**: Include tests as a part of the code review process to ensure their quality and share best practices within the team.
- **Collaborative Approach to Testing**: Encourage a culture where all team members contribute to and value testing.

Performance Monitoring

- **Monitor Test Performance**: Keep an eye on the execution time of tests. Slow tests can become a bottleneck in the development process.

Stay Updated with Jest

- **Keep Jest Updated**: Regularly update Jest to benefit from the latest features, performance improvements, and bug fixes.

By adhering to these best practices, you can leverage Jest to effectively assess and improve the quality of your codebase, while ensuring that it remains robust, scalable, and maintainable.

Conclusion

We started with setting up and configuring Jest, while learning how it easily integrates into projects and adapts to different needs. Then we covered the basics of writing and running tests, using matchers, and creating snapshots. Finally, we looked at code coverage to see how well our tests protect the code, which further shows how Jest helps keep applications reliable and maintainable.

Further Reading

- https://jestjs.io/docs/getting-started
- https://jestjs.io/docs/configuration
- https://jestjs.io/docs/cli
- https://jestjs.io/docs/configuration#collectcoverage-boolean
- https://jestjs.io/docs/expect#matchers
- https://jestjs.io/docs/expect#custom-matchers-api

CHAPTER 3

Introduction to React and React Testing Library

Introduction

In this chapter, we will focus on React Testing Library (RTL), which is a modern and powerful tool for testing React applications. While the book covers the broader landscape of React development and testing, this chapter specifically zooms in on RTL, while emphasizing its role, capabilities, and how it integrates seamlessly with React and Jest. Our aim is to provide a deep and practical understanding of RTL, which makes it an indispensable resource for developers who want to write reliable, maintainable, and effective tests for their React components.

Structure

This chapter covers the following topics:

- Introduction to React
- React Testing Library Introduction
- Configuring Jest with React Testing Library
- React Testing Library Functionalities
- Rendering Components and Event Triggering in Testing
- Enhancing Element Selection with ARIA Roles

Introduction to React

React is a popular JavaScript library for building user interfaces and is especially useful for web applications. Developed by Facebook, React stands out for its efficiency and flexibility, which enable developers to create interactive and dynamic user interfaces.

Overview and Fundamentals

Here is a basic introduction to the foundational concepts of React:

Components: At its core, React is built around components. These are reusable, self-contained pieces of code that represent a part of the user interface. Each component can have its own state and props and can be nested within other components to build complex interfaces. Components can be written as JavaScript functions or classes.

JSX (JavaScript XML): React introduces JSX, a syntax extension for JavaScript. It allows you to write HTML structures in the same file as your JavaScript code. This makes the code more readable and easier to write. JSX is transpiled to regular JavaScript at runtime.

State and Props:

- **State** is a data structure that starts with a default value which can be changed over time. It is local to the component and can be updated using the **`setState`** function in class components or the **`useState`** hook in functional components.
- **Props** (short for properties) are read-only components that must be passed to the component, much like parameters to a function. They are used to pass data from one component to another, typically from a parent to a child component.

Lifecycle Methods: In class components, React provides several lifecycle methods that are called at different stages of a component's life in the DOM. These include mounting, updating, and unmounting phases, allowing developers to perform specific actions at each stage.

Hooks: Introduced in React 16.8, hooks allow you to use state and other React features in functional components. Hooks like **`useState`**, **`useEffect`**, and **`useContext`** provide a more straightforward and cleaner way to write components.

Virtual DOM: React uses a virtual DOM, which is a lightweight copy of the actual DOM. It allows React to optimize rendering by minimizing the number of updates to the real DOM, which is a costly operation. This results in improved performance and a smoother user experience.

These foundational elements make React a powerful tool for developing efficient and maintainable web applications. React's component-based architecture and its efficient update mechanism through the virtual DOM enable developers to build large-scale applications with relative ease.

Building Your First React Project with Vite

A fast, modern, and developer-friendly way to kickstart your application, combining React's flexibility with Vite's blazing speed and simplicity.

Opening the Terminal/Command Prompt

1. Run the following command to create a new React project using Vite's JavaScript template:

   ```
   npm create vite@latest my-react-app -- --template react
   ```

2. Replace `my-react-app` with your desired project name.
3. Filling Out Project Details: Choose the framework as react.
4. Once the process is complete, run the following commands:

   ```
   cd my-react-app
   npm install
   npm run dev
   ```

Install Dependencies: Your project will come with the necessary dependencies for a React project. However, if you need to add additional libraries, you can install them using npm here:

```
npm install <library-name>
```

Explore and Modify Your React App: Vite sets up a basic project structure for you. You can start editing the files under the `src` directory to build your React components.

Run Your Application: To start the development server, run:

```
npm run dev
```

This will start the local development server and you can view your application by clicking on this URL: `http://localhost:3000`

By following these steps, you will have a fully set up React application using Vite, which is ready for development.

Creating Your First React Component

Let us create a simple component named Greeting that displays a greeting message to the user through the following steps:

- **Create a New File:** Create a new file named **`Greeting.jsx`** inside your project's **`src`** directory.
- **Import React:** At the top of your **`Greeting.jsx`** file, import React from the **`'react'`** package. This import statement allows you to use JSX, a syntax extension for JavaScript that looks similar to HTML.

```
import React from 'react';
```

- **Define the Component:** Define the Greeting component as a functional component. Functional components are simpler and recommended for most cases. It will accept a name prop and display a personalized greeting.

```
import React from 'react';

function Greeting({ name }) {
  return <h1>Hello, {name}!</h1>;
}
```

- **Export the Component:** Finally, export the Greeting component so it can be used in other parts of your application.

```
export default Greeting;
```

- **Using Your Component:** To use the Greeting component, import it into another component or your application's entry point, typically **`App.jsx`**, and render it with the desired props.

```
import React from 'react';
import Greeting from './Greeting';

function App() {
 return (
  <div>
   <Greeting name="Alice" />
  </div>
 );
}

export default App;
```

This renders the Greeting component within the App component, displaying "**`Hello, Alice!`**" on the page.

React Testing Library Introduction

React Testing Library simplifies the way we test React components by focusing on user interactions and behavior, ensuring that applications are validated the same way real users experience them.

Overview of React Testing Library

React Testing Library is a popular utility for testing React components. It promotes a minimal, user-focused approach instead of poking into component internals.

RTL is built on top of **`react-dom`** and **`@testing-library/dom`**. It helps you write tests that:

- Render components
- Interact with them via the DOM
- Assert what the user actually sees

Instead of testing internal implementation details (state, instance methods, and so on), RTL encourages testing the resulting DOM by:

- Selecting elements by text, labels, or roles
- Only falling back to **`data-testid`** when necessary

Because tests are written from the user's perspective, they tend to be:

- More resilient to refactors
- Less fragile when implementation changes but behavior does not

RTL is often used as a more modern alternative to tools like **Enzyme**, which focus heavily on component internals. RTL intentionally pushes you away from this style of testing.

Here are some important points to remember:

- RTL is not a test runner; it is a helper library used with a test runner.
- It works with Jest, Vitest, and other runners.
- It is built on top of the DOM Testing Library, which powers all of its query logic.

Key Features

- **Lightweight:** RTL is focused on testing components from the perspective of the users, rather than the implementation details. This approach encourages better testing practices and results in more maintainable tests.
- **Accessibility-Focused**: By encouraging the selection of elements based on their role or text, RTL naturally steers developers towards building more accessible applications.
- **Integration with Jest**: While RTL can be used with any test runner, it integrates seamlessly with Jest and offers a comprehensive testing solution out of the box.

- **Custom Jest Matchers**: It extends Jest with additional custom matchers and makes it easier to write tests for DOM elements.
- **Support for Hooks and Events**: RTL provides utilities to test custom hooks and simulate user events (clicks, typing, and so on), while enabling comprehensive testing scenarios.

Key Differences from Other Testing Libraries

React Testing Library differs from libraries like Enzyme in both design and philosophy in the following ways:

- **Focuses on User Interactions, Not Internals:** RTL tests simulate how users interact with the app: clicking buttons, typing in inputs, reading text. It does not expose component instances or lifecycle methods.
- **Works Directly with the DOM:** RTL returns DOM nodes, not React component instances. You assert on actual rendered output, not internal state.
- **Smaller, Simpler API:** Enzyme exposes many helpers to inspect and manipulate internals; RTL keeps the API small and focused on queries and events. This naturally discourages implementation-heavy tests.
- **Accessibility-First Querying:** RTL promotes `getByRole`, `getByLabelText`, and visible text queries. This nudges you to build more accessible UIs while writing your tests.
- **No Shallow Rendering:** Enzyme supports shallow rendering; RTL does not. Enzyme's shallow rendering stops at the component boundary, meaning child components are not rendered or interacted with. This can hide integration issues and give a false sense of confidence because you are testing implementation details rather than real behavior. React Testing Library intentionally avoids shallow rendering and renders components in a full DOM using `jsdom`. This forces tests to interact with components the same way users do—through rendered output, events, and accessibility roles—ensuring that parent and child components work together correctly in real usage scenarios.

Overall, RTL's design leads to test suites that are more durable and relevant to real user behavior.

Core Principles of React Testing Library

React Testing Library is built around several core principles that guide its design and usage. These principles focus on improving the quality and maintainability of tests by ensuring they closely resemble the way users interact with applications. Here is an outline of these core principles:

- **Test From the User's Perspective**: The primary principle of React Testing Library is to test the application as users would use it. This means focusing on the user interface and user interactions rather than the internal implementation of the components. By adhering to this principle, tests become more robust and less likely to break with implementation changes that don't affect user experience.
- **Avoid Testing Implementation Details:** Tests should not rely on the internal workings of components, such as state, props, or lifecycle methods. Testing implementation details can lead to fragile tests that break with refactoring, even when the user-facing functionality remains unchanged. React Testing Library encourages writing tests that only interact with the components' outputs (that is, the DOM and any side effects).
- **Be Accessible:** Encouraging the selection of elements by accessible queries such as role, labels, and text content, not only makes tests more resilient but also nudges developers towards creating more accessible applications. This principle aligns with the idea that good testing practices should complement good development practices, which benefits the end-users.
- **Lightweight Wrapper Around the DOM**: React Testing Library acts as a lightweight wrapper around the DOM, while providing utilities to interact with it as a user would. This approach ensures that the library remains simple and focused on user-centric testing rather than offering a broad suite of tools for manipulating component internals.
- **Async and Event-based Testing:** As modern web applications are highly interactive and often rely on asynchronous operations, React Testing Library offers first-class support for testing asynchronous code and user events. This makes it easier to write tests for a wide range of user interactions, including those that involve fetching data, updating the DOM, and handling user inputs.
- **Integration Over Unit Testing**: While React Testing Library can be used for unit testing, its principles and tools are geared more towards integration and functional testing. By encouraging tests that cover how different parts of the application work together from the user's perspective, it helps ensure that the system works as intended in real-world scenarios.

These principles lead to tests that are meaningful, maintainable, and stable as your app evolves.

Installation and Setup for React Testing Library

While React Testing Library itself provides the utilities for rendering components and interacting with them in tests, Jest is the recommended testing framework to run your tests, and **@testing-library/jest-dom** offers custom matchers that make it easier to write assertions.

To start using React Testing Library in a JavaScript React project, install:

```
npm install --save-dev jest @testing-library/react @testing-library/
jest-dom jest-environment-jsdom
```

- **jest**: Test runner and assertion library
- **@testing-library/react**: Core React testing utilities
- **@testing-library/jest-dom**: Extra DOM matchers like **toBeInTheDocument**
- **jest-environment-jsdom**: Simulated browser environment for Jest

If you are using **Vite**, you can still use Jest, but Vitest is often simpler. We will cover Vitest briefly after Jest.

Jest Configuration

Create **jest.config.cjs** in your project root as follows:

```
module.exports = {
  testEnvironment: 'jsdom',
  setupFilesAfterEnv: ['<rootDir>/setupTests.js'],
   testMatch: ['<rootDir>/src/**/*.test.jsx', '<rootDir>/src/**/*.test.
js'],
};
```

Then create **setupTests.js** which is demonstrated here:

```
import '@testing-library/jest-dom';
```

Add a test script to **package.json** as shown:

```
"scripts": {
  "test": "jest"
}
```

Now you can run tests with the following command:

```
npm test
```

Understanding "No tests found"

If Jest prints the following message:

`No tests found`

It means that no files matched its test patterns (**`testMatch`** / **`testRegex`**).

Some common reasons behind this message might be the following:

- Your test file is not named correctly (for example, **`GreetingTest.js`** instead of **`Greeting.test.js`**)
- The test file is not under **`src/`**, when Jest expects it to be there.
- **`testMatch`** is misconfigured.

For example, if you use:

```
testMatch: ['<rootDir>/src/**/*.test.jsx', '<rootDir>/src/**/*.test.js'],
```

Then Jest will only detect tests like:

- **`src/Greeting.test.jsx`**
- **`src/components/Header.test.js`**

Rename or move your files to match these patterns.

Crafting Your First Test with Jest + React Testing Library

Assuming Jest is configured as above and you already have **`Greeting.jsx`**:

Create a test file next to it as shown here:

```
// src/Greeting.test.jsx
import { render, screen } from '@testing-library/react';
import '@testing-library/jest-dom';
import Greeting from './Greeting';

describe('Greeting component', () => {
  test('renders the correct greeting text', () => {
    const testName = 'Jest';

    render(<Greeting name={testName} />);

    const greetingElement = screen.getByText(`Hello, ${testName}!`);
    expect(greetingElement).toBeInTheDocument();
  });
});
```

This test performs the following functions via the indicated terms:

- **`render`**: Mounts the Greeting component into a jsdom DOM
- **`screen.getByText`**: Finds the **`<h1>`** element by its text content
- **`expect(...).toBeInTheDocument()`**: Asserts that the element exists in the rendered output

Run: `npm test`

Jest should discover **`Greeting.test.jsx`** and execute this test.

Alternative: Using Vitest with React Testing Library

If you are using **Vite**, **Vitest** is usually the smoother choice `and can be installed via:t": "jest"`

```
npm install --save-dev vitest @testing-library/react @testing-library/
jest-dom jsdom
```

Add to **`package.json`** the following:

```
"scripts": {
  "test": "vitest"
}
```

You can also add a basic **`vitest.config.js`** (if you want explicit setup) via:

```
import { defineConfig } from 'vitest/config';

export default defineConfig({
  test: {
    environment: 'jsdom',
    setupFiles: './setupTests.js',
  },
});
```

Your test code (like **`Greeting.test.jsx`**) stays exactly the same; only the runner changes (**`jest → vitest`**).

React Testing Library Functionalities

React Testing Library (RTL) provides a focused set of utilities that help you test React components based on how users actually interact with the UI. Instead of exposing component internals, RTL gives you tools to render components, query the DOM, fire user actions, and handle asynchronous updates.

Core Functions

At the heart of React Testing Library are several core functions that form the backbone of most testing scenarios. These are mentioned as follows:

- **render:** This is your starting point. The render function takes a React component and mounts it into a simulated DOM. This enables you to question and interact with it in your tests. It is akin to placing a component on a test bench, which is ready for examination and interaction.

```
render(<MyComponent />);
```

- **screen:** Think of screen as your toolbox for finding elements within the rendered output. It provides access to various query functions that mimic how users find elements on the page by text, role, label, and so on. Using screen encourages a user-centric approach to testing, focusing on what is actually visible and accessible to users.

```
screen.getByText('Submit');
screen.getByRole('button', { name: /save/i });
```

- **fireEvent:** To simulate user actions like clicking a button or entering text into an input field, RTL offers **fireEvent**. This function allows you to dispatch browser events to elements, while effectively mimicking user interactions in a controlled test environment.

```
fireEvent.click(button);
fireEvent.change(input, { target: { value: 'Hello' } });
```

- **waitFor**: Modern web applications often involve asynchronous operations like fetching data from an API. **waitFor** is a utility that pauses your test until certain conditions are met or elements appear, while ensuring that asynchronous state changes or DOM updates are accounted for before assertions are made.

```
await waitFor(() => {
  expect(screen.getByText('Loaded')).toBeInTheDocument();
});
```

Query Types

RTL's querying functions are designed to mimic the way users find elements on the screen, while supporting a wide range of queries based on text content, display value, role, test IDs, and more. These queries are divided into several categories such as:

- **getBy***: It returns the first matching node for a given query, while throwing an error if no elements match or if more than one match is found. It is ideal for when an element is expected to be present in the DOM.

```
screen.getByText('Hello');
```

- **getAllBy***: It is similar to getBy*, but returns an array of all matching nodes. It is useful for asserting multiple elements are present.
  ```
  screen.getAllByRole('listitem');
  ```
- **queryBy***: It is like getBy*, but returns null if no elements match. This is useful for asserting an element is not present in the document.
  ```
  expect(screen.queryByText('Error')).toBeNull();
  ```
- **queryAllBy***: It returns an array of all matching nodes or an empty array if no elements are found. It is useful for querying multiple items without causing a test to fail if they are absent.
  ```
  screen.queryAllByRole('button');
  ```
- **findBy***: It returns a promise that is resolved when an element is found or rejected if no element is found after a timeout. These queries are useful for dealing with elements that appear as a result of asynchronous operations.
  ```
  const item = await screen.findByText('Data Loaded');
  ```

Cleanup and Teardown Functions

To ensure that tests are isolated and do not affect each other, RTL automatically cleans up after each test and removes the rendered components from the test environment. This cleanup mechanism prevents tests from inadvertently interacting with each other through shared state or lingering DOM elements. Additionally, RTL provides utilities like cleanup for manual cleanup in more complex scenarios, which ensures a fresh start for each test.

These tools help you write tests that are:

- User-focused
- More reliable
- Less dependent on implementation details
- Easier to maintain as components evolve

By sticking to RTL's principles and using these core functions correctly, your test suite remains aligned with real-world usage and avoids fragile, internal-detail-driven testing.

Rendering Components and Event Triggering in Testing

React Testing Library makes it straightforward to render components, simulate user interactions, mock dependencies, and test asynchronous UI updates. These are the core operations used in almost every React test.

Rendering Components: Use **`render()`** to mount your component into a simulated DOM as follows:

```
render(<MyComponent />);
```

This allows you to interact with the UI exactly the way a user would.

Mocking Dependencies: Components often rely on external modules or APIs. Mock these dependencies using **`jest.mock()`** or **`jest.fn()`** to isolate component behavior as shown here:

```
jest.mock('../api/userApi');
const mockFn = jest.fn();
```

Simulating User Interactions: RTL provides **`fireEvent`** and **`userEvent`** for simulating interactions in the following manner:

```
fireEvent.click(button);
await userEvent.type(input, 'Hello');
```

Prefer **`userEvent`** for realistic typing, clicking, and keyboard interactions.

Handling Async UI Updates: Many components update UI asynchronously. Use **`findBy*`** queries or **`waitFor()`** to wait for updates:

```
const item = await screen.findByText('Loaded');
await waitFor(() => expect(screen.getByText('Done')).
toBeInTheDocument());
```

This ensures that your assertions happen after the UI finishes updating.

Enhancing Element Selection with ARIA Roles

React Testing Library encourages selecting elements using the same semantics that assistive technologies use. ARIA roles make components more accessible and make tests more reliable and readable.

Why ARIA Roles Matter

ARIA roles describe the semantic meaning of UI elements for assistive technologies like screen readers.

A few examples include:

- Button
- Textbox
- Link

- Alert
- Dialog

Using proper roles ensures that your application is accessible and allows RTL to query elements in a user-centric way.

Leveraging ARIA Roles for Element Selection

Leveraging ARIA roles allows tests to query elements the same way assistive technologies and users do. This approach improves test resilience by avoiding brittle selectors like class names or IDs that change frequently. Role-based queries are especially useful in forms, dialogs, modals, navigation menus, and interactive components, ensuring both accessibility compliance and behavior correctness are validated together.

Using `getByRole` and `queryByRole` Functions

RTL provides the **`getByRole`** and **`queryByRole`** among its querying functions that allow you to select elements based on their ARIA role. We have explained these functions as follows:

- **`getByRole`:** Use this when you expect the element to be present in the DOM. It throws an error if the element is not found, which makes it ideal for asserting that an element with a specific role exists.

  ```
  screen.getByRole('button', { name: /submit/i });
  ```

- **`queryByRole`**: This is the safer option when you are not sure if the element will be present. It returns null if the element is not found, which allows you to assert the absence of an element without causing your test to fail immediately.

  ```
  expect(screen.queryByRole('alert')).toBeNull();
  ```

Best Practices for ARIA Role Integration

- **Use Semantic HTML:** Whenever possible, use semantic HTML5 elements (like **`<button>`**, **`<nav>`**, **`<header>`**, **`<footer>`**, **`<article>`**, and **`<section>`**) that inherently carry the correct ARIA roles. This practice reduces the need to explicitly define ARIA roles and improve your application's accessibility.

- **Explicit Roles When Necessary:** For custom components or when semantic HTML elements cannot convey the exact role of an element (for instance, a div used as a button), explicitly set ARIA roles to ensure the element's purpose is clear.

  ```
  <div role="button" aria-label="Close modal">×</div>
  ```

- **Test for Accessibility:** Incorporate accessibility checks into your testing routine. Tools like Axe or Lighthouse can automate accessibility testing, while helping you identify and fix issues related to ARIA roles and other accessibility concerns.
- **Reflect User Interactions:** When writing tests, select elements by their roles to mimic how users, including those with disabilities, interact with your application. This approach not only improves test reliability but also reinforces the importance of building accessible web applications.

By integrating ARIA roles into both your application and testing practices, you can enhance the accessibility of your web application and ensure your tests validate the most user-centric aspects of your UI. This alignment between testing and accessibility best practices not only benefits users but also fosters a more inclusive web environment.

Conclusion

React Testing Library provides a practical, user-focused way to test React applications. Instead of relying on internal component details, RTL emphasizes how users actually interact with your UI through visible text, roles, inputs, and events. When combined with Jest or Vitest, it offers a fast, reliable testing environment that mirrors real browser behavior.

By learning how to render components, query the DOM, trigger user actions, and handle asynchronous updates, you now have the core tools needed to build stable and maintainable test suites. This approach ensures your tests remain accurate even as your implementation evolves, resulting in cleaner code, fewer regressions, and a more predictable development workflow.

With these fundamentals in place, you're ready to move toward writing more advanced tests, integrating mocks, and testing complex user flows with confidence.

Explore Jest and React Testing Library documentation (https://testing-library.com/docs/) for more advanced testing techniques and best practices.

CHAPTER 4

Advanced Testing Techniques

Introduction

We will begin this chapter by exploring advanced Jest techniques for sophisticated testing, where we will unveil the power of Snapshot Testing with advanced configurations. This section also covers the strategic use of Parameterized Tests with **`test.each`** for data-driven testing and the creation of Custom Matchers and Assertions to articulate specific testing criteria. These techniques enhance the clarity and expressiveness of your tests.

We will also delve into the art of simulating functionality by transitioning to Jest Mocking. We will explore the basics of mocking functions using **`jest.fn()`** and **`jest.mock`**. Additionally, we will discuss the nuances of spying on function calls with **`jest.spyOn()`**. This section also addresses the challenges of mocking external libraries and modules and equips you with the techniques to isolate your tests from external dependencies.

Lastly, we will learn to handle third-party libraries in tests via comprehensive strategies. Whether it is mocking API calls using **`jest.mock()`** for Axios or Fetch, simulating database interactions, or dealing with non-standard modules through **`setupFiles`** and **`moduleNameMapper`**, these strategies will ensure that your tests are both resilient and adaptable. Moreover, they will be capable of handling the complexities of modern JavaScript development.

Structure

This chapter covers the following topics:

- Advanced Jest Techniques
- Jest Mocking: Functions and Libraries
- Jest Handling of Third-Party Libraries in Tests
- Handling Non-Standard Modules: **`setupFiles`** and **`moduleNameMapper`**

Advanced Jest Techniques

Advanced Jest techniques help teams move beyond basic assertions and build test suites that scale with application complexity. Features like snapshot testing, parameterized tests, and custom matchers reduce duplication, improve readability, and make test intent explicit. Together, they enable faster maintenance, clearer failures, and more reliable long-term testing.

Snapshot Testing

Snapshot testing is a technique in software development used to ensure that a piece of code continues to produce the expected output over time. It works by taking a "**`snapshot`**" of the output (often UI components) and comparing it against a reference snapshot previously recorded. If there are any discrepancies between the two, the test fails, which indicates a change or a potential error. Within Jest's testing ecosystem, snapshot testing plays a crucial role by providing a straightforward and efficient method to track changes in the application's output. This helps developers quickly identify and address unintended modifications. This approach fits seamlessly into Jest's broader suite of testing tools and is designed to offer a comprehensive testing solution that emphasizes simplicity and ease of use.

Snapshot testing captures the expected state of your application's UI and compares it against future outputs to detect changes. It is pivotal for maintaining UI consistency as it automatically alerts developers to any unintended modifications. By ensuring that changes to the UI only occur when explicitly intended, snapshot testing preserves the user experience and helps in preventing regressions.

Basic Snapshot Testing

Imagine that you have a simple React component called **`ButtonComponent`**, which is shown here:

```
import React from 'react';
```

```
const ButtonComponent = ({ label }) => {
 return <button>{label}</button>
}

export default ButtonComponent;
```

A basic snapshot test using Jest might look like this:

```
import React from 'react';
import { render } from '@testing-library/react';
import ButtonComponent from './ButtonComponent';

it('Button renders correctly 1', () => {

 const { asFragment } = render(<ButtonComponent label="Click me" />);
 expect(asFragment()).toMatchSnapshot();

});
```

This test renders a Button component, takes a snapshot, and compares it to a reference snapshot stored alongside the test.

How Jest Matches Rendered Output with a Snapshot

- **Render → Serialize**: Your test renders the component (for example, with **`@testing-library/react`**). The result (a tree) is serialized via Jest's pretty-format into a stable string.
- **Locate Snapshot Entry**: Jest looks for a matching key in the snapshot file located at **`__snapshots__/ButtonComponent.test.jsx.snap`**.
    - The key is built from the test name (for example, "**`Button renders correctly 1`**").
- **Compare Strings**: Jest compares the current serialized string to the stored snapshot string byte-for-byte (whitespace included).
- **`Pass/Fail` and `Diff`**:
    - If they match, they pass.
    - If not, then Jest prints a unified **`diff`** (using **`jest-diff`**) to highlight additions/removals.
- **First Run/Missing Snapshot**: If no snapshot exists, Jest creates one.
- **Update Flow**: When legitimate UI changes occur, run with **`-u/--updateSnapshot`** (or press **`u`** in watch mode) to update snapshots.
- **Inline vs External**: **`toMatchSnapshot()`** writes to a .snap file; **`toMatchInlineSnapshot()`** stores the snapshot inline inside your test for tighter coupling.

When you run your test the first time, Jest writes a .snap like this:_

```
exports[`Button renders correctly 1 1`] = `
 <DocumentFragment>
   <button>
     Click me
   </button>
 </DocumentFragment>`;
```

The file is auto-generated; do not hand-edit. Each export corresponds to a single **`expect(...).toMatchSnapshot()`** call in your test.

Advanced configurations in snapshot testing allow for more nuanced control over how tests capture and compare snapshots, especially vital for complex applications with dynamic content such as dates and user-specific information. These configurations enable developers to fine-tune snapshot tests to ignore or replace certain variable elements, while ensuring that tests remain robust and relevant. For sophisticated applications, these advanced settings are crucial for maintaining high accuracy in tests as they accommodate the variability without sacrificing the integrity of the snapshot testing process.

Advanced Configurations for Dynamic Content

Dynamic content such as timestamps and randomized data presents a unique challenge to snapshot testing by introducing variability that can cause tests to fail even when the application is functioning correctly. Strategies to handle these elements include using mock functions or libraries to generate consistent output during tests, employing custom serializers to normalize dynamic content, or leveraging Jest's ability to ignore or replace specific parts of the snapshot. These approaches maintain the effectiveness of snapshot tests in applications where content changes frequently.

For a component displaying dynamic content, such as a Timestamp component that shows the current time, consider the following example:

```
import React from 'react';

const Timestamp = () => {
 return <div>{new Date().toString()}</div>;
};
```

You might use mock functions to freeze time within your test.:

```
import React from 'react';
import { render } from '@testing-library/react';
import Timestamp from './Timestamp';

beforeAll(() => {
```

```
  jest.useFakeTimers().setSystemTime(new Date('2020-01-01T00:00:00Z'));
 });
 afterAll(() => {
  jest.useRealTimers();
 });
 it('renders a consistent timestamp', () => {
   const { asFragment } = render(<Timestamp />);
   expect(asFragment()).toMatchSnapshot();
 });
```

This approach ensures that the timestamp in your snapshot remains consistent across tests. Serializers in Jest allow for custom formatting of snapshot data, while enabling the testing framework to handle complex data structures or specific data formats gracefully. By customizing serializers, developers can ensure that their snapshots accurately represent the state of their application's UI or data in a way that's both meaningful and manageable. This customization is particularly useful for dealing with unique data types or formats that require normalization or specific handling to maintain consistency across tests. For instance, a custom serializer could be designed to convert complex objects into a simplified, test-friendly format, which ensures that snapshots remain relevant and readable despite the underlying complexity.

Custom Serializers

If your application includes a component that renders complex data structures, you could use a custom serializer to simplify the snapshot. For instance, for a **`UserProfile`** component might look like this:

```
const UserProfile = ({ user }) => (
 <div>
  <h1>{user.name}</h1>
  <h3>{user.id}</h3>
  <p>{user.email}</p>
 </div>
);
```

You might write a serializer that simplifies the user object here, as shown:

```
expect.addSnapshotSerializer({
 test: (val) =>
   val != null &&
   typeof val === 'object' &&
   'name' in val &&
   'email' in val,
 print: (val) =>
```

```
  `User: ${val.name}, Email: ${val.email.substring(0, 10)}...`,
});
```

Property Matchers with Snapshot Tests

Property matchers in snapshot tests enhance test precision by allowing developers to specify how certain parts of the snapshot should be matched or ignored. This is particularly useful for dynamic data within snapshots, like dates or random values, as it ensures that the focus remains on the significant parts of the output. By employing property matchers, tests can ignore or replace specific snapshot data, which makes them more robust and focused on the actual areas of interest. This approach significantly improves the effectiveness of snapshot testing for complex applications.

For components with parts of their output that are unpredictable or irrelevant for the test, such as IDs or timestamps, you can use property matchers to focus on the important parts, such the ones shown here:

```
import React from 'react';
import { render } from '@testing-library/react';
import UserProfile from './UserProfile';

it('matches the user profile, ignoring dynamic fields', () => {
  const user = {
    id: Math.random(), // dynamic
    name: 'John Doe',
    email: 'john@example.com',
  };

  expect(user).toMatchSnapshot({
    id: expect.any(Number),
  });
});
```

- **Commit Snapshots:** Snapshots should be committed to your version control system. This allows you to track changes over time and ensures that every team member is working with the latest version.
- **Review Snapshot Diffs:** Always review the diffs of updated snapshots during code review processes. This helps catch unintentional changes and keeps your snapshots meaningful.
- **Keep Snapshots Small and Focused**: Large snapshots can be difficult to decipher when they fail. If possible, break down components into smaller, more testable units to keep snapshots understandable and manageable.

- **Update Snapshots with Intention**: When a snapshot test fails due to intentional changes in the component, update the snapshot only after verifying that the change is correct and as expected.

Update all snapshots using:

- ```
  One-shot update
  npx jest --updateSnapshot
  ```
- ```
  or shorthand
  npx jest -u
  ```

Update a single file (recommended) using:

- ```
  Limit to the test file
  npx jest path/to/UserProfile.test.jsx -u
  ```

Update a single test within a file using:

- ```
  Use a name pattern to target exactly one test
  npx jest path/to/UserProfile.test.jsx -t="renders user profile" -u
  ```
- **Use Descriptive Test Names:** Clearly name your snapshot tests to reflect what they are testing. This makes it easier to identify the purpose of a snapshot when reading test files or reviewing failed tests.
- **Integrate Snapshot Testing with Other Test Types:** Do not rely solely on snapshot testing. Combine it with other types of tests (unit, integration, end-to-end) for comprehensive coverage.
- **Handle Dynamic Data**: For components displaying dynamic content (for example, dates, random IDs), use mock functions or Jest's functionalities to ensure consistency across test runs.
- **Regularly Prune Old Snapshots**: Remove snapshots for deleted or refactored components to keep the snapshot directory clean and up-to-date.
- **Over-Reliance on Snapshots:** While snapshot tests are useful, they should not be your only form of testing as they cannot catch logic errors or verify interactive functionalities effectively.
- **Snapshot Noise**: Frequently updated components (due to dynamic content) can lead to frequent snapshot updates, which creates noise and potentially hides meaningful changes. Use mocking and static data wherever appropriate.
- **Ignoring Snapshot Updates:** Automatically updating snapshots without reviewing changes can lead to missed regressions. Always inspect snapshot updates carefully.

- **Large and Unwieldy Snapshots**: Large snapshots can be hard to review and understand. Focus on testing smaller, isolated parts of your components to make snapshots more meaningful and manageable.
- **UI Regression Testing:** Snapshot tests are ideal for detecting unintended changes in UI components to ensure that updates to the codebase are not regressing the visual output of your components.
- **Component Output Verification:** Verify that components render correctly given a set of props or state, while capturing the rendered output to confirm it meets expectations.
- **Refactoring Validation:** After refactoring a component, use snapshot tests to validate that the output remains consistent. This ensures that the refactoring hasn't introduced any regressions.

Parameterized Tests with `test.each`

Parameterized testing allows for the efficient execution of the same test logic across multiple sets of data. Jest's **`test.each`** function is a powerful tool that supports this approach and enables developers to write concise and readable tests for varied input and output combinations. This technique simplifies the testing process for functions that should behave consistently across a range of values, reducing redundancy, and potential for error in test code. By preparing a table of test cases, where each row represents a different set of arguments and expected results, developers can leverage **`test.each`** to iterate over these cases while significantly increasing test coverage without a proportional increase in code complexity.

Parameterized tests allow you to run the same test with different inputs. Jest's **`test.each`** method is a powerful feature for this purpose, as it enables you to easily test multiple scenarios with a table of arguments. This is particularly useful when you want to ensure that your function or component behaves correctly across a range of conditions.

The **`test.each`** method can be used in two formats: array of arrays or tagged template literal.

Array of arrays looks like this:

```
describe('multiply function', () => {
  test.each([
    [1, 2, 2],
    [2, 3, 6],
    [3, 4, 12],
  ])('multiply %i by %i equals %i',
```

```
    (a, b, expected) => {
      expect(a * b).toBe(expected);
    });
});
```

In this example, each sub-array represents a set of arguments to be passed to the test function. %i is used as a placeholder in the test name for each argument.

Tagged template literal looks like this:

```
describe('add function', () => {
  test.each`
    a    | b    | expected
    ${1} | ${2} | ${3}
    ${2} | ${3} | ${5}
    ${4} | ${5} | ${9}
  `('adds $a + $b to equal $expected', ({ a, b, expected }) => {
    expect(a + b).toBe(expected);
  });
});
```

This format makes it easy to see the table of parameters and expected results. The variables (a, b, expected) are enclosed in ${} within the template string.

Advanced Usage for React Components

Parameterized tests can also be beneficial for testing React components with different props. For example, if you have a Button component with a prop size that can be either "**`small`**", "**`medium`**", or "**`large`**", you could use **`test.each`** to test all sizes in the following way:

```
import { render } from '@testing-library/react';
import Button from './Button';

describe('Button component sizes', () => {
  test.each`
    size
    ${'small'}
    ${'medium'}
    ${'large'}
  `('renders a $size button', ({ size }) => {
   const { getByTestId } = render(<Button size={size}>Click me</Button>);
    const button = getByTestId('button');
    expect(button).toHaveClass(size);
  });
});
```

This assumes your Button component uses the size prop to determine a class name that affects its styling, and that you have set `data-testid="button"` on the button element.

- **Clearly Define Test Cases:** Structure your test cases clearly within the `test.each` table or array. This makes it easier to understand what each test case is verifying.
- **Use Descriptive Test Names**: Use the placeholders (`%s`, `%i`, `%p`, and so on.) provided by Jest to include variable data in your test names. This makes test reports more informative and helps quickly identify failing cases.
- **Limit Scope per Test**: Each parameterized test should focus on a single aspect or behavior of the function/component. Avoid combining unrelated assertions just because they can be parameterized together.
- **Keep Data Close to Tests**: Define your test data as close to your tests as possible to avoid jumping around files or code blocks to understand the test. This improves readability and maintainability.
- **Avoid Overly Large Data Sets**: While `test.each` is powerful for handling multiple test cases, excessively large datasets can make tests hard to maintain and slow down test execution. Focus on representative data points and edge cases.
- **Use Tagged Template Literal for Complex Data**: When dealing with multiple parameters or needing a clear layout of the test cases, prefer the tagged template literal syntax for better readability.
- **Testing Across Various Inputs**: Use parameterized tests for functions that are expected to yield different results for different inputs. For example, test a function that calculates tax based on income levels.
- **Handling Edge Cases**: Efficiently cover edge cases for your functions, like testing how your function behaves with zero, negative, or extremely large values.
- **Validating Data Transformations**: When testing functions that transform input data in various ways (for example, parsing, formatting), parameterized tests can help you verify correctness across a range of inputs.
- **UI Component Variants**: In React applications, test that a component correctly renders with different props, such as testing different sizes, themes, or configurations of a UI component to ensure that each variant behaves as expected.
- **Form Validation Functions**: Test form validation logic for a variety of inputs to ensure that validations are correctly identifying valid and invalid inputs.

- **Internationalization and Localization:** Verify that UI components or functions correctly handle different locales, currencies, date formats, and so on, by parameterizing the tests with locale-specific cases.
- **Redundancy in Test Cases**: Avoid duplicating test cases with slight variations that do not add value or cover new paths in your code.
- **Complexity in Test Data:** While **`test.each`** supports complex data structures, overly complex test cases can make tests hard to read and maintain. Simplify wherever possible.
- **Neglecting Other Types of Tests**: Parameterized tests are powerful, but they should not be the only tool in your testing toolkit. Use them in combination with unit, integration, and end-to-end tests for comprehensive coverage.

By adhering to these practices and being mindful of the common use cases and pitfalls, you can leverage Jest's **`test.each`** to write efficient, comprehensive, and maintainable tests for a wide range of scenarios in your applications.

Custom Matchers and Assertions

Custom Matchers and Assertions extend Jest's built-in expectation library, which allows developers to tailor the testing framework to suit their specific needs. Creating custom matchers can streamline tests by encapsulating complex assertion logic into reusable functions. This not only improves test readability but also enhances the expressiveness of test suites, which makes it easier to understand what each test is verifying. Custom matchers are particularly useful when dealing with domain-specific logic or when the default assertions provided by Jest do not meet the unique requirements of your project. By employing custom matchers, developers can create a more intuitive and maintainable testing suite that precisely reflects the intentions behind each test.

Jest allows the extension of its expect API by adding custom matchers. This is done using the **`expect.extend(matchers)`** method, where matchers is an object containing one or more custom matcher functions.

Creating a Custom Matcher

Suppose you are frequently testing if numbers are even in your test suite. You can create a custom matcher **`toBeEven`** to simplify these assertions as shown here:

```
expect.extend({
  toBeEven(received) {
    const pass = received % 2 === 0;
    if (pass) {
      return {
```

```
        message: () => `expected ${received} not to be even`,
        pass: true,
      };
    } else {
      return {
        message: () => `expected ${received} to be even`,
        pass: false,
      };
    }
  },
});

test('2 is even', () => {
  expect(2).toBeEven();
});
test('3 is not even', () => {
  expect(3).not.toBeEven();
});
```

- **Clarity**: Custom matchers can make tests more readable and expressive, making it clear what you are testing for.
- **Reusability**: You can encapsulate repetitive assertion logic in a single, reusable matcher.
- **Domain-Specific**: You can create matchers specific to your application's domain, which will make your tests more aligned with your business logic.

Custom Assertions with Testing Libraries

In addition to Jest's built-in functionality, other testing libraries, such as those used with React (for example, React Testing Library), also support the use of custom matchers. For example, **@testing-library/jest-dom** offers a set of custom matchers to use in testing DOM elements, while enhancing readability and expressiveness when working with React components.

```
import React from 'react';
import { render } from '@testing-library/react';
import '@testing-library/jest-dom';

test('renders a visible element', () => {
  const { getByText } = render(<div>Visible Content</div>);
  const element = getByText('Visible Content');
  expect(element).toBeVisible();
});
```

In this example, **`toBeVisible`** is a custom matcher provided by **`@testing-library/jest-dom`** that makes it straightforward to test if an element is rendered and visible to the user.

- **Clearly Define Use Cases:** Only create custom matchers for repetitive assertions that enhance readability and reduce boilerplate. Avoid creating them for one-off tests where they do not add value.
- **Ensure Readability**: The names and messages of your custom matchers should make tests more understandable. Prefer expressive names that clearly state the expectation, such as **`toBeEven`** for checking if a number is even.
- **Provide Informative Error Messages**: Custom matchers should return helpful error messages that clearly explain why a test failed. This makes it easier for developers to diagnose issues.
- **Maintain Consistency**: Apply custom matchers consistently across your test suite. Inconsistent use can lead to confusion and reduce the overall benefit of having them.
- **Write Tests for Your Matchers**: Since custom matchers are part of your testing infrastructure, they should be reliable. Write tests for your matchers to ensure that they work as expected and remain reliable as you update your codebase.
- **Document Your Custom Matchers**: Ensure that your team knows about the available custom matchers, how and when to use them, and their benefits. Documentation helps in maintaining consistency and maximizing their usage.
- **Over-Engineering**: Creating overly complex matchers for simple assertions can introduce unnecessary complexity into your tests. Aim for simplicity and readability.
- **Overuse**: While custom matchers can be powerful, not every assertion needs to be abstracted behind a custom matcher. Overuse can lead to a bloated testing suite that is hard to understand and maintain.
- **Lack of Maintenance**: As your application evolves, your custom matchers may need to be updated or refined. Neglecting to maintain them can lead to misleading test failures or false positives.
- **Poor Error Messaging**: Vague or misleading error messages from custom matchers can make debugging failed tests difficult. Ensure error messages accurately describe the expectation and the reason for failure.

- **Ignoring Context**: Custom matchers should be meaningful in the context of your application. Creating matchers that are too generic or unrelated to your domain can reduce the clarity and relevance of your tests.
- **Creating Redundant Matchers:** Before creating a new custom matcher, check if a matcher exists already (either built-in or from a third-party library) and meets your needs. Redundant matchers can clutter your test suite and confuse team members.

By following these practices, you can leverage custom matchers and assertions to build a more robust, readable, and maintainable test suite. These tools can significantly enhance your testing strategy and improve the quality of your software when used judiciously.

Jest Mocking: Functions and Libraries

Jest offers powerful mocking capabilities that are essential for isolating tests and controlling the behavior of dependencies. Mocking in Jest can be applied to functions, modules, and even entire libraries, which enables developers to simulate the behavior of real objects in a controlled environment. This ensures that tests are deterministic and not influenced by external factors such as network requests, file system operations, or interactions with databases.

Mocking Functions with `jest.fn()`

`jest.fn()` allows you to create a mock function that can be used in place of a real function in your tests. This is particularly useful when you want to assert that a function is called with the correct arguments, a specific number of times, or to manually specify a function's return value or implementation for the purpose of a test.

```
const mockCallback = jest.fn();
mockCallback.mockReturnValue('I am a mock!');

console.log(mockCallback()); // Outputs: "I am a mock!"

// Assert that the mock function was called
expect(mockCallback).toHaveBeenCalled();
```

You can also use `jest.spyOn()` to mock a module's method within a test, which will allow you to control the return value or implementation detail of that method:

```
import * as myModule from './myModule';

test('mock implementation of a module function', () => {
 const someFunctionMock = jest
```

```
    .spyOn(myModule, 'someFunction')
    .mockImplementation(() => 'mock value');

  expect(myModule.someFunction('input')).toBe('mock value');
  expect(someFunctionMock).toHaveBeenCalledWith('input');

  someFunctionMock.mockRestore();
});
```

Mocking Modules with `jest.mock()`

`jest.mock()` is used to mock entire modules. This is particularly useful when a module has side effects just from importing it or when you want to mock the module's exports with specific values or implementations.

When you call **`jest.mock('moduleName')`**, Jest replaces the module's exports with a mocked version, thereby allowing you to specify return values or implementations for any of its exported functions.

Assume you have a module named math.js with a function add, as shown here:

```
// math.js
const add = (a, b) => a + b;
module.exports = { add };
```

You can mock this entire module as follows:

```
// In your test file
jest.mock('./math.js', () => ({
  add: jest.fn().mockReturnValue('mocked add'),
}));

import { add } from './math.js';

test('adds numbers using a mocked implementation', () => {
  expect(add(1, 2)).toBe('mocked add');
  expect(add).toHaveBeenCalledWith(1, 2);
});
```

Use **`jest.fn()`** when:

- You need to create a mock function in isolation.
- You want to mock a function passed as a prop in React components.
- You are testing how a function interacts with other parts of your code (for example, was it called, what arguments was it called with).

Use **`jest.mock()`** when:

- You need to mock an entire module or package.

- You want to set up default mock implementations for all exports of a module, possibly with specific behaviors for certain tests.
- You dealing with modules that have side effects upon importing and wish to avoid those during tests.

Mocking Return Values and Implementation

Mocking functions and libraries in Jest is a powerful feature that allows developers to replace complex, unpredictable, or external dependencies with simplified versions that produce controlled outputs. This capability is crucial for writing unit tests that are deterministic, fast, and focused on testing a specific piece of code without interference from other parts of the system. Here is an overview focusing on how to mock return values and implementations.

Mocking Return Values

Mocking return values and implementation details in Jest is a key aspect of unit testing that allows you to simulate the behavior of functions and modules to ensure your tests are both isolated and focused. This process enables you to specify what mocked functions return or how they behave when invoked, which makes it easier to test components or functions under specific conditions without relying on their real implementations or external systems.

You can specify what a mock function should return using **`.mockReturnValue()`** or **`.mockReturnValueOnce()`**, as shown here:

```
 const mockFunction = jest.fn();
mockFunction.mockReturnValue('default value');

// For specific calls
mockFunction.mockReturnValueOnce('first call');
mockFunction.mockReturnValueOnce('second call');

console.log(mockFunction()); // "first call"
console.log(mockFunction()); // "second call"
console.log(mockFunction()); // "default value"
```

Mocking Implementations

Instead of just returning values, you can also define a custom implementation for a mock function using **`.mockImplementation()`** or **`.mockImplementationOnce()`** as done in the example here:

```
const mockFunction = jest.fn();

 // Define a custom implementation
```

```
mockFunction.mockImplementation((x, y) => x + y);

// For specific calls
mockFunction.mockImplementationOnce(() => 'first call');
mockFunction.mockImplementationOnce(() => 'second call');

console.log(mockFunction());      // "first call"
console.log(mockFunction());      // "second call"
console.log(mockFunction(5, 3));  // 8
```

When dealing with entire modules, you can use **`jest.mock()`** to override their exports with mocked functions, including specific return values or implementations. This is demonstrated here:

```
// Mocking an entire module
jest.mock('myModule', () => {
  return {
    fetchData: jest.fn(() => Promise.resolve('mock data')),
  };
});

// Now, when myModule.fetchData is called anywhere in your tests,
// it will return 'mock data'
```

- **Clear Mocks: Use `jest.clearAllMocks()`** or **`mockFunction.mockClear()`** to clear any previously stored calls and results. This is important for tests that rely on the mock function's call history.
- **Restore Originals**: If you override a module using **`jest.mock()`**, consider restoring the original module in your test teardown using **`jest.resetModules()`** or **`jest.restoreAllMocks()`** to ensure that other tests are not affected by the mocked state.
- **Keep Tests Focused**: Mock out only the necessary parts of your dependencies to keep your tests focused on the code being tested. Over-mocking can lead to tests that can no longer effectively validate the real-world scenario.

Mocking functions and modules in Jest is a cornerstone of writing effective unit tests in JavaScript, which allows developers to create isolated and deterministic tests by controlling the behavior of dependencies.

Spying on Function Calls: `jest.spyOn()`

Spying on function calls is a technique used in testing to observe and interact with the behavior of functions without necessarily altering their implementations. Jest's **`spyOn()`** function is a powerful tool for this purpose, enabling you to track calls to object methods and access data about those calls, such as how many times they were called, what arguments were passed, and what values were returned. Additionally, **jest.spyOn()** allows you to change the implementation of the spied method, either temporarily for the scope of a test or for the duration of the entire test suite, depending on how it is used.

Suppose you have an object calculator with a method add that you want to test:

```
// A simple calculator object
const calculator = {
  add: (a, b) => a + b,
};
```

You can use **jest.spyOn()** to observe calls to **calculator.add**:

```
describe('calculator.add', () => {
it('calls the add method', () => {
 const addSpy = jest.spyOn(calculator, 'add');
 const result = calculator.add(2, 3);
 expect(addSpy).toHaveBeenCalledWith(2, 3);
 expect(result).toBe(5);
addSpy.mockRestore(); // Optional: Restores the original implementation
});
});
```

Mocking Return Values and Implementations with jest.spyOn()

While spying, you might want to temporarily alter the behavior of the spied method:

```
describe('mock implementation of add', () => {
 it('can mock the implementation', () => {
 const addMock = jest.spyOn(calculator, 'add').mockImplementation(() =>
'mocked value');

  expect(calculator.add(5, 2)).toBe('mocked value');
  expect(addMock).toHaveBeenCalled();
  addMock.mockRestore(); // Restores the original implementation
 });
});
```

- **Verifying Call Counts and Arguments**: Spy on methods to assert they were called the correct number of times and with the expected arguments. This is useful for callbacks and event handler testing.

- **Intercepting Return Values**: Alter the return value of a method in your tests to simulate different scenarios such as error conditions or edge cases without changing the actual method.
- **Testing the Interaction Between Objects**: Ensure that objects interact correctly by spying on method calls and verifying that these interactions happen as expected.
- **Restoration**: Always restore the original implementation after your test if you change the behavior of the spied method. This can be done using `mockRestore()` or by cleaning up in an `afterEach` block.
- **Isolation**: Use spying to test the interaction between parts of your application in isolation, without relying on the actual implementation of external services or modules.
- **Minimal Interference**: Prefer using `spyOn()` when you want to observe the behavior of a function without modifying its implementation, while keeping your tests as close to real-world scenarios as possible.
- **Overuse:** Relying too heavily on spies for every test can lead to brittle tests that break with implementation changes. Focus on the public API and outcomes rather than internal methods.
- **Forgetting to Restore:** Not restoring the original implementation after a test can lead to unexpected behavior in subsequent tests, which might result in difficult-to-diagnose errors.
- `jest.spyOn()` is an essential tool in the Jest ecosystem for creating flexible and robust tests, which allows developers to monitor and modify the behavior of functions in a controlled testing environment whenever deemed necessary.

Mocking External Libraries and Modules

Mocking external libraries and modules is a common practice in unit testing to isolate the code under test from external dependencies. This approach allows you to control and simulate the behavior of these dependencies, thereby ensuring that your tests are focused on the internal logic of your application while avoiding side effects and interactions with external systems. Jest provides a powerful and flexible system for mocking external libraries and modules. Here is how to do it:

`jest.mock()` is used to automatically mock the entire module. When you mock a module, all its methods are replaced with mock functions that have no implementation.

Mocking a Module

Suppose you have a module math.js that you use in your application:

```
// math.js
const add = (a, b) => a + b;
const subtract = (a, b) => a - b;

module.exports = {
  add,
  subtract
};
```

You will use this module in your application: `const doAdd = (a, b) => math.add(a, b);`

```
// app.js
// app.js
const math = require('./math');

const doAdd = (a, b) => math.add(a, b);
const doSubtract = (a, b) => math.subtract(a, b);

module.exports = {
  doAdd,
  doSubtract,
};
```

To mock **`math.js`** in a test file for **`app.js`**, use:

```
 // app.test.js
jest.mock('./math'); // This replaces math with a mock module

const app = require('./app');
const math = require('./math');

// Mock implementations
math.add.mockImplementation(() => 3);
math.subtract.mockImplementation(() => -1);

test('doAdd adds numbers', () => {
  expect(app.doAdd(1, 2)).toBe(3);
  expect(math.add).toHaveBeenCalledWith(1, 2);
});

test('doSubtract subtracts numbers', () => {
  expect(app.doSubtract(1, 2)).toBe(-1);
  expect(math.subtract).toHaveBeenCalledWith(1, 2);
});
```

In the example above, **`jest.mock('./math')`** tells Jest to use the mock math module instead of the real one. The **`.mockImplementation()`** method is then used to define custom implementations for the mocked functions.

Mocking Node Modules

To mock Node modules or npm packages, the process is similar. Suppose you are using axios for HTTP requests and want to mock it with a mock module like this one:

```
// fetchData.test.js
jest.mock('axios'); // Automatically replaces axios with a mock

const axios = require('axios');

// Function under test
const fetchData = () => axios.get('/my/data');

// Mock implementation
axios.get.mockResolvedValue({ data: 'some data' });

test('fetchData fetches data', async () => {
  const data = await fetchData();
  expect(data).toEqual({ data: 'some data' });
  expect(axios.get).toHaveBeenCalledWith('/my/data');
});
```

- **Mock at the Right Level:** Mock dependencies at the highest level that makes sense for your test. For unit tests, this often means mocking external modules or libraries your unit of code interacts with directly.
- **Return Realistic Data:** Ensure that your mocks return data that closely mimics what the actual library or module would return. This helps maintain the validity of your tests against real-world scenarios.
- **Reset/Clear Mocks:** Use Jest's **`mockClear`**, **`mockReset`**, and **`mockRestore`** methods appropriately to clear, reset, or restore mocks. This is crucial for ensuring that the state of mocks does not leak between tests, while maintaining test isolation.
- **Keep Mocks Close to Usage:** Define mocks as close to their usage as possible for clarity, unless a mock is shared across multiple test files. Shared mocks can be extracted to a separate file but should be documented clearly.
- **Avoid Over-Mocking:** While mocking is powerful, over-mocking can lead to tests that are disconnected from reality. Strive to balance between mocking for isolation and keeping tests representative of real-world usage.

- **External API Calls:** When your application makes calls to external services or APIs (for example, using axios or fetch), you can mock these calls to prevent actual requests during testing. This allows you to simulate various response scenarios such as success, failure, or timeouts, without relying on external services.
- **Database Access:** Similar to external APIs, direct database calls can be mocked to avoid interactions with a real database. This is crucial for ensuring tests do not affect production data or rely on the state of a database, thereby making tests more deterministic.
- **Complex Libraries:** Libraries that perform complex operations, like file manipulation, network requests, or hardware access (for example, accessing the filesystem, making HTTP requests), are ideal candidates for mocking. This simplifies tests by focusing on the behavior in response to these operations rather than the operations themselves.
- **Over-Reliance on Implementation Details:** Mocking should not rely too heavily on the internal implementation details of the module being mocked. Tests should focus on the interface and behavior rather than how the behavior is achieved.
- **Ignoring Async Behavior:** When mocking async functions or modules, ensure to mock their asynchronous nature accurately. Neglecting to do so can lead to false positives or negatives in your tests.
- **Complex Mock Logic:** Avoid creating complex logic within your mocks. If a mock requires significant logic to simulate behavior, it may be a sign that your test or the component being tested is too complex and should be simplified or broken down.
- **Forgetting to Mock:** A common pitfall is forgetting to mock a dependency that makes external calls, which can lead to unintended side effects like altering a database or making real network requests during tests.
- **Mocking Too Much:** Excessive mocking, especially beyond direct dependencies of the unit under test, can lead to brittle tests that break easily with any change in the codebase, even if those changes are not directly related to the functionality being tested.

Tracking Calls in Jest Mocks

All Jest mocks, whether they are created with `jest.fn()`, `jest.mock()`, or `jest.spyOn()`, automatically record detailed information about how they are called and what they return.

You can access this history via the **.mock** property, which exposes:

- **mock.calls** → Array of arguments for each call
- **mock.results** → Return values or thrown errors for each call
- **mock.instances** → Instances created with new when mocking constructors

Tracking Calls with jest.fn():

```
const mockFn = jest.fn((x, y) => x + y);

mockFn(1, 2);
mockFn(5, 10);

console.log(mockFn.mock.calls);
// [[1, 2], [5, 10]]

console.log(mockFn.mock.results);
// [{ type: 'return', value: 3 }, { type: 'return', value: 15 }]

expect(mockFn).toHaveBeenCalledTimes(2);
expect(mockFn).toHaveBeenCalledWith(5, 10);
expect(mockFn.mock.results[1].value).toBe(15);
```

Tracking Calls with jest.mock()

Suppose you mock an entire module such as the one here:

```
// math.js
export const add = (a, b) => a + b;

// math.test.js
jest.mock('./math.js', () => ({
  add: jest.fn((a, b) => `mocked:${a + b}`),
}));

const { add } = require('./math.js');
test('tracks calls on mocked module function', () => {
  add(2, 3);
  add(10, 20);

  console.log(add.mock.calls);
  // [[2, 3], [10, 20]]

  console.log(add.mock.results);
  // [{ type: 'return', value: 'mocked:5' }, { type: 'return', value:
'mocked:30' }]

  expect(add).toHaveBeenCalledTimes(2);
  expect(add).toHaveBeenCalledWith(10, 20);
});
```

Tracking Calls with `jest.spyOn()`

`jest.spyOn` wraps a real function, letting you track calls and optionally override behavior, which is shown here:

```
// user.test.js
const user = {
  greet: (name) => `Hello, ${name}`,
};

test('tracks spy calls', () => {
  const spy = jest.spyOn(user, 'greet');

  user.greet('Alice');
  user.greet('Bob');

  // Inspect call arguments
  console.log(spy.mock.calls);
  // [['Alice'], ['Bob']]

  // Inspect return values
  console.log(spy.mock.results);
  // [
  //   { type: 'return', value: 'Hello, Alice' },
  //   { type: 'return', value: 'Hello, Bob' }
  // ]

  expect(spy).toHaveBeenCalledTimes(2);
  expect(spy).toHaveBeenCalledWith('Bob');

  spy.mockRestore(); // restore original implementation
});
```

No matter how you create a **`mock–fn`**, **`mock`**, or **`spy–Jest`** gives you full introspection into calls and return values. This makes your tests not only assert correctness but also inspect behavior deeply. Doing so is essential for debugging and verifying complex interactions.

Jest Handling of Third-Party Libraries in Tests

Modern applications rely heavily on third-party libraries for networking, state management, storage, and backend communication. While these libraries are essential in production, they should not control or slow down your unit tests. Jest allows you to isolate your code from external dependencies by mocking third-party libraries, ensuring tests remain fast, deterministic, and focused only on the logic you own.

Strategies for Handling Third-Party Libraries

Handling third-party libraries in tests often requires special consideration, especially in a unit testing context where isolation from external dependencies is crucial. Jest provides several features to help manage and mock third-party libraries effectively, while ensuring that your tests remain focused on the code you write. Here is how to handle third-party libraries in Jest tests, along with some best practices.

Mocking API Calls(Axios): Axios is a popular HTTP client in the JavaScript ecosystem. You can mock Axios using Jest's **`jest.mock()`** function, which replaces the Axios module with mock functions. This is shown here:

```
// First, call jest.mock to replace axios with Jest's mock
jest.mock('axios');

const axios = require('axios');

// Function under test
const fetchData = () => axios.get('/some_endpoint');

// In your test, specify what axios.get() should return when it is
called
test('fetches data successfully from an API', async () => {
  const mockData = { data: 'some data' };
  axios.get.mockResolvedValue(mockData);

  await expect(fetchData()).resolves.toEqual(mockData);
  expect(axios.get).toHaveBeenCalledWith('/some_endpoint');
});
```

Mocking Fetch: If you are using the Fetch API for HTTP requests, you can mock it by overriding **`global.fetch`**, just like it is shown here:

```
// Mock the global fetch function
global.fetch = jest.fn(() =>
  Promise.resolve({
    json: () => Promise.resolve({ data: 'some data' }),
  })
);

test('fetches data successfully from an API', async () => {
  const response = await fetch('/some_endpoint');
  const data = await response.json();
```

```
  expect(data).toEqual({ data: 'some data' });
  expect(global.fetch).toHaveBeenCalledWith('/some_endpoint');
});
```

Mocking Database or Storage Dependencies

Mocking databases or storage systems like MongoDB, Firebase, or **localStorage** in Jest requires a slightly different approach, as these systems have more complex interactions and states.

Mocking Mongoose/MongoDB: For MongoDB, especially when using Mongoose, you can use libraries like **mockoose** or manually mock Mongoose models.

```
// Using jest.mock to mock mongoose model
jest.mock('../models/userModel');

const { UserModel } = require('../models/userModel');
const { getUser } = require('../services/userService');

test('gets user by id', async () => {
  const mockUser = { id: '1', name: 'John Doe' };

  // Mock implementation of findById
  UserModel.findById.mockResolvedValue(mockUser);

  const user = await getUser('1');

  expect(user).toEqual(mockUser);
  expect(UserModel.findById).toHaveBeenCalledWith('1');
});
```

Mocking Firebase: For Firebase, you can create manual mocks for the Firebase SDK functions you use. Place these mocks in the **__mocks__** directory if you want to apply them globally or use **jest.mock()** in individual test files.

```
// Mocking Firebase auth in a __mocks__/firebase.js file
const auth = jest.fn(() => ({
 createUserWithEmailAndPassword: jest.fn(() => Promise.resolve({ user: {
uid: '123'    }})),}));

module.exports = { auth };
```

Mocking localStorage: LocalStorage can be mocked by creating a mock implementation of its API, as shown here:

```
beforeAll(() => {
 global.localStorage = {
 getItem: jest.fn(),
```

```
  setItem: jest.fn(),
  clear: jest.fn(),
  };
});
```

Use Realistic Mock Data: Ensure that the data returned by your mocks closely resembles what the actual API or database would return.

Isolate Tests: Use mocks to ensure each test is isolated, not relying on the state from previous tests or actual external dependencies.

Cleanup: Reset or clear your mocks between tests to avoid state leakage using **`beforeEach`**, **`afterEach`** with methods like **`jest.resetAllMocks()`**.

Over-Mocking: Avoid mocking everything to the point where you are no longer testing how your application interacts with the actual libraries.

Ignoring Error Handling: Ensure that you mock and test error pathways, as handling errors correctly is often a critical part of your application's functionality.

Stale Mocks: Keep your mock implementations up-to-date with the third-party libraries' APIs. Outdated mocks can lead to tests that pass incorrectly or miss issues.

By applying these strategies and considerations, you can effectively mock third-party libraries in Jest, while creating a robust and isolated testing environment for your application.

Handling Non-Standard Modules: `setupFiles` and `moduleNameMapper`

When working with Jest to test JavaScript applications, you might encounter situations where your project uses non-standard modules or file formats that are not inherently understood by Jest. This can include CSS modules, images, or other static assets referenced in your JavaScript code, as well as custom alias paths defined in your project configuration. Jest provides tools to handle these scenarios, notably through **`setupFiles`** and **`moduleNameMapper`** configurations.

Handling Non-Standard Modules with `setupFiles`

The **`setupFiles`** configuration in Jest allows you to specify files that will be executed before the test framework is installed in the environment. This is particularly useful for setting up global mocks or configurations that need to be in place for all tests.

For example, if your application code uses browser-specific APIs (like **`localStorage`** or **`sessionStorage`**) that are not available in Jest's Node environment, you can create a setup file to mock these APIs globally, as shown here:

```
// jest.setup.js
global.localStorage = {
  getItem: jest.fn(),
  setItem: jest.fn(),
  removeItem: jest.fn(),
  clear: jest.fn(),
};

global.sessionStorage = {
  ...global.localStorage,
};

// jest.config.js
module.exports = {
  setupFiles: ['./jest.setup.js'],
};
```

Handling Non-Standard Modules with moduleNameMapper

The **moduleNameMapper** configuration allows you to define custom paths or alias mappings, similar to webpack's alias feature, or to mock out resources like CSS modules and images with dummy modules.

When your code imports CSS files or images (which Jest cannot process by default), you can use **moduleNameMapper** to map these imports to a mock module or an empty file, just like we have done here:

```
// jest.config.js
module.exports = {
  moduleNameMapper: {
    '\\.(css|less|scss|sass)$': 'identity-obj-proxy',
    '\\.(jpg|jpeg|png|gif|webp|svg)$': '<rootDir>/__mocks__/fileMock.js',
  },
};
```

For CSS modules, identity-obj-proxy (which needs to be installed via **npm** or **yarn**) can mock CSS imports to return an object, which allows you to simulate the use of CSS module classes in your tests without any errors.

For images and other assets, you can create a simple mock file (for example, **fileMock.js**) that exports a string or a simple object, and map all image extensions to this mock, just like we have done here:

```
// __mocks__/fileMock.js
module.exports = 'test-file-stub';
```

- **Keep Configuration Clean:** Only include necessary setup files and mappings. Overuse can make the configuration hard to maintain and understand.
- **Document Your Configuration:** Especially when using `moduleNameMapper` to handle aliases or mock out static assets, make sure you document why and how these mappings are used for future reference.
- **Consistent Mocking Strategy:** Ensure that the way you mock APIs, modules, or assets is consistent across your test suite to avoid confusion and potential test fragility.
- **Over-Mocking:** While it is necessary to mock non-standard modules or browser APIs, avoid mocking everything indiscriminately. Over-mocking can lead to tests that do not accurately reflect real-world scenarios.
- **Ignoring Module Mapping in Refactoring:** When refactoring your project's structure or updating dependencies, ensure that your Jest configuration, especially `moduleNameMapper`, is updated to reflect these changes.

Conclusion

In this chapter, you learned how to take full control of your tests using Jest's mocking and snapshot capabilities. You now know how to isolate modules, intercept functions, control return values, track calls, and replace entire dependencies with predictable mocks. You also learned how to use snapshot testing effectively and safely to capture UI output, track changes over time, and avoid brittle tests by focusing only on what matters.

You have seen how to mock everything from simple utilities and module functions to React components, Node modules, browser APIs like `localStorage`, and even CSS or asset imports that Jest can't process natively. You also learned the importance of consistency in module systems (CommonJS vs ESM), how to avoid unsafe patterns like reassigning ES module imports, and how to structure mocks cleanly, so that your tests stay readable and deterministic.

At this point, you should be able to Create targeted mocks using `jest.fn`, `jest.spyOn`, and `jest.mock`; Control and verify function behavior without touching real implementations; Mock non-standard imports and browser APIs; Use snapshot tests responsibly and understand what they are actually validating; and Build tests that are stable, maintainable, and independent of external factors.

With these tools, you will no longer be dependent on real modules or unpredictable environment behavior. You can shape your test environment exactly the way you need it. This is the foundation for writing fast, isolated, and trustworthy tests in real-world JavaScript and React applications.

Chapter 5
Testing React Hooks and Asynchronous Operations

Introduction

This chapter focuses on testing React hooks and the dynamic behavior they drive in components, especially with hooks like **`useState`**, **`useEffect`**, and **`useReducer`**. As hooks are now the core of modern React, knowing how to test them thoroughly is essential for reliability and performance. We will also look at testing asynchronous data fetching with Axios and validating Redux logic that depends on async flows and shared state.

Structure

This chapter covers the following topics:

- Testing React Hooks
- Testing Asynchronous Operations with Axios
- Testing Redux

Testing React Hooks

Testing React hooks is not just about ensuring the correctness of a component's output, but also about verifying that it responds appropriately to user interactions and asynchronous events. This is a challenge that requires a thoughtful approach and the right tools. React hooks, which were introduced in React 16.8, allow functional components to harness state and lifecycle features previously only available in class components. Hooks such as **useState**, **useEffect**, and **useReducer** enable developers to write cleaner, more modular code. However, testing components using these hooks can be tricky due to their inherent reliance on the React component lifecycle and external data sources.

Writing Tests for useState Hook

Testing components that use the **useState** hook involves verifying that the component behaves correctly as the state changes. These tests often simulate user interactions or lifecycle events to trigger state changes and then assert the expected outcomes in the component's output. In this section, we will explore how to write tests for components using the **useState** hook with examples that illustrate these concepts.

Testing useState

Let us consider a simple component called Counter that uses the **useState** hook to manage its count state. It has two buttons to increment and decrement the count, which display the current count to the user, as shown here:

```
import React, { useState } from 'react';
function Counter() {
 const [count, setCount] = useState(0);
 return (
   <div>
     <p>Current Count: {count}</p>
     <button onClick={() => setCount(count + 1)}>Increment</button>
     <button onClick={() => setCount(count - 1)}>Decrement</button>
   </div>
 );
}
export default Counter;
```

The goal is to test if the Counter component correctly responds to user interactions by incrementing and decrementing the count.

Initial Render: First, verify that the component correctly displays the initial count, such as in the code here:

```
import { render, screen } from '@testing-library/react';
import Counter from './Counter';
```

```
test('initial count is 0', () => {
  render(<Counter />);
  const countElement = screen.getByText(/current count:/i);
  expect(countElement).toHaveTextContent('Current Count: 0');
});
```

Increment Button: Next, test if clicking the "**Increment**" button increases the count, as shown here:

```
import { render, screen, fireEvent } from '@testing-library/react';
import Counter from './Counter';
test('increments count by 1 when increment button is clicked', () => {
 render(<Counter />);
 const incrementButton = screen.getByText(/increment/i);
 fireEvent.click(incrementButton);
 expect(screen.getByText(/current count:/i)).toHaveTextContent('Current
Count: 1');
});
```

Decrement Button: Similarly, verify that the "**Decrement**" button decreases the count.

```
import { render, screen, fireEvent } from '@testing-library/react';
import Counter from './Counter';
test('decrements count by 1 when decrement button is clicked', () => {
 render(<Counter />);
 // First, increment to ensure the test is independent of order
 fireEvent.click(screen.getByText(/increment/i));
 // Now, decrement
 fireEvent.click(screen.getByText(/decrement/i));
 expect(screen.getByText(/current count:/i)).toHaveTextContent('Current
Count: 0');
});
```

- **Isolate the Test Cases:** Each test should independently test a single behavior to avoid dependencies between tests.
- **Simulate User Interactions:** Use **fireEvent** or the newer **userEvent** library to simulate clicks and other user interactions.
- **Assert the Expected Outcome:** After triggering state changes, assert the expected changes in the component's output, whether it be text, classes, or other attributes.

By following these steps and principles, you can effectively write tests for React components using the **useState** hook and ensure that they behave as expected in response to user interactions and state changes.

Testing useEffect Hook: Side Effects and Cleanup

Testing components that utilize the **useEffect** hook requires a slightly different approach compared to testing state changes with **useState**. The **useEffect** hook is used for side effects in functional components, such as fetching data, directly manipulating the DOM, setting up subscriptions, or cleanup activities. Here is how you can test components that use **useEffect** for side effects and cleanup operations:

Understanding useEffect in Testing Context

When testing components that use **useEffect**, you are often interested in two aspects:

- **Side Effects:** For instance, data fetching and how the component behaves when the data is received or when an error occurs.
- **Cleanup Functions:** Sometimes, **useEffect** returns a function for cleanup activities, like unsubscribing from a service or clearing timeouts/intervals.

To test side effects, you often need to mock external dependencies, such as API calls, which is shown here:

```
// Component that fetches and displays user data
function UserProfile({ userId }) {
 const [user, setUser] = useState(null);

 useEffect(() => {
  const fetchData = async () => {
   const response = await fetch(`https://api.example.com/
users/${userId}`);
   const userData = await response.json();
   setUser(userData);
  };

  fetchData();
 }, [userId]);

 if (!user) {
  return <div>Loading...</div>;
 }
```

```
  return <div>{user.name}</div>;
}
```

Explanation:

- **Mock Fetch:** Use Jest to mock fetch to control the response.
- **Render Component:** Use React Testing Library to render the component.
- **Assert Side Effects**: Check that `fetch` is called with the correct URL and that the component eventually renders the fetched user's name.

```
import { render, screen, waitFor } from '@testing-library/react';
import UserProfile from './UserProfile';

 global.fetch = jest.fn(() =>
  Promise.resolve({
    ok: true,
    json: async () => ({ name: 'John Doe' }),
  })
 );

test('loads and displays user data', async () => {
 render(<UserProfile userId="123" />);
 await waitFor(() =>
  expect(global.fetch).toHaveBeenCalledWith('https://api.example.
com/users/123')
 );
 await waitFor(() => screen.getByText('John Doe'));
});
```

If your **useEffect** hook has a cleanup function, you can simulate component unmounting to test if the cleanup works correctly. Now, assume that **useEffect** sets up a subscription that needs to be cleaned up:

```
useEffect(() => {
  const subscription = dataSource.subscribe();
  return () => {
  // Cleanup subscription
    subscription.unsubscribe();
  };
}, []);
```

To test the cleanup, you can use React Testing Library's unmount function:

```
import { render } from '@testing-library/react';
import MyComponent from './MyComponent';
```

```
import { dataSource } from '../path/to/dataSource'; // Adjust the path
accordingly
test('cleans up on unmount', () => {
  // Mock the unsubscribe function
  const unsubscribeMock = jest.fn();
  dataSource.subscribe = jest.fn(() => ({ unsubscribe: unsubscribeMock
}));

  const { unmount } = render(<MyComponent />);
  unmount();
  expect(unsubscribeMock).toHaveBeenCalled();
});
```

Testing components with **useEffect** involves mocking external dependencies for side effects and possibly simulating component lifecycle for cleanup. Using Jest and React Testing Library together provides a powerful set of tools to test these aspects effectively.

Testing Custom Hooks

When building React applications, custom hooks are a powerful tool for encapsulating logic and reusability. Testing these hooks is crucial to ensure their functionality. In this chapter, we will explore how to create custom hooks and effectively test them using Jest, which is a popular testing framework.

Custom hooks in React are functions that use React hooks internally. They allow you to extract component logic into reusable functions. Let us create a simple custom hook called **useCounter** that manages a counter state:

```
// useCounter.js
import { useState } from 'react';

const useCounter = (initialValue = 0) => {
   const [count, setCount] = useState(initialValue);
   const increment = () => { setCount(count + 1); };
   const decrement = () => { setCount(count - 1); };
   return { count, increment, decrement };
};

export default useCounter;
```

Testing custom hooks involves testing their behavior in isolation. We will use Jest along with React Testing Library to test our **useCounter** hook, in the manner shown here:

```
// useCounter.test.js
import { renderHook, act } from '@testing-library/react';
```

```
import useCounter from './useCounter';
describe('useCounter', () => {
 it('should increment the count', () => {
  const { result } = renderHook(() => useCounter());
  act(() => {
   result.current.increment();
  });
  expect(result.current.count).toBe(1);
 });
it('should decrement the count', () => {
  const { result } = renderHook(() => useCounter(2));
  act(() => {
   result.current.decrement();
  });
  expect(result.current.count).toBe(1);
 });
it('should initialize count with initial value', () => {
  const initialValue = 5;
  const { result } = renderHook(() => useCounter(initialValue));
  expect(result.current.count).toBe(initialValue);
 });
});
```

Explanation:

- We use **renderHook** from React Testing Library to render the hook within a test environment.
- **act** is used to perform actions like calling the increment or decrement functions.
- Assertions are made using Jest's expect function to ensure that the hook behaves as expected.

Testing custom hooks is essential for maintaining the reliability of your React application. By following the examples provided in this chapter, you can confidently create and test your own custom hooks and ensure that they function correctly in various scenarios.

Mocking Dependencies in Custom Hook Testing

When testing custom hooks in React, it is common to encounter scenarios where the hook depends on external dependencies such as APIs, libraries, or even other hooks. Mocking these dependencies is essential to isolate the hook's behavior and ensure reliable testing results. In this section, we will explore strategies for effectively mocking dependencies in custom hook testing using Jest, a powerful testing framework.

Let us consider a custom hook called **useFetchData**, which fetches data from an external API using fetch. We want to test this hook's behavior without making actual network requests, in the manner shown here:

```
// useFetchData.js
import { useState, useEffect } from 'react';
const useFetchData = (url) => {
 const [data, setData] = useState(null);
 const [loading, setLoading] = useState(true);
 const [error, setError] = useState(null);
 useEffect(() => {
   const fetchData = async () => {
   try {
    const response = await fetch(url);
    if (!response.ok) {
    throw new Error('Failed to fetch data');
   }
    const result = await response.json();
    setData(result);
   } catch (error) {
      setError(error);
   } finally {
     setLoading(false);
   }
  };
  fetchData();
 }, [url]);
 return { data, loading, error };
};
export default useFetchData;
```

Testing with Mocked Fetch: We will use Jest's mocking capabilities to mock the fetch function and simulate its behavior within our test environment, as shown here:

```
// useFetchData.test.js
import { renderHook, waitFor } from '@testing-library/react';
import useFetchData from './useFetchData';
```

```
beforeEach(() => {
  global.fetch = jest.fn(() =>
    Promise.resolve({
      ok: true,
      json: async () => ({ name: 'John Doe' }),
    })
  );
});

afterEach(() => {
  jest.clearAllMocks();
});

describe('useFetchData', () => {
  it('should fetch data from the API', async () => {
    const { result } = renderHook(() =>
      useFetchData('https://example.com/data')
    );

    // Initial state
    expect(result.current.loading).toBe(true);
    expect(result.current.data).toBe(null);
    expect(result.current.error).toBe(null);

    // Wait for fetch + state update
    await waitFor(() =>
      expect(result.current.data).toEqual({ name: 'John Doe' })
    );

    expect(result.current.loading).toBe(false);
    expect(result.current.error).toBe(null);
    expect(global.fetch).toHaveBeenCalledWith('https://example.com/
data');
  });
});
```

Explanation:

a. **Mocking Fetch Function**: We use **jest.fn()** to mock the fetch function globally. This ensures that any calls to fetch within the tested component or hook are intercepted and replaced with our mock implementation.

b. **Simulating Fetch Response**: The mocked fetch function returns a Promise resolving to an object with the properties ok and json, while simulating a successful API response.

c. **Testing the Hook**: Within the test case, we will render the hook using **`renderHook`** from React Testing Library. We will then assert the hook's behavior before and after the API call, checking loading states, fetched data, and error handling.

d. **Mocking Complex Dependencies**: For more complex dependencies like libraries or other hooks, you may need to create manual mocks or use Jest's manual mocking capabilities to provide custom behavior.

e. **Cleaning Up Mocks**: It is essential to clean up any mocks after each test to avoid interference with subsequent tests. Jest provides lifecycle hooks like **`beforeEach`** and **`afterEach`** for this purpose.

Mocking dependencies effectively in custom hook testing allows developers to isolate the hook's behavior and ensure reliable and predictable test results. By leveraging Jest's mocking capabilities and following best practices, developers can confidently test custom hooks with external dependencies, which will lead to more robust and maintainable React applications.

Testing Asynchronous Operations with Axios

Testing asynchronous operations, such as API calls made with Axios, is a common scenario in React applications. When testing custom hooks or components that use Axios for data fetching, it is essential to ensure that these asynchronous operations are tested thoroughly. Let us now explore how to test such scenarios using Jest and Axios mock adapter.

Configuring Jest for asynchronous testing involves setting up Jest to handle asynchronous operations such as API requests, timers, and promises effectively. Jest provides several configuration options and utilities to handle asynchronous code. Let us explore how to configure Jest for asynchronous testing:

Setting Timeout: By default, Jest has a timeout for asynchronous operations (for example, API requests) to complete. You can adjust this timeout in the Jest configuration to accommodate longer-running tests, just like it is done here:

```
// jest.config.js
module.exports = {
  testTimeout: 10000, // 10 seconds
};
```

This configuration sets the timeout for each test file to 10 seconds.

Using `async/await`: Jest supports **`async/await`** syntax for handling asynchronous code. You can use async functions in your test cases and await for asynchronous operations.

```
test('async test', async () => {
 const result = await asyncFunction();
 expect(result).toBe(expectedValue);
});
```

Testing Promises: Jest provides utilities like resolves and rejects to test promises. You can use these utilities to assert whether a promise resolves or rejects as expected.

```
test('promise resolves', () => {
 return expect(asyncFunction()).resolves.toBe(expectedValue);
});

test('promise rejects', () => {
 return expect(asyncFunction()).rejects.toThrow(errorMessage);
});
```

Mocking Timers: When testing code with timers (for example, `setTimeout`, `setInterval`), Jest's timer mocks can be used to control the passage of time.

```
jest.useFakeTimers();
test('timer test', () => {
 const callback = jest.fn();
 setTimeout(callback, 1000);
 jest.advanceTimersByTime(1000);
 expect(callback).toHaveBeenCalled();
});
```

Using Mock Functions: For mocking asynchronous functions such as API requests, you can use Jest's mock functions (`jest.fn()`) and mock implementation (`mockImplementation`) to simulate different responses.

```
const fetchData = jest.fn().mockResolvedValue({ data: 'test' });
 test('fetchData resolves with data', async () => {
 const result = await fetchData();
 expect(result).toEqual({ data: 'test' });
});
```

Cleaning Up: Ensure that asynchronous operations are properly cleaned up after each test to prevent interference between test cases. Jest provides lifecycle methods (`beforeEach`, `afterEach`) for setup and teardown tasks.

```
beforeEach(() => {
 // Setup tasks
});

afterEach(() => {
 // Teardown tasks
});
```

By configuring Jest to handle asynchronous testing effectively and utilizing its built-in utilities for promises, timers, and mocks, you can write comprehensive tests for asynchronous code in your React applications. This ensures the reliability and correctness of your codebase, leading to more robust and maintainable applications.

Mocking Axios for Unit Tests

Mocking Axios for unit tests involves intercepting HTTP requests made by Axios and providing mock responses. By doing so, you can isolate your tests from external APIs and ensure predictable behavior. Jest provides utilities to achieve this, while allowing you to create mock implementations of Axios and simulate various scenarios such as successful responses, errors, and timeouts. Let us walk through the process of mocking Axios for unit tests:

Mocking Axios with Jest: Jest provides a simple way to mock modules, including Axios. You can create a manual mock for Axios by creating a **`__mocks__ directory`** adjacent to your **`node_modules`** directory and placing a file named axios.js inside it. This file will contain your mocked Axios module.

```
// __mocks__/axios.js
export default {
 get: jest.fn(() => Promise.resolve({ data: {} })),
 post: jest.fn(() => Promise.resolve({ data: {} })),
 // Add other Axios methods as needed
};
```

In this mock implementation, we define mocked versions of Axios methods like get and post, with each returning a resolved promise with a mock response. You can customize these responses according to your test scenarios.

Writing Unit Tests: With Axios mocked, you can now write unit tests for functions or components that make HTTP requests using Axios. Here is an example of how you can test a function that makes a GET request using Axios:

```
import axios from 'axios';
import fetchData from './fetchData'; // Function that makes Axios GET
request
jest.mock('axios'); // Mock Axios module
describe('fetchData', () => {
 it('fetches data successfully', async () => {
   const mockData = { id: 1, name: 'Test' };
   axios.get.mockResolvedValueOnce({ data: mockData });
   const data = await fetchData('/api/data');
   expect(data).toEqual(mockData);
```

```
    expect(axios.get).toHaveBeenCalledWith('/api/data');
  });
  it('handles errors', async () => {
    const errorMessage = 'Error fetching data';
    axios.get.mockRejectedValueOnce(new Error(errorMessage));
    await expect(fetchData('/api/data')).rejects.toThrow(errorMessage);
    expect(axios.get).toHaveBeenCalledWith('/api/data');
  });
});
```

In these unit tests, we are mocking the Axios module using **`jest.mock('axios')`**. Then, within each test case, we have used **`axios.get.mockResolvedValueOnce`** or **`axios.get.mockRejectedValueOnce`** to define the behavior of the mocked Axios get method. This allows us to simulate both successful responses and errors, while verifying that our code handles these scenarios correctly.

Cleanup: It is important to reset the Axios mock after each test to prevent interference between test cases. You can achieve this using Jest's **`afterEach`** hook, as shown here:

```
afterEach(() => {
 jest.clearAllMocks();
});
```

By clearing all mocks after each test, you can ensure that each test starts with a clean slate, avoiding any unintended interactions from previous tests.

Mocking Axios for unit tests allows you to write tests that are fast, deterministic, and independent of external dependencies. By defining mock responses for Axios methods, you can simulate different scenarios and thoroughly test your code's behavior under various conditions.

Testing Async Functions and Promises

Testing asynchronous functions and promises is a fundamental aspect of unit testing in JavaScript. It ensures that your code behaves correctly when dealing with asynchronous operations such as API requests, timeouts, or async computations. Jest provides utilities to handle testing asynchronous code effectively. Let us explore how to test async functions and promises using Jest:

Testing Async Functions with `async/await`: Jest supports the use of **`async/await`** syntax for testing asynchronous functions. You can mark your test functions as async and use await to wait for asynchronous operations to complete.

```
// asyncFunction.js
const asyncFunction = async () => {
```

```
 return new Promise(resolve => {
   setTimeout(() => {
     resolve('Async Result');
   }, 1000);
 });
};
// asyncFunction.test.js
import asyncFunction from './asyncFunction';
test('async function resolves with expected value', async () => {
 const result = await asyncFunction();
 expect(result).toBe('Async Result');
});
```

In this example, we have defined an asynchronous function **asyncFunction** that resolves a promise after a delay of 1 second. In the test case, we have used async/await to wait for the function to complete and then assert the resolved value using Jest's expect.

Testing Promises with .resolves and .rejects: Jest provides matcher functions **.resolve**s and **.reject**s to test promises. You can use these matcher functions to assert whether a promise resolves or rejects as expected.

```
// asyncFunction.js
const asyncFunction = () => {
 return new Promise((resolve, reject) => {
   setTimeout(() => {
     resolve('Async Result');
   }, 1000);
 });
};

// asyncFunction.test.js
import asyncFunction from './asyncFunction';
test('promise resolves with expected value', () => {
 return expect(asyncFunction()).resolves.toBe('Async Result');
});
test('promise rejects with expected error message', () => {
 return expect(asyncFunction()).rejects.toThrow('Error');
});
```

In this example, we test that the promise returned by **asyncFunction** resolves with the expected value using .resolves. We also test that it rejects with the expected error message using **.rejects.toThrow**.

Testing with Mock Timers: If your asynchronous code involves timers (for example, **`setTimeout`**, **`setInterval`**), Jest's timer mocks can be used to control the passage of time and test time-dependent behavior.

```
// timerFunction.js
const timerFunction = (callback) => {
 setTimeout(() => {
   callback('Timer Result');
 }, 1000);
};

// timerFunction.test.js
import timerFunction from './timerFunction';
jest.useFakeTimers();

test('timer function calls callback after 1 second', () => {
 const callback = jest.fn();
 timerFunction(callback);
 jest.advanceTimersByTime(1000);
 expect(callback).toHaveBeenCalledWith('Timer Result');
});
```

In this example, we use Jest's timer mocks to test a function **`timerFunction`** that calls a callback after a delay of 1 second. We use **`jest.advanceTimersByTime`** to manually advance the timer by 1 second and then assert that the callback is called with the expected value.

By leveraging Jest's utilities for testing async functions, promises, and timers, you can write comprehensive tests for your asynchronous code, while ensuring its correctness and reliability.

Handling Axios Mocks for Different Scenarios

When testing code that makes HTTP requests using Axios, it is common to need different mock responses for different scenarios such as success, error, or timeout. Jest provides mechanisms for creating mock implementations of modules like Axios and controlling their behavior to simulate various scenarios. Let us explore how to handle Axios mocks for different scenarios in unit tests:

Mocking Axios with Jest: Before diving into different scenarios, let us set up a basic mock for Axios that will intercept HTTP requests and return mock responses:

```
// __mocks__/axios.js
const axiosMock = jest.genMockFromModule('axios');
axiosMock.create = jest.fn(() => axiosMock);
export default axiosMock;
```

This mock intercepts all Axios requests and returns a mock Axios instance.

Mocking Different Scenarios: Now, let us look at how to mock different scenarios such as success, error, and timeout for Axios requests:

```
// fetchData.js
import axios from 'axios';

const fetchData = async () => {
 try {
  const response = await axios.get('/api/data');
  return response.data;
 } catch (error) {
  throw new Error('Failed to fetch data');
 }
};
```

In this example, **`fetchData`** is a function that makes a GET request to **`/api/data`** using Axios. Let us write unit tests for different scenarios:

```
// fetchData.test.js
 import axios from 'axios';
 import fetchData from './fetchData';
 jest.mock('axios');

 describe('fetchData', () => {
  afterEach(() => {
   jest.clearAllMocks();
  });

 it('fetches data successfully', async () => {
  const mockData = { id: 1, name: 'Test' };
  axios.get.mockResolvedValueOnce({ data: mockData });
  const data = await fetchData();
  expect(data).toEqual(mockData);
  expect(axios.get).toHaveBeenCalledWith('/api/data');
 });

 it('handles error', async () => {
  axios.get.mockRejectedValueOnce(new Error('Request failed'));
  await expect(fetchData()).rejects.toThrow('Failed to fetch data');
  expect(axios.get).toHaveBeenCalledWith('/api/data');
 });

 it('times out', async () => {
  jest.useFakeTimers();

  axios.get.mockImplementationOnce(() =>
    new Promise((resolve, reject) => {
```

```
      setTimeout(() => reject(new Error('timeout')), 6000);
    })
  );

  const promise = fetchData();

  // Fast-forward the timer instead of really waiting 6 seconds
  jest.advanceTimersByTime(6000);

  await expect(promise).rejects.toThrow('timeout');
  expect(axios.get).toHaveBeenCalledWith('/api/data');

  jest.useRealTimers();
 });
});
```

In these test cases:

- The first test simulates a successful response by mocking **axios.get** to return a resolved promise with mock data.
- The second test simulates an error response by mocking **axios.get** to return a rejected promise.
- The third test simulates a timeout scenario by using Jest's fake timers and a rejected promise after a delay, which allows the test to fast-forward time without actually waiting.

By mocking different scenarios for Axios requests in your unit tests, you can thoroughly test the behavior of your code under various conditions, while ensuring its reliability and correctness.

Testing Redux

Redux is a powerful state management library, and testing it is crucial to ensure the stability and consistency of an application's state. Here's how to tackle testing Redux, particularly for complex scenarios:

When dealing with Redux setups, it is important to focus on integration testing. This helps ensure that the various components like actions, reducers, and the store are interacting correctly.

Consider a Redux setup for an e-commerce application. It has actions like "**ADD_TO_CART**", "**REMOVE_FROM_CART**", and "**CHECKOUT**". Here is how you can structure tests:

```
import { createStore } from 'redux';
import rootReducer from '../reducers';
import { addToCart, removeFromCart, checkout } from '../actions';
describe('E-commerce Redux Application', () => {
```

```
 let store;
 beforeEach(() => {
  store = createStore(rootReducer);
 });
it('should add an item to the cart', () => {
 store.dispatch(addToCart({ id: 1, name: 'Item 1', price: 100 }));
 const state = store.getState();
 expect(state.cart.items).toContainEqual({ id: 1, name: 'Item 1', price:
100 });
});
it('should remove an item from the cart', () => {
 store.dispatch(addToCart({ id: 1, name: 'Item 1', price: 100 }));
 store.dispatch(removeFromCart(1));
 const state = store.getState();
 expect(state.cart.items).not.toContainEqual({ id: 1, name: 'Item 1',
price: 100 });
});
it('should handle checkout correctly', () => {
 store.dispatch(addToCart({ id: 1, name: 'Item 1', price: 100 }));
 store.dispatch(checkout());
 const state = store.getState();
 expect(state.cart.items).toHaveLength(0);
});
});
```

This example shows how integration testing can help ensure that actions, reducers, and the store work cohesively.

Edge Cases and Error Handling: Redux applications often involve edge cases. For example, an action might trigger multiple state changes, or a reducer might need to handle an unexpected state.

Continuing with the e-commerce app, consider how the checkout action might fail if there are no items in the cart, which might look like this:

```
it('should not allow checkout with an empty cart', () => {
 store.dispatch(checkout());
 const state = store.getState();
 expect(state.cart.items).toHaveLength(0);
 expect(state.errors).toContain('Cart is empty');
});
```

This tests that the application handles errors gracefully, while maintaining robustness.

Testing Redux Actions: Simple and Async

Actions are the driving force behind Redux applications. They trigger changes in the store by calling reducers. Here is how to test both simple and asynchronous actions:

Simple actions return plain objects. Testing them involves checking that they produce the expected output.

Suppose there is a simple action to add an item to the cart:

```
import { addToCart } from '../actions';
describe('Simple Actions', () => {
 it('should create an action to add an item to the cart', () => {
  const item = { id: 1, name: 'Item 1', price: 100 };
  const expectedAction = { type: 'ADD_TO_CART', payload: item };
  expect(addToCart(item)).toEqual(expectedAction);
 });
});
```

Asynchronous Actions: Redux `Thunk` is often used to handle asynchronous actions. Testing these actions requires mocking the asynchronous behavior, usually with libraries like Jest. For instance, suppose there is an asynchronous action to fetch product data, like the one here:

```
import { configureStore } from '@reduxjs/toolkit';
import thunk from 'redux-thunk';
import rootReducer from '../reducers';
import { fetchProduct } from '../actions';
import * as api from '../api';

describe('Asynchronous Actions', () => {
  it('should fetch product data and update state', async () => {
    const product = { id: 1, name: 'Product 1', price: 50 };

    jest.spyOn(api, 'getProduct').mockResolvedValue(product);

    const store = configureStore({
      reducer: rootReducer,
      middleware: (getDefaultMiddleware) =>
        getDefaultMiddleware().concat(thunk),
    });

    await store.dispatch(fetchProduct(1));

    const state = store.getState();
    // Adjust this to match your real state shape
```

```
    expect(state.products.items).toContainEqual(product);
  });
});
```

This example uses Jest to mock an API call and verify that the store state is updated correctly after the async action runs.

Testing Redux Reducers: State Changes

Reducers define how actions transform the state. Testing them involves simulating various actions and checking the resulting state.

Let us consider a reducer managing an e-commerce cart:

```
import { cartReducer } from '../reducers';
import { addToCart, removeFromCart } from '../actions';
describe('Cart Reducer', () => {
 it('should handle adding an item to the cart', () => {
  const initialState = { items: [] };
  const action = addToCart({ id: 1, name: 'Item 1', price: 100 });
  const newState = cartReducer(initialState, action);
  expect(newState.items).toContainEqual({ id: 1, name: 'Item 1', price:
100 });
 });

 it('should handle removing an item from the cart', () => {
  const initialState = { items: [{ id: 1, name: 'Item 1', price: 100 }] };
  const action = removeFromCart(1);
  const newState = cartReducer(initialState, action);
  expect(newState.items).not.toContainEqual({ id: 1, name: 'Item 1',
price: 100 });
 });
});
```

This example demonstrates how to test state transformations directly.

Mocking the Redux Store for Unit Tests

For unit tests, isolating components from the Redux store is essential. Mocking the store simplifies this process. To unit test a component that interacts with Redux, such as a cart component like this example, you can use the following code:

```
import React from 'react';
import { render, screen, fireEvent } from '@testing-library/react';
import { Provider } from 'react-redux';
import { configureStore } from '@reduxjs/toolkit';
```

```
import cartReducer from '../reducers/cartReducer';
import Cart from '../components/Cart';

function renderWithStore(ui, { preloadedState } = {}) {
  const store = configureStore({
    reducer: { cart: cartReducer },
    preloadedState,
  });

  return {
    ...render(<Provider store={store}>{ui}</Provider>),
    store,
  };
}

describe('Cart Component', () => {
  it('should render cart items', () => {
    const preloadedState = {
      cart: { items: [{ id: 1, name: 'Item 1', price: 100 }] },
    };

    renderWithStore(<Cart />, { preloadedState });

    expect(screen.getByText('Item 1')).toBeInTheDocument();
  });

  it('should handle removing items', () => {
    const preloadedState = {
      cart: { items: [{ id: 1, name: 'Item 1', price: 100 }] },
    };

    const { store } = renderWithStore(<Cart />, { preloadedState });

    const removeButton = screen.getByText('Remove');
    fireEvent.click(removeButton);

    const state = store.getState();
    expect(state.cart.items).toHaveLength(0);
  });
});
```

This example shows how to mock a Redux store to test a component in isolation.

Integration Testing for Action Creators and Reducers

Integration testing ensures that actions and reducers work cohesively. This involves triggering actions and verifying that the state updates as expected.

Let us revisit the e-commerce app to integrate action creators and reducers:

```
import { createStore } from 'redux';
import rootReducer from '../reducers';
import { addToCart, checkout } from '../actions';
describe('Integration Testing', () => {
 let store;
 beforeEach(() => {
  store = createStore(rootReducer);
 });

it('should handle checkout process correctly', () => {
 store.dispatch(addToCart({ id: 1, name: 'Item 1', price: 100 }));
 store.dispatch(checkout());

 const state = store.getState();
 expect(state.cart.items).toHaveLength(0);
 expect(state.orders).toContainEqual({ id: 1, name: 'Item 1', price: 100
});
});

});
```

This example demonstrates how integration testing ensures that actions and reducers work together seamlessly. In summary, testing Redux involves a variety of approaches that range from simple unit tests for actions and reducers to integration tests that ensure components interact correctly. By combining these approaches, you can ensure the stability and reliability of your Redux applications.

Conclusion

Testing React hooks and asynchronous operations is not optional anymore; it is a core skill for building stable, predictable React applications. Hooks shift most of a component's logic into isolated, reusable functions that makes it easier to test only if you understand how to control state updates, effects, and async flows.

In this chapter, you learned how to test custom hooks with **`renderHook`**, **`waitFor`**, and predictable state assertions; handle asynchronous UI updates without relying on fragile timing assumptions; Mock fetch, Axios, timers, and external services in a consistent and reliable way; test failure paths, timeouts, race conditions, and side effects; validate Redux logic using real stores instead of outdated mock-store tools; and combine hook logic, API calls, and Redux updates in integration tests to ensure behavior matches real user flows.

The main idea is simple:

If your component or hook depends on async behavior, you must test the full lifecycle—trigger, loading, success, failure, and cleanup included.

CHAPTER 6

Redux Thunk and Context

Introduction

This chapter delves into the intricacies of testing applications that can help you leverage Redux Thunk for handling complex asynchronous logic and React Context for managing state across components. Readers will gain a comprehensive understanding of Redux Thunk, explore its role in facilitating asynchronous operations within Redux, and learn effective testing strategies for Redux action creators that employ Thunk middleware. Additionally, the chapter addresses the testing of React Context and covers scenarios where context is used with embedded state to manage application-wide data.

Structure

This chapter covers the following topic:

- Redux Thunk for Asynchronous Logic
- Complex Redux Actions with Thunk
- Testing React Context

Redux Thunk for Asynchronous Logic

As your applications grow in complexity, you will often need to handle asynchronous operations such as fetching data from an API, handling timers, or interacting with a database. Redux Toolkit (RTK) automatically includes Redux Thunk by default when you create a store with **configureStore**. Redux Toolkit simplifies asynchronous state management by standardizing patterns that are widely adopted in production-grade applications.

Redux Thunk Middleware

This middleware allows you to write logic that performs asynchronous tasks such as fetching data before dispatching actions to update the Redux state.

First, let us set up a basic Redux store with Redux Thunk middleware.

```
// src/store.js
import { configureStore } from '@reduxjs/toolkit';
import dataReducer from './features/dataSlice';

export const store = configureStore({
  reducer: { data: dataReducer },
});
```

Since the store already includes Thunk middleware, you can directly dispatch async actions inside Jest tests without extra setup, while making the flow both testable and predictable.

Asynchronous Action Creators

Asynchronous action creators are functions that return a function instead of an action. These functions allow you to perform asynchronous operations such as API calls before dispatching actions to the Redux store. This is especially useful for handling side effects in a Redux application.

To define asynchronous actions in Redux Toolkit, use **createAsyncThunk**. It wraps async logic and automatically dispatches three lifecycle actions: pending, fulfilled, and rejected.

```
// src/features/dataThunk.js
import { createAsyncThunk } from '@reduxjs/toolkit';

export const fetchData = createAsyncThunk(
  'data/fetchData',
  async (_, { rejectWithValue }) => {
```

```
    try {
      const response = await fetch('https://api.example.com/data');
      if (!response.ok) {
        const message = await response.text().catch(() => response.
statusText);
        return rejectWithValue(message || 'Failed to fetch');
      }
      return await response.json();
    } catch (error) {
      return rejectWithValue(error.message);
    }
  });
```

Each async operation is encapsulated in a single, testable function that can be dispatched in your app or directly tested in Jest.

Every async Thunk dispatches multiple actions automatically throughout its lifecycle. These are discussed in the following table:

Stage	Action	Description
1	data/fetchData/pending	Triggered when the request starts
2	data/fetchData/fulfilled	Triggered when data is successfully fetched
3	data/fetchData/rejected	Triggered if an error occurs during the request

Table 6.1: *Actions*

Testing Asynchronous Action Creators with Jest

With Redux Toolkit (RTK), you define async action creators using **`createAsyncThunk`**. It automatically emits pending, fulfilled, and rejected actions. In Jest, you simply mock **`global.fetch`**, dispatch the Thunk on a real RTK store, and assert the result action and final Redux state.

Data Slice

```
// src/features/dataSlice.js
import { createSlice } from '@reduxjs/toolkit';
import { fetchData } from './dataThunk';

const initialState = { status: 'idle', data: null, error: null };

const dataSlice = createSlice({
  name: 'data',
```

```
  initialState,
  reducers: { reset: () => initialState },
  extraReducers: (b) => {
    b.addCase(fetchData.pending, (s) => {
      s.status = 'loading';
      s.error = null;
    });
    b.addCase(fetchData.fulfilled, (s, a) => {
      s.status = 'succeeded';
      s.data = a.payload;
    });
    b.addCase(fetchData.rejected, (s, a) => {
      s.status = 'failed';
      s.error = a.payload ?? a.error?.message ?? 'Unknown error';
    });
  },
});

export const { reset } = dataSlice.actions;
export default dataSlice.reducer;
```

Here is what we are testing:

- **Success Path**: Thunk dispatches fulfilled, while the state becomes successful with payload.
- **Network Error**: Thunk dispatches rejected, while state captures thrown error message.
- **Non-OK HTTP**: Thunk dispatches rejected with payload (from **`rejectWithValue`**).
- (Optional) Reset brings state back to idle.

This is how we will test:

- Mock **`global.fetch`** per test case.
- Dispatch **`fetchData()`** on a fresh RTK store.
- Assert the result action type and final Redux state.

```
// src/features/dataThunk.int.test.js
import { configureStore } from '@reduxjs/toolkit';
import dataReducer, { reset } from './dataSlice';
import { fetchData } from './dataThunk';

const makeStore = () => configureStore({ reducer: { data: dataReducer }
});
```

```
describe('Testing Asynchronous Action Creators with Jest (RTK)', () => {
  const originalFetch = global.fetch;

  afterEach(() => {
    jest.resetAllMocks();
    if (originalFetch) {
     global.fetch = originalFetch;
    } else {
     delete global.fetch;
    }
  });

  test('success: fulfilled updates state with payload', async () => {
    const mock = { data: 'some data' };
    global.fetch = jest.fn().mockResolvedValue({ ok: true, json: async
() => mock });

    const store = makeStore();
    const action = await store.dispatch(fetchData());

    expect(action.type).toBe(fetchData.fulfilled.type);

    const state = store.getState().data;
    expect(state.status).toBe('succeeded');
    expect(state.data).toEqual(mock);
    expect(state.error).toBeNull();
  });

  test('network error: rejected puts error message in state', async ()
=> {
    global.fetch = jest.fn().mockRejectedValue(new Error('Network
down'));

    const store = makeStore();
    const action = await store.dispatch(fetchData());

    expect(action.type).toBe(fetchData.rejected.type);

    const state = store.getState().data;
    expect(state.status).toBe('failed');
    expect(state.error).toBe('Network down');
  });

  test('non-OK response: rejected with payload from server text', async
() => {
    global.fetch = jest.fn().mockResolvedValue({
      ok: false,
      statusText: 'Bad Request',
```

```
      text: async () => 'Invalid query',
    });

    const store = makeStore();
    const action = await store.dispatch(fetchData());

    expect(action.type).toBe(fetchData.rejected.type);
    expect(action.payload).toBe('Invalid query');

    const state = store.getState().data;
    expect(state.status).toBe('failed');
    expect(state.error).toBe('Invalid query');
  });

  test('reset brings state back to idle', () => {
    const store = makeStore();
    store.dispatch({ type: fetchData.fulfilled.type, payload: { data: 'x'
} });
    store.dispatch(reset());
    expect(store.getState().data).toEqual({ status: 'idle', data: null,
error: null });
  });
});
```

Multiple Actions in Thunks

Sometimes one async flow needs more than one action. For example, there might be a file upload that reports start → progress → success/failure. With Redux Toolkit you can:

- Create a slice with small, focused reducers (**`uploadStarted`**, **`uploadProgress`**, **`uploadSucceeded`**, **`uploadFailed`**).
- Write a custom Thunk that dispatches those actions over time. We will simulate an upload that ticks progress every 200ms, then succeeds (or fails at a chosen step).

Upload Slice (state + actions): For these tests, we create a minimal Redux store that includes only the upload slice (state + actions), allowing us to isolate and verify the thunk behavior without involving unrelated reducers or application-wide configuration.

```
// src/features/uploadSlice.js
import { createSlice } from '@reduxjs/toolkit';

const initialState = {
  inFlight: false,
  progress: 0, // 0..100
```

```
  error: null,
  done: false,
};

const uploadSlice = createSlice({
  name: 'upload',
  initialState,
  reducers: {
    uploadStarted(state) {
      state.inFlight = true;
      state.progress = 0;
      state.error = null;
      state.done = false;
    },
    uploadProgress(state, action) {
      state.progress = action.payload; // 0..100
    },
    uploadSucceeded(state) {
      state.inFlight = false;
      state.done = true;
    },
    uploadFailed(state, action) {
      state.inFlight = false;
      state.error = action.payload;
    },
    resetUpload() {
      return initialState;
    },
  },
});

export const {
  uploadStarted,
  uploadProgress,
  uploadSucceeded,
  uploadFailed,
  resetUpload,
} = uploadSlice.actions;

export default uploadSlice.reducer;
```

Upload Thunk (involves dispatching multiple actions): This thunk represents a real-world asynchronous workflow where a single operation triggers multiple state transitions, such as starting an upload, reporting progress over time, and finally resolving with success or failure.

```
// src/features/uploadThunks.js
```

```
import {
  uploadStarted,
  uploadProgress,
  uploadSucceeded,
  uploadFailed,
} from './uploadSlice';

const sleep = (ms) => new Promise((resolve) => setTimeout(resolve, ms));

export const uploadFile = (file, options = {}) => {
  return async (dispatch) => {
    try {
      dispatch(uploadStarted());

      for (let p = 0; p <= 100; p += 20) {
        await sleep(200);
        if (options.failAt === p) {
          throw new Error(`Upload failed at ${p}%`);
        }
        dispatch(uploadProgress(p));
      }

      // pretend server finalize
      // await api.finalize(file);
      dispatch(uploadSucceeded());
    } catch (e) {
      const message = e instanceof Error ? e.message : String(e);
      dispatch(uploadFailed(message));
    }
  };
};
```

Store (for these tests): For testing purposes, the store is intentionally limited to the upload slice (state and actions) so the tests focus purely on how the thunk dispatches multiple actions and transitions state over time.

```
// src/store.js
import { configureStore } from '@reduxjs/toolkit';
import dataReducer from './features/dataSlice';

export const store = configureStore({
  reducer: { data: dataReducer },
});

// In a pure JS setup we skip explicit type exports.
```

Here is what we are testing:

- Start → progress ticks → success
- Failure path at a chosen step
- Optional: Progress values occur in order

This is how we will test:

- Use Jest fake timers to control the delays.
- Dispatch the Thunk and advance timers to simulate time passing.
- Assert final state (and optionally the sequence of progress updates).

```
// src/features/upload.int.test.js
import { configureStore } from '@reduxjs/toolkit';
import uploadReducer, { resetUpload } from './uploadSlice';
import { uploadFile } from './uploadThunks';

describe('Multiple Actions in Thunks (upload progress)', () => {
  // Use fake timers to control setTimeout in the thunk
  beforeAll(() => {
    jest.useFakeTimers();
  });
  afterAll(() => {
    jest.useRealTimers();
  });

  const makeStore = () =>
    configureStore({
      reducer: { upload: uploadReducer },
    });

  test('success: progress ticks to 100 and succeeds', async () => {
    const store = makeStore();

    // Optional: track progress sequence for readers
    const progressLog = [];
    const unsubscribe = store.subscribe(() => {
      const p = (store.getState().upload).progress;
      // only push when progress actually changes
      if (progressLog[progressLog.length - 1] !== p) {
        progressLog.push(p);
      }
    });

    // Dispatch the thunk (returns a promise)
    const promise = store.dispatch(uploadFile(new Blob(['content'])));
```

```
    // 6 ticks: 0,20,40,60,80,100 – each after 200ms
    for (let i = 0; i < 6; i++) {
      jest.advanceTimersByTime(200);
      await Promise.resolve(); // flush microtasks
    }

    // Wait for thunk to complete
    await promise;
    unsubscribe();

    const s = store.getState().upload;
    expect(s.inFlight).toBe(false);
    expect(s.done).toBe(true);
    expect(s.error).toBeNull();
    expect(s.progress).toBe(100);

    // Nice for learners: prove the order of progress
    expect(progressLog).toEqual([0, 20, 40, 60, 80, 100]);
  });

  test('failure: throws at a chosen step and records error', async () =>
{
    const store = makeStore();

    // Fail at 40%
    const promise = store.dispatch(
      uploadFile(new Blob(['content']), { failAt: 40 })
    );

    // tick 0% and 20%
    jest.advanceTimersByTime(200);
    await Promise.resolve();
    jest.advanceTimersByTime(200);
    await Promise.resolve();

    // tick 40% → will throw
    jest.advanceTimersByTime(200);
    await Promise.resolve();

    await promise; // thunk catches and dispatches uploadFailed

    const s = store.getState().upload;
    expect(s.inFlight).toBe(false);
    expect(s.done).toBe(false);
    expect(s.progress).toBe(20); // last successful progress before
failure
```

```
    expect(s.error).toBe('Upload failed at 40%');
  });

  test('resetUpload: returns to initial state', () => {
    const store = makeStore();
    store.dispatch(resetUpload());
    const s = store.getState().upload;
    expect(s).toEqual({ inFlight: false, progress: 0, error: null, done:
false });
  });
});
```

Complex Redux Actions with Thunk

Testing complex Redux actions, especially those involving asynchronous operations, can be challenging. Redux Thunk, a middleware that allows you to write action creators that return a function instead of an action, is particularly useful for handling such asynchronous logic. This chapter will guide you through structuring complex actions with Thunk, coordinating multiple asynchronous operations, handling errors in Thunk actions, and testing these actions using Jest with proper examples.

Coordinating Multiple Async Operations

In more complex scenarios, you might need to coordinate multiple asynchronous operations. Redux Thunk allows you to chain or parallelize these operations within a single action creator, as shown here:

```
// src/features/orderThunks.js
import { createAsyncThunk } from '@reduxjs/toolkit';

export const fetchOrder = createAsyncThunk(
  'order/fetchOrder',
  async (orderId, { rejectWithValue }) => {
    try {
      const res = await fetch(`/api/orders/${orderId}`);
      if (!res.ok) {
        const msg = (await res.text().catch(() => res.statusText)) ||
'Failed';
        return rejectWithValue(msg);
      }
      return await res.json();
    } catch (e) {
      const message = e instanceof Error ? e.message : String(e);
      return rejectWithValue(message);
```

```
    }
  }
);

// src/features/userThunks.js
import { createAsyncThunk } from '@reduxjs/toolkit';

export const fetchUser = createAsyncThunk(
  'user/fetchUser',
  async (userId, { rejectWithValue }) => {
    try {
      const res = await fetch(`/api/users/${userId}`);
      if (!res.ok) {
        const msg = (await res.text().catch(() => res.statusText)) ||
'Failed';
        return rejectWithValue(msg);
      }
      return await res.json();
    } catch (e) {
      const message = e instanceof Error ? e.message : String(e);
      return rejectWithValue(message);
    }
  }
);

// src/features/orderUserThunks.js
import { createAsyncThunk } from '@reduxjs/toolkit';
import { fetchOrder } from './orderThunks';
import { fetchUser } from './userThunks';

export const fetchOrderAndUser = createAsyncThunk(
  'flow/fetchOrderAndUser',
  async (orderId, { dispatch, rejectWithValue }) => {
    try {
      const order = await dispatch(fetchOrder(orderId)).unwrap();
      await dispatch(fetchUser(order.userId)).unwrap();
      // no return needed; void payload
    } catch (e) {
      const message = e instanceof Error ? e.message : String(e);
      return rejectWithValue(message);
    }
  }
);
```

This is what we are doing here (intuition):

- We have split the problem into two single-purpose **`thunks (fetchOrder, fetchUser)`** and a coordinator **`Thunk (fetchOrderAndUser)`** that sequences them.
- **`.unwrap()`** is key: if **`fetchOrder`** fails, the coordinator throws immediately and you do not proceed to **`fetchUser`**. That is a clean "**`fail fast`**" control flow.

This is why we have structured it in such a manner (design):

- Each low-level thunk is independently testable and reusable.
- The coordinator focuses only on orchestration, not raw fetching.
- Slices stay simple: they react to the Thunk they care about.

Test (and why it proves correctness)

```
// src/features/orderUserThunks.int.test.js
import { configureStore } from '@reduxjs/toolkit';
import orderReducer from './orderSlice';
import userReducer from './userSlice';
import { fetchOrderAndUser } from './orderUserThunks';

const makeStore = () =>
  configureStore({ reducer: { order: orderReducer, user: userReducer }
});

describe('Coordinating Multiple Async Operations: order → user (chain)',
() => {
  const originalFetch = global.fetch;

  afterEach(() => {
   jest.clearAllMocks();
   if (originalFetch) {
     global.fetch = originalFetch;
   } else {
     delete global.fetch;
   }
  });

  test('success: order then user both load', async () => {
    const order = { id: 1, userId: 7, total: 25 };
    const user = { id: 7, name: 'Jane' };

    global.fetch = jest.fn((url: string) => {
      if (url === '/api/orders/1') return Promise.resolve({ ok: true,
```

```
json: async () => order });
      if (url === '/api/users/7') return Promise.resolve({ ok: true,
json: async () => user });
      return Promise.reject(new Error('Not Found'));
    });

    const store = makeStore();
    const result = await store.dispatch(fetchOrderAndUser(1));

    expect(result.type).toBe('flow/fetchOrderAndUser/fulfilled');

    const os = store.getState().order;
    const us = store.getState().user;
    expect(os.status).toBe('succeeded');
    expect(os.entity).toEqual(order);
    expect(us.status).toBe('succeeded');
    expect(us.entity).toEqual(user);
  });

  test('failure: order call fails → entire flow rejected', async () => {
    global.fetch = jest.fn().mockRejectedValue(new Error('Order API
down'));

    const store = makeStore();
    const result = await store.dispatch(fetchOrderAndUser(1));

    expect(result.type).toBe('flow/fetchOrderAndUser/rejected');
    expect(result.payload).toBe('Order API down');

    const os = store.getState().order;
    expect(os.status).toBe('failed');
    expect(os.error).toBe('Order API down');

  });
});
```

Here is what we are testing:

- **Happy Path**: Both requests resolve; each slice ends in success with the right data.
- **Early Failure**: The first step fails; the coordinator rejects and the order slice shows failed.

This is how the test works (mechanics):

- We mock **`global.fetch`** to return different JSON for each URL.
- We build a real RTK store (no mock store) and dispatch the coordinator **`thunk`**.

- We assert the result action type (fulfilled/rejected) and the final slice states.

Error Handling in Thunk Actions

Use **createAsyncThunk** with **rejectWithValue** to attach friendly, typed error messages to rejected actions. Your slice reads **action.payload** to store that message.

Enhanced Error Handling

```
// src/features/productThunks.js
import { createAsyncThunk } from '@reduxjs/toolkit';

export const fetchProduct = createAsyncThunk(
  'product/fetchProduct',
  async (productId, { rejectWithValue }) => {
    try {
      const res = await fetch(`/api/products/${productId}`);
      if (!res.ok) {
        if (res.status === 404) {
          return rejectWithValue('Product not found');
        }
        const msg =
          (await res.text().catch(() => res.statusText)) || 'Unexpected
error';
        return rejectWithValue(msg);
      }
      return await res.json();
    } catch (e) {
      return rejectWithValue('An unexpected error occurred');
    }
  }
);
```

What and Why:

- Map known server states (for example, 404) to clear messages with **rejectWithValue**.
- Catch unexpected failures once and return a generic fallback.

Slice—store friendly errors from **rejected.payload**, as shown here:

```
// src/features/productSlice.js
import { createSlice } from '@reduxjs/toolkit';
import { fetchProduct } from './productThunks';
```

```
const initialState = {
  status: 'idle',
  entity: null,
  error: null,
};

const productSlice = createSlice({
  name: 'product',
  initialState,
  reducers: {
    resetProduct: () => initialState,
  },
  extraReducers: (builder) => {
    builder.addCase(fetchProduct.pending, (state) => {
      state.status = 'loading';
      state.error = null;
    });
    builder.addCase(fetchProduct.fulfilled, (state, action) => {
      state.status = 'succeeded';
      state.entity = action.payload;
    });
    builder.addCase(fetchProduct.rejected, (state, action) => {
      state.status = 'failed';
      state.error =
        action.payload ??
        action.error?.message ??
        'Unknown error';
    });
  },
});

export const { resetProduct } = productSlice.actions;
export default productSlice.reducer;
```

Minimal store for tests looks like:

```
// src/store.product.js
import { configureStore } from '@reduxjs/toolkit';
import productReducer from './features/productSlice';

export const makeProductStore = () =>
  configureStore({
    reducer: { product: productReducer },
});
```

`ProductThunks.int.test.js` looks like:

```
// src/features/productThunks.int.test.js
import { makeProductStore } from '../../store.product';
import { fetchProduct } from './productThunks';

describe('Error Handling in Thunk Actions (RTK)', () => {
  const originalFetch = global.fetch;

  afterEach(() => {
    jest.clearAllMocks();
    if (originalFetch) {
      global.fetch = originalFetch;
    } else {
      delete global.fetch;
    }
  });

  test('success: fulfilled stores product and clears error', async () =>
{
    const product = { id: 1, name: 'Product A' };
    global.fetch = jest.fn().mockResolvedValue({
      ok: true,
      json: async () => product,
    });

    const store = makeProductStore();
    const action = await store.dispatch(fetchProduct(1));

    expect(action.type).toBe(fetchProduct.fulfilled.type);

    const s = store.getState().product;
    expect(s.status).toBe('succeeded');
    expect(s.entity).toEqual(product);
    expect(s.error).toBeNull();
  });

  test('404 → rejected with friendly payload', async () => {
    global.fetch = jest.fn().mockResolvedValue({
      ok: false,
      status: 404,
      statusText: 'Not Found',
      text: async () => 'Not Found',
    });

    const store = makeProductStore();
    const action = await store.dispatch(fetchProduct(999));
```

```
    expect(action.type).toBe(fetchProduct.rejected.type);
    expect(action.payload).toBe('Product not found');

    const s = store.getState().product;
    expect(s.status).toBe('failed');
    expect(s.error).toBe('Product not found');
  });

  test('unexpected exception → generic message', async () => {
    global.fetch = jest.fn().mockRejectedValue(new Error('socket hang
up'));

    const store = makeProductStore();
    const action = await store.dispatch(fetchProduct(1));

    expect(action.type).toBe(fetchProduct.rejected.type);
    expect(action.payload).toBe('An unexpected error occurred');

    const s = store.getState().product;
    expect(s.status).toBe('failed');
    expect(s.error).toBe('An unexpected error occurred');

  });
});
```

Here is what we are testing:

- **Success**: Slice becomes succeeded, product stored, error cleared.
- **404**: Thunk rejected with payload "**`Product not found`**" and the slice stores that.
- **Unexpected**: A generic and friendly message is used.

Here is how we are testing:

- Mock **`global.fetch`** per scenario.
- Dispatch **`fetchProduct()`** on a fresh RTK store.
- Assert the result action and the final slice state.

Testing React Context

With Redux Thunk fully covered, we can now switch to the other major shared, which is the state mechanism in React and is called Context. Unlike Redux, Context is not about async logic but about testing components that depend on shared values.

Introduction to React Context Testing

React Context is a powerful feature for managing global state in a React application. Testing components that rely on context can be challenging, but with the right approach, it becomes manageable and efficient. In this chapter, we will cover the essentials of testing React Context, including setting up the context for testing, testing context providers and consumers, and mocking context values for isolation.

React Context allows you to share data across the component tree without passing props down manually at every level. While this simplifies state management, it also adds complexity to testing. Properly testing components that use context ensures that your application behaves as expected and makes your codebase more maintainable.

Setting Up Context for Testing

To test components that use React Context, you will need to create a test environment that mirrors your application's context setup. Here is a step-by-step guide to setting up a context for testing:

Create the Context

Define your context in a separate file, as shown here:

```
// context/MyContext.js
import React, { createContext, useState } from 'react';

export const MyContext = createContext(undefined);

export const MyProvider = ({ children }) => {
  const [state, setState] = useState('default value');

  return (
    <MyContext.Provider value={{ state, setState }}>
      {children}
    </MyContext.Provider>
  );
};
```

Set Up the Test Environment

Wrap your test components with the context provider, as shown here:

```
// __tests__/MyComponent.test.js
import React from 'react';
import { render, screen } from '@testing-library/react';
```

```
import '@testing-library/jest-dom';
import MyComponent from '../MyComponent';
import { MyProvider } from '../context/MyContext';

const renderWithProvider = (ui) => {
  return render(<MyProvider>{ui}</MyProvider>);
};

test('it renders with context', () => {
  renderWithProvider(<MyComponent />);
  expect(screen.getByText('default value')).toBeInTheDocument();
});
```

Testing Context Providers and Consumers

Testing context providers and consumers involves verifying that the context value is passed down correctly and that consumers behave as expected based on the context value.

Testing Context Provider

Ensure the provider updates the context value correctly, which is demonstrated here:

```
// __tests__/MyProvider.test.js
import React from 'react';
import { render, screen } from '@testing-library/react';
import '@testing-library/jest-dom';
import { MyProvider, MyContext } from '../context/MyContext';

const ConsumerComponent = () => {
  const value = React.useContext(MyContext);
  if (!value) return null;
  const { state } = value;
  return <div>{state}</div>;
};

test('provider updates the context value', () => {
  render(
    <MyProvider>
      <ConsumerComponent />
    </MyProvider>
  );
  expect(screen.getByText('default value')).toBeInTheDocument();
});
```

Testing Context Consumer

Verify that the consumer behaves correctly based on the context value, as shown here:

```
// __tests__/MyComponent.test.js
import React from 'react';
import { render } from '@testing-library/react';
import '@testing-library/jest-dom'; // remove if already set up globally
import MyComponent from '../MyComponent';
import { MyProvider } from '../context/MyContext';

test('consumer uses context value', () => {
  const { getByText } = render(
    <MyProvider>
      <MyComponent />
    </MyProvider>
  );
  expect(getByText('default value')).toBeInTheDocument();
});
```

Mocking Context Values for Isolation

In some cases, you may want to isolate the component you are testing from the actual context implementation. This is particularly useful for unit testing. You can mock the context values to test the component in isolation.

Mocking Context

Use a mock context provider to supply custom values for testing, as shown here:

```
// __tests__/MyComponent.mockContext.test.js
import React from 'react';
import { render, screen } from '@testing-library/react';
import '@testing-library/jest-dom';
import MyComponent from '../MyComponent';
import { MyContext } from '../context/MyContext';

const MockProvider = ({ children, value }) => (
  <MyContext.Provider value={value}>{children}</MyContext.Provider>
);

test('it renders with mock context value', () => {
  const mockValue = { state: 'mock value', setState: jest.fn() };
```

```
  render(
    <MockProvider value={mockValue}>
      <MyComponent />
    </MockProvider>
  );

  expect(screen.getByText('mock value')).toBeInTheDocument();
});
```

By following these techniques, you can effectively test components that rely on React Context. Properly testing context ensures that your global state management is reliable and your components are interacting correctly with the context values. This chapter has provided you with a solid foundation for testing React Context, which will make your testing process more robust and your codebase more maintainable.

Conclusion

Redux Thunk enables you to model real-world asynchronous workflows where a single user action triggers multiple state transitions over time. This pattern is widely used in applications such as dashboards, e-commerce platforms, fintech systems, and enterprise tools, where API coordination, progress tracking, retries, and error handling are essential. As applications evolve, the challenge shifts from merely writing async logic to testing it reliably and maintaining it at scale. The next chapter builds on this foundation by focusing on Jest best practices and capabilities that help keep these complex async tests stable, readable, and resilient as your test suite grows.

CHAPTER 7
Jest Best Practices and Capabilities

Introduction

This chapter is dedicated to exploring best practices encouraged by React Testing Library and unlocking the full potential of Jest, the powerful testing framework. In this chapter, readers will discover and adopt best practices for writing effective tests using React Testing Library, besides learning to leverage Jest's capabilities such as mocking and restoring individual properties of modules and gaining insights into controlling test execution and running test suites with different data. The chapter also addresses common pitfalls in testing and provides tips to avoid them.

Structure

This chapter covers the following topics:

- Best Practices in React Testing Library
- Mocking and Restoring Module Properties
- Test Execution Control: .skip and .only
- Diverse Data Testing with .each in Jest
- Avoiding Common Testing Pitfalls

Best Practices in React Testing Library

While exploring the React Testing Library, here is how you can test it like a seasoned user: query by accessible **`roles/labels/text`** (not IDs); interact with user-event; use **`findBy/waitFor`** for **`async`**, and assert visible outcomes, instead of focusing on implementation details.

Prefer Queries Based on User Perspective

When writing tests with React Testing Library, it is crucial to think from a user's perspective. The library is designed to encourage this approach, which leads to more robust and maintainable tests. Instead of selecting elements based on their internal implementation, like class names or IDs, make sure to focus on how users interact with your application.

For instance, use queries like **`getByText`**, **`getByLabelText`** and **`getByPlaceholderText`** to select elements. These queries are more resilient to changes in your codebase because they rely on the content and accessibility attributes that users see and interact with. This approach ensures that your tests remain stable even if you refactor your component's internal structure.

```
// Preferable approach:
const submitButton = screen.getByRole('button', { name: /submit/i });
await userEvent.click(submitButton);

// Avoid this:
const legacyButton = document.querySelector('.submit-button');
legacyButton.click(); // direct DOM click (not recommended)
```

Let us say you have a login form component, which looks like this:

```
function LoginForm() {
 return (
   <form>
     <label htmlFor="username">Username</label>
     <input id="username" placeholder="Enter username" />

     <label htmlFor="password">Password</label>
     <input id="password" type="password" placeholder="Enter password"
/>

     <button type="submit">Login</button>
   </form>
 );
}
```

Now, we will test it from the user's perspective via this code:

```
import { render, screen } from '@testing-library/react';
import LoginForm from './LoginForm';
import userEvent from '@testing-library/user-event';

test('allows the user to log in', async () => {
  render(<LoginForm />);

  // Select elements based on user interactions
  await userEvent.type(
    screen.getByPlaceholderText(/enter username/i),
    'testuser'
  );
  await userEvent.type(
    screen.getByPlaceholderText(/enter password/i),
    'password'
  );

  await userEvent.click(
    screen.getByRole('button', { name: /login/i })
  );

  // Add assertions here to verify login behavior
});
```

Avoid Direct Interaction with Implementation Details

Directly interacting with implementation details can make your tests brittle and tightly coupled to the internal structure of your components. Instead, focus on testing the component's behavior and how it interacts with the user.

Avoid selecting elements by class names or IDs specific to your implementation. These can change frequently during refactoring or design updates and might cause tests to break unnecessarily. Stick to queries that reflect the user's experience, while ensuring that your tests are more meaningful and less prone to breaking.

```
// Preferable approach:
const loginButton = screen.getByRole('button', { name: /login/i });
fireEvent.click(loginButton);

// Avoid this:
const loginButton = document.getElementById('login-button');
fireEvent.click(loginButton);
```

Consider the same login form example. Avoid this approach here:

```
import { render, fireEvent } from '@testing-library/react';
import LoginForm from './LoginForm';

test('allows the user to log in', () => {
  render(<LoginForm />);

  // Directly interacting with implementation details
  const usernameInput = document.getElementById('username');
  const passwordInput = document.getElementById('password');
  const loginButton = document.getElementById('login-button');

  fireEvent.change(usernameInput, { target: { value: 'testuser' } });
  fireEvent.change(passwordInput, { target: { value: 'password' } });
  fireEvent.click(loginButton);

  // Add assertions here to verify login behavior
});
```

Instead, use queries that reflect user interactions, as shown here:

```
import { render, screen } from '@testing-library/react';
import userEvent from '@testing-library/user-event';
import LoginForm from './LoginForm';

test('allows the user to log in', async () => {
  render(<LoginForm />);

  // Interacting with elements as a user would
  await userEvent.type(
    screen.getByPlaceholderText(/enter username/i),
    'testuser'
  );

  await userEvent.type(
    screen.getByPlaceholderText(/enter password/i),
    'password'
  );

  await userEvent.click(
    screen.getByRole('button', { name: /login/i })
  );

  // Add assertions here to verify login behavior
});
```

Leverage getByRole for Accessibility Testing

Using **getByRole** is one of the best ways to ensure your application is accessible. This query helps you select elements based on their roles, which are critical for accessibility. It aligns with the ARIA (Accessible Rich Internet Applications) standards and allows you to test the application's accessibility features.

By using **getByRole**, you can not only test the presence of elements, but also verify that they are correctly labeled and accessible to users relying on assistive technologies.

```
// Checking a button's existence and label:
const addButton = screen.getByRole('button', { name: /add item/i });
expect(addButton).toBeInTheDocument();

// Verifying an input field:
const nameInput = screen.getByRole('textbox', { name: /name/i });
expect(nameInput).toBeInTheDocument();
```

Consider a component with various interactive elements:

```
function UserProfile() {
 return (
   <div>
     <h1>User Profile</h1>
     <img src="user.jpg" alt="User Profile Picture" />
     <button>Save</button>
     <a href="/edit-profile">Edit Profile</a>
   </div>
 );
}
```

It might look like this when you test the component for accessibility:

```
import { render, screen } from '@testing-library/react';
import UserProfile from './UserProfile';

test('displays user profile correctly', () => {
 render(<UserProfile />);

 // Verifying roles and accessibility attributes
 expect(screen.getByRole('heading', { name: /user profile/i })).
toBeInTheDocument();
 expect(screen.getByRole('img', { name: /user profile picture/i })).
toBeInTheDocument();
 expect(screen.getByRole('button', { name: /save/i })).
```

```
toBeInTheDocument();
 expect(screen.getByRole('link', { name: /edit profile/i })).toBeInTheDocument();
});
```

Utilize `waitFor` for Asynchronous Operations

React applications often involve asynchronous operations such as fetching data from an API or updating state based on user interactions. Therefore, while testing these scenarios, it is essential to use **`waitFor`** to handle asynchronous behavior.

The **`waitFor`** utility allows you to wait for an element or a condition to appear or change in the DOM before proceeding with assertions. This ensures that your tests are reliable and do not fail due to timing issues.

Suppose you have a component that fetches and displays user data like this:

```
import { useState, useEffect } from 'react';

function UserProfile({ userId }) {
 const [user, setUser] = useState(null);

 useEffect(() => {
   async function fetchUser() {
     const response = await fetch(`/api/users/${userId}`);
     const data = await response.json();
     setUser(data);
   }
   fetchUser();
 }, [userId]);

 if (!user) {
   return <div>Loading...</div>;
 }

 return (
   <div>
     <h1>{user.name}</h1>
     <p>{user.email}</p>
   </div>
 );
}
```

It might look like this when you test it for asynchronous behavior:

```
import { render, screen, waitFor } from '@testing-library/react';
import '@testing-library/jest-dom/extend-expect';
```

```
import UserProfile from './UserProfile';

test('loads and displays user profile', async () => {
 // Mocking fetch response
 global.fetch = jest.fn(() =>
   Promise.resolve({
     json: () => Promise.resolve({ name: 'John Doe', email: 'john@
example.com' }),
   })
 );

 render(<UserProfile userId="123" />);

 // Waiting for the user name to be displayed
 await waitFor(() => expect(screen.getByText(/john doe/i)).
toBeInTheDocument());

 // Verifying email display
 expect(screen.getByText(/john@example.com/i)).toBeInTheDocument();

 // Restoring the original fetch
 global.fetch.mockRestore();
});
```

Prefer findBy* for async elements (React Testing Library best practice)

When an element appears after an asynchronous update (fetch, delayed render, user typing, API call), React Testing Library recommends using **findBy*** queries instead of wrapping a **getBy*** call inside **waitFor**. All **findBy*** queries return a Promise. Therefore, you must always await them.

findBy* is simply:

- A **getBy*** query
- Wrapped automatically in a waitFor
- With built-in retries
- With better error messages

Here is an example of a preferred approach:

```
// Instead of waiting manually
await waitFor(() =>
  expect(screen.getByText(/john doe/i)).toBeInTheDocument()
);

// Use findBy* directly
expect(await screen.findByText(/john doe/i)).toBeInTheDocument();
```

Here is a short table that suggests you the occasions when you can use each command:

Use this	When
findBy*	You expect an element to appear asynchronously
waitFor	You are waiting for something that is not an element, such as:** **• a state change** **• a disabled → enabled toggle** **• a function call** **• an element count changing

Table 7.1: *Choosing Between findBy* and waitFor in React Testing Library*

This keeps your async tests predictable, stable, and aligned with RTL's recommended practices.

By incorporating these best practices into your tests, you can create a more reliable and maintainable test suite. React Testing Library encourages a developer to think from the user's perspective, which leads to better test coverage and improved application quality.

Mocking and Restoring Module Properties

Override module exports with **jest.mock** (or a single function with **jest.spyOn**), then restore real implementations via **jest.resetModules/jest.restoreAllMocks**, so that each test stays isolated.

Mocking Module Properties with jest.mock

When you want to test a part of your code that relies on a configuration or constant values from a module, you might want to replace those values with something else during the test. This is called mocking module properties. Imagine that you have a configuration file **config.js**, which looks like:

```
// config.js
module.exports = {
 apiEndpoint: 'https://api.example.com',
 timeout: 5000,
};
```

You want to test a function that uses these properties without depending on the real values. It might look like:

```
// myFunction.js
const config = require('./config');
```

```
function getApiEndpoint() {
  return config.apiEndpoint;
}

module.exports = { getApiEndpoint };
```

This is how you can mock module properties:

```
// myFunction.test.js
jest.mock('./config', () => ({
  apiEndpoint: 'https://mock-api.example.com',
  timeout: 1000,
}));

const { getApiEndpoint } = require('./myFunction');

test('should use mocked config properties', () => {
  expect(getApiEndpoint()).toBe('https://mock-api.example.com');
});
```

Restoring Original Module Properties

To use the original module properties again, you can reset the modules as shown here:

```
// myFunction.test.js
beforeEach(() => {
 jest.resetModules(); // Clears the cache and resets all mocks
});

test('should use original config properties', () => {
  const config = require('./config');
  const { getApiEndpoint } = require('./myFunction');
  expect(config.apiEndpoint).toBe('https://api.example.com');
  expect(getApiEndpoint()).toBe('https://api.example.com');
});
```

Mocking Specific Functions and Methods

Sometimes, you might want to mock only specific functions or methods within a module.

Consider a **`math.js`** module here:

```
// math.js
module.exports = {
  add: (a, b) => a + b,
```

```
  subtract: (a, b) => a - b,
};
```

You want to mock the add method while keeping the subtract method unchanged. This might look like:

```
// testFile.spec.js
const math = require('./math');

jest.spyOn(math, 'add').mockImplementation((a, b) => a * b);

test('should use mocked add method', () => {
  expect(math.add(2, 3)).toBe(6); // Mocked implementation
  expect(math.subtract(5, 3)).toBe(2); // Original implementation
});

afterEach(() => {
  jest.restoreAllMocks(); // Restore all mocks to their original
implementations
});
```

Mocking Dependencies for Isolated Testing

Mocking dependencies is crucial for isolated testing, as it ensures that your tests only cover the functionality of the module being tested and not the behavior of its dependencies. Assume you have a **`userService.js`** that relies on an `apiClient.js`. It might look like:

```
// apiClient.js
module.exports = {
 fetchUser: (id) => {
   // Simulates an API call
   return { id, name: 'John Doe' };
 },
};

// userService.js
const apiClient = require('./apiClient');

module.exports = {
 getUser: async (id) => {
   const user = await apiClient.fetchUser(id);
   return user;
 },
};
```

You would want to test `userService.js` without actually making API calls. This might look like:

```
// userService.spec.js
const userService = require('./userService');
const apiClient = require('./apiClient');

jest.mock('./apiClient', () => ({
 fetchUser: jest.fn(),
}));

test('should fetch user using mocked apiClient', async () => {
 const mockUser = { id: 1, name: 'Jane Doe' };
 apiClient.fetchUser.mockResolvedValue(mockUser);

 const user = await userService.getUser(1);
 expect(user).toEqual(mockUser);
 expect(apiClient.fetchUser).toHaveBeenCalledWith(1);
});
```

Mocking and Restoring with `jest.mock` and `jest.restoreAllMocks`

Combining mocking and restoring functionalities ensures that your tests are independent and do not affect each other. It might show up as:

```
// myModule.js
module.exports = {
 getData: () => 'real data',
};

// myModule.spec.js
const myModule = require('./myModule');

jest.mock('./myModule', () => ({
 getData: jest.fn(),
}));

beforeEach(() => {
 jest.clearAllMocks(); // Clear any previous mock calls
});

afterEach(() => {
 jest.restoreAllMocks(); // Restore original implementations
});
```

```
test('should use mocked getData method', () => {
 myModule.getData.mockReturnValue('mock data');
 expect(myModule.getData()).toBe('mock data');
});

test('should use original getData method', () => {
 expect(myModule.getData()).toBe('real data');
});
```

By following these practices, you can ensure that your tests are modular, maintainable, and isolated from external dependencies, which makes them more reliable and easier to understand.

Test Execution Control: `.skip` and `.only`

In Jest, you can control the execution of your tests using **`.skip`** and **`.only`**. These features allow you to skip certain tests or focus on running specific tests, which can be very helpful during development and debugging. Let us explore each of these in detail.

Skipping Tests with `.skip`

When you use `.skip`, the specified test will be skipped and will not run during the test execution. This is useful when you have tests that are not ready to be executed or are temporarily broken. Consider the following example:

```
// myTests.test.js
test.skip('this test will be skipped', () => {
 expect(true).toBe(false); // This assertion will not be executed
});

test('this test will run', () => {
 expect(true).toBe(true);
});
```

In this example, the first test is skipped and only the second test will run.

Running Specific Tests with `.only`

When you use **`.only`**, only the specified test(s) will be run, and all other tests will be skipped. This is useful when you want to focus on a particular test or a group of tests. Consider this example:

```
// myTests.test.js
test.only('this test will run', () => {
 expect(true).toBe(true);
```

```
});

test('this test will be skipped', () => {
 expect(true).toBe(false);
});
```

In this example, only the first test will run, and the second test will be skipped.

Conditional Test Execution

Sometimes, you may want to conditionally skip or run tests based on certain conditions, such as the environment or specific configurations. In these cases, consider the following example:

```
// myTests.test.js
const isProduction = process.env.NODE_ENV === 'production';

(isProduction ? test.skip : test)('this test will run only in non-
production environments', () => {
 expect(true).toBe(true);
});

(isProduction ? test : test.skip)('this test will run only in production
environments', () => {
 expect(true).toBe(true);
});
```

In this example, the first test will run only if the environment is not production and the second test will run only if the environment is production. Here are a few tips that will help you during this step of the process:

- **Use `.only` Sparingly**: **`.only`** is very powerful but should be used sparingly. Remember to remove or comment it out before committing your code to avoid accidentally running a subset of your tests.
- **Document Reasons for Skipping Tests**: When using `.skip`, it is good practice to document why the test is being skipped. This will allow other developers (or your future self) to understand the reason behind it.

  ```
  test.skip('this test is skipped because the feature is under
  development', () => {
        expect(true).toBe(false);
        });
  ```

- **Use Conditional Execution Wisely**: Conditional test execution should be used wisely to ensure that all necessary tests run in appropriate environments. Clearly document the conditions under which tests should run or be skipped.

- **Cleanup Before Committing**: Ensure that no `.only` or unnecessary `.skip` remains in your tests before committing code. This ensures that the full test suite runs in CI/CD pipelines and other environments.

Diverse Data Testing with `.each` in Jest

Data-driven testing allows you to run the same test logic against different sets of input data. Jest provides a powerful feature called `.each` that makes it easy to write parameterized tests. This is especially useful for testing functions with a variety of inputs to ensure that they behave as expected in different scenarios.

Introduction to Data-Driven Testing

Data-driven testing involves running the same test logic with multiple sets of data inputs. This helps in verifying that the function or component works correctly with a diverse range of data.

Creating Data Sets with `.each`

Jest's `.each` allows you to define test cases in a table-like format. Each row in the table represents a different set of inputs and expected outputs.

```
// mathFunctions.js
function add(a, b) {
 return a + b;
}

module.exports = { add };


// mathFunctions.test.js
const { add } = require('./mathFunctions');

test.each([
 [1, 1, 2],
 [2, 3, 5],
 [4, 5, 9],
 [-1, 1, 0]
])('adds %i and %i to get %i', (a, b, expected) => {
 expect(add(a, b)).toBe(expected);
});
```

In this example, the `add` function is tested with multiple sets of inputs and expected outputs. The **`test.each`** function takes an array of arrays, where each inner array represents a test case.

Parameterized Testing with Multiple Data Sets

You can use `.each` to run parameterized tests with multiple data sets, which is useful for more complex scenarios. Consider the following code:

```
// mathFunctions.js
function multiply(a, b) {
 return a * b;
}

module.exports = { multiply };


// mathFunctions.test.js
const { multiply } = require('./mathFunctions');

test.each([
 { a: 2, b: 3, expected: 6 },
 { a: -1, b: 5, expected: -5 },
 { a: 0, b: 7, expected: 0 },
 { a: 4, b: 4, expected: 16 }
])('multiplies $a and $b to get $expected', ({ a, b, expected }) => {
 expect(multiply(a, b)).toBe(expected);
});
```

In this example, each test case is represented as an object, which makes the test more readable and allows for more complex data structures.

Dynamic Test Generation with `.each`

You can also dynamically generate tests using `.each`. This is useful when the test data is generated or fetched dynamically.

```
// stringFunctions.js
function toUpperCase(str) {
 return str.toUpperCase();
}

module.exports = { toUpperCase };


// stringFunctions.test.js
const { toUpperCase } = require('./stringFunctions');

const testCases = [
 ['hello', 'HELLO'],
```

```
 ['world', 'WORLD'],
 ['jest', 'JEST'],
 ['test', 'TEST']
];

test.each(testCases)('converts %s to %s', (input, expected) => {
 expect(toUpperCase(input)).toBe(expected);
});
```

- **Keep Test Cases Readable**: Use descriptive variable names and structure your test cases for readability. This helps in developing a robust understanding of the purpose of each test case.
- **Document Test Cases:** Comment on complex test cases or data sets to explain the reasoning behind them.
- **Use Descriptive Test Titles:** When using `.each`, make sure the test title is descriptive and includes variables to provide context in test reports.
- **Combine with Other Jest Features:** Use `.each` in combination with other Jest features like mock functions and snapshots to create comprehensive test suites.

By leveraging Jest's `.each` feature, you can create robust and comprehensive test suites that cover a wide range of input scenarios, while ensuring that your functions and components behave correctly under various conditions.

Avoiding Common Testing Pitfalls

Effective testing is crucial for maintaining robust and reliable code. However, there are several common pitfalls that developers often encounter. Let us explore these pitfalls and how to avoid them.

Overusing Mocks and Fixtures

Mocks and fixtures are useful tools for isolating tests and simulating dependencies, but overusing them can lead to brittle tests that do not accurately reflect real-world scenarios.

Here are a few strategies to solve this issue:

- **Use Real Implementations When Possible:** Try to use real implementations, especially for integration tests, to ensure the system works as expected in a real environment.
- **Limit the Scope of Mocks:** Use mocks only for the specific part of the system you need to isolate. Avoid mocking everything in your tests.

- **Maintain Realistic Mocks:** Ensure your mocks behave similarly to the real implementations. This can prevent unexpected issues when the real system behaves differently.

Instead of mocking everything in a simple function test, try this:

```
// Overusing mock
const fetchData = jest.fn(() => Promise.resolve('mocked data'));

test('should process fetched data', async () => {
 const result = await processData(fetchData);
 expect(result).toBe('processed mocked data');
});
```

Use real implementations wherever you deem it appropriate, like in this example:

```
// Using real implementation
const fetchData = () => Promise.resolve('real data');

test('should process fetched data', async () => {
 const result = await processData(fetchData);
 expect(result).toBe('processed real data');
});
```

Neglecting Code Coverage Analysis

When code coverage is neglected, critical execution paths may never be exercised during testing, allowing defects to slip into production unnoticed. These hidden bugs often surface under edge conditions, leading to runtime failures, incorrect data processing, or degraded user experience. Over time, this erodes system reliability, increases production incidents, and raises the cost of maintenance as failures become harder to trace and fix. Regular coverage analysis helps teams identify blind spots early and ensures the system behaves correctly under both expected and unexpected conditions.

Solution:

- **Use Code Coverage Tools:** Use tools like Jest's built-in code coverage reports to identify untested parts of your code.
- **Aim for High Coverage:** Strive for high code coverage, but do not sacrifice test quality for the sake of numbers. Ensure that your tests are meaningful and cover important scenarios.
- **Review Coverage Regularly:** Make code coverage analysis a part of your CI/CD pipeline to ensure that new changes are covered by tests.

Enable code coverage in Jest by running this command:

```
jest --coverage
```

Review the generated coverage report to identify gaps.

Not Considering Edge Cases

When edge cases are ignored, the system may fail under uncommon but realistic conditions such as invalid input, extreme values, or unexpected user behavior. These failures often appear in production rather than during development, causing crashes, data corruption, or inconsistent behavior that undermines system stability and user trust.

Solution:

- **Identify Edge Cases:** Think about boundary conditions, invalid inputs, and unusual situations your code might encounter.
- **Write Tests for Edge Cases:** Ensure your tests cover these edge cases to validate that your code handles them correctly.

Instead of only testing typical inputs like this:

```
// Typical test
test('should add two positive numbers', () => {
 expect(add(1, 2)).toBe(3);
});
```

Test edge cases to validate if your code handles them correctly:

```
// Edge case tests
test('should add a positive and a negative number', () => {
 expect(add(1, -2)).toBe(-1);
});

test('should add zero', () => {
 expect(add(0, 0)).toBe(0);
});

test('should add large numbers', () => {
 expect(add(1000000, 1000000)).toBe(2000000);
});
```

Failing to Update Tests with Code Changes

When code changes, tests can become outdated and may no longer accurately reflect the current behavior of the system. This can lead to false positives or negatives.

Follow these strategies to overcome this barrier:

- **Update Tests with Code Changes:** Ensure that tests are updated whenever the code changes. This includes changing existing tests and adding new ones as necessary.
- **Automate Test Execution:** Use CI/CD pipelines to run tests automatically when code changes are made. This helps detect issues early on.
- **Refactor Tests:** Regularly refactor tests to keep them maintainable and relevant.

  When you are refactoring a function like this:

  ```
  // Original function
  function greet(name) {
   return `Hello, ${name}!`;
  }

  // Updated function
  function greet(name, greeting = 'Hello') {
   return `${greeting}, ${name}!`;
  }
  ```

Update the tests accordingly, as shown here:

```
// Original test
test('should greet with name', () => {
 expect(greet('Alice')).toBe('Hello, Alice!');
});

// Updated tests
test('should greet with name and default greeting', () => {
 expect(greet('Alice')).toBe('Hello, Alice!');
});

test('should greet with name and custom greeting', () => {
 expect(greet('Alice', 'Hi')).toBe('Hi, Alice!');
});
```

- **Avoid Overusing Mocks and Fixtures:** Use real implementations where possible and keep mocks realistic and limited in scope.
- **Analyze Code Coverage:** Use code coverage tools to identify untested parts of your code and aim for high, meaningful coverage.
- **Consider Edge Cases:** Identify and test edge cases to ensure your code handles all possible scenarios.

- **Update Tests with Code Changes:** Ensure tests are updated alongside code changes and automate test execution with CI/CD.

By being mindful of these common pitfalls and implementing these solutions, you can improve the effectiveness and reliability of your tests.

Conclusion

In this chapter, you learned to test the way users actually use your app. These strategies included querying by **`roles/labels/text`**, interacting with user-event, and waiting for async UI with **`findBy/waitFor`**. You also leveled up your Jest skills: you learned to mock or spy only at the edges, restore originals (**`jest.restoreAllMocks`**, **`jest.resetModules`**) to keep tests isolated, focus runs with **`.only/.skip`** sparingly, and drive breadth with data tables via **`.each`**. A good rule of thumb will be to keep suites fast and deterministic by creating fresh state per test, aiming for meaningful coverage (not just a percentage), and guarding against over-mocking. Do not forget edge cases and to evolve tests with the code. In conclusion, these habits will yield readable, resilient tests that are capable of catching real regressions and scaling with your codebase.

CHAPTER 8

Testing Real-World React Applications

Introduction

In this chapter, we will move ahead from isolated examples and learn about real-world React applications. You will test full user flows, authentication and routing, dynamic state changes, API-driven UIs, and performance-sensitive lists. The goal is to mirror how testing actually looks in production apps, not just in toy examples.

Structure

This chapter covers the following topics:

- Testing Real-World React App
- Testing Authentication and Routing
- Challenges in Testing Dynamic Applications

Testing Real-World React Applications

Real-world React applications are composed of multiple components, shared state, routing, and asynchronous interactions that work together to deliver user-facing features. Testing these applications requires validating complete user flows—such as form submissions, data fetching, and navigation—rather than isolated component internals. By exercising the app the way users interact with it, integration-focused tests catch issues that unit tests often miss, including broken workflows, incorrect state transitions, and unexpected side effects. This approach ensures the application behaves correctly in production-like scenarios and provides higher confidence during releases.

Writing Integration Tests for Components

Integration tests verify that different parts of the application work together as expected. In React, this means testing how components interact with each other and with other parts of the system such as APIs or context providers. You must therefore consider the following factors while writing integration tests:

- **Test User Interactions, Not Implementation Details**: Focus on how a user would interact with the app rather than on the component's internal structure.
- **Use React Testing Library**: It encourages testing components from the user's perspective, while ensuring that tests are resilient against refactoring.

Consider a simple form component that allows users to input their name and email, as shown here:

```
// SignupForm.jsx
import React, { useState } from 'react';

export default function SignupForm() {
  const [name, setName] = useState('');
  const [email, setEmail] = useState('');

  function handleSubmit(e) {
    e.preventDefault();
    console.log({ name, email }); // pretend API call
  }

  return (
    <form onSubmit={handleSubmit}>
      <label htmlFor="name">Name</label>
      <input id="name" value={name} onChange={(e) => setName(e.target.
value)} />

      <label htmlFor="email">Email</label>
      <input
        id="email"
        type="email"
```

```
        value={email}
        onChange={(e) => setEmail(e.target.value)}
      />

      <button type="submit">Sign Up</button>
    </form>
  );
}
```

Integration test for this form component using React Testing Library will look like:

```
// SignupForm.int.test.jsx
import { render, screen } from '@testing-library/react';
import userEvent from '@testing-library/user-event';
import SignupForm from './SignupForm';

afterEach(() => {
  jest.restoreAllMocks();
});

test('allows the user to submit the form', async () => {
  const user = userEvent.setup();
  const logSpy = jest.spyOn(console, 'log').mockImplementation(() =>
{});

  render(<SignupForm />);

  await user.type(screen.getByLabelText(/name/i), 'John Doe');
  await user.type(screen.getByLabelText(/email/i), 'john@example.com');
  await user.click(screen.getByRole('button', { name: /sign up/i }));

  expect(logSpy).toHaveBeenCalledWith({
    name: 'John Doe',
    email: 'john@example.com',
  });
});
```

- **User Perspective**: Notice how the test interacts with the form just like a user would by using `getByLabelText` and `getByRole`.
- **Resilience**: The test is resilient to changes in internal implementation, such as changing the input IDs or button classes.

Mocking API Calls and External Services

Mocking is essential in testing because it allows you to simulate API calls and other external services without making actual network requests. This isolation helps ensure that tests are fast, reliable, and focus on the component's behavior rather than on external dependencies.

- **Use Mock Service Worker (MSW)**: MSW allows to mock API calls by intercepting requests at the network level, while providing more realistic testing scenarios.
- **Avoid Over-Mocking**: Mock only what is necessary to avoid creating tests that are too detached from real-world scenarios.

Let us say that we have a component that fetches user data from an API, which looks like this:

```
// UserProfile.jsx
import React, { useEffect, useState } from 'react';

export default function UserProfile({ userId }) {
  const [user, setUser] = useState(null);

  useEffect(() => {
    async function run() {
      const res = await fetch(`/api/users/${userId}`);
      const data = await res.json();
      setUser(data);
    }
    run();
  }, [userId]);

  if (!user) return <div>Loading...</div>;

  return (
    <div>
      <h1>{user.name}</h1>
      <p>{user.email}</p>
    </div>
  );
}
```

Here is how to test **UserProfile** component using MSW to mock the API call:

```
// UserProfile.int.test.jsx
import { render, screen } from '@testing-library/react';
import { rest } from 'msw';
import { setupServer } from 'msw/node';
import UserProfile from './UserProfile';

const server = setupServer(
  rest.get('/api/users/:userId', (_req, res, ctx) =>
```

```
    res(ctx.json({ name: 'John Doe', email: 'john@example.com' }))
  )
);

beforeAll(() => server.listen());
afterEach(() => server.resetHandlers());
afterAll(() => server.close());

test('loads and displays user profile', async () => {
  render(<UserProfile userId="123" />);
  expect(await screen.findByText(/john doe/i)).toBeInTheDocument();
  expect(screen.getByText(/john@example.com/i)).toBeInTheDocument();
});
```

For truly unit-level tests you can also inject a `**fetchData**` function as a prop (as shown later in `**DataFetchingComponent**`) and mock that function directly instead of mocking `**fetch**` or using MSW.

Testing Authentication and Routing

Authentication and routing form the backbone of most real-world React applications, directly controlling access, navigation, and user experience. Even small mistakes in these areas can expose protected content, break navigation flows, or trap users in invalid states. Testing authentication and routing together ensures that permission boundaries, redirects, and session-driven UI changes behave correctly under real user conditions. By simulating auth states and navigation paths, these tests validate not just correctness, but also security, reliability, and consistency across the entire application lifecycle.

Testing Authentication Flows: Login, Logout

Authentication is a critical part of any application. Testing authentication flows such as login and logout ensures that users can securely access the necessary parts of the application. This section will cover how to write tests that simulate user interactions with authentication processes.

- Focus on how users interact with the login and logout functionalities, rather than testing internal implementation details.
- Make sure that you cover successful logins, failed logins due to incorrect credentials, and logouts.

A login component allows users to enter their credentials and submit them to an API, as shown here:

```
// LoginForm.jsx
```

```
import React, { useState } from 'react';

export default function Login({ onLogin }) {
  const [username, setUsername] = useState('');
  const [password, setPassword] = useState('');

  async function handleSubmit(e) {
    e.preventDefault();
    const res = await fetch('/api/login', {
      method: 'POST',
      headers: { 'Content-Type': 'application/json' }, // realistic
header
      body: JSON.stringify({ username, password }),
    });
    if (res.ok) onLogin();
    // else set error state and render a message users can see
  }

  return (
    <form onSubmit={handleSubmit}>
      <label htmlFor="username">Username</label>
      <input
        id="username"
        placeholder="Username"
        value={username}
        onChange={(e) => setUsername(e.target.value)}
      />

      <label htmlFor="password">Password</label>
      <input
        id="password"
        placeholder="Password"
        type="password"
        value={password}
        onChange={(e) => setPassword(e.target.value)}
      />

      <button type="submit">Login</button>
    </form>
  );
}
```

A test for the login flow using React Testing Library will look like this:

```
// LoginForm.test.jsx
```

```
import { render, screen, waitFor } from '@testing-library/react';
import userEvent from '@testing-library/user-event';
import Login from './Login';

afterEach(() => {
  jest.restoreAllMocks();
});

test('allows the user to log in (happy path)', async () => {
  const user = userEvent.setup();
  const mockOnLogin = jest.fn();

  const fetchSpy = jest
    .spyOn(global, 'fetch')
    .mockResolvedValue({
      ok: true,
      json: async () => ({ token: 'abc' }),
    });

  render(<Login onLogin={mockOnLogin} />);

  await user.type(screen.getByPlaceholderText(/username/i), 'testuser');
  await user.type(screen.getByPlaceholderText(/password/i),
'password123');
  await user.click(screen.getByRole('button', { name: /login/i }));

  expect(fetchSpy).toHaveBeenCalledWith(
    '/api/login',
    expect.objectContaining({
      method: 'POST',
      body: JSON.stringify({ username: 'testuser', password:
'password123' }),
    })
  );

  await waitFor(() => expect(mockOnLogin).toHaveBeenCalled());
});

test('shows error / does not call onLogin on failed credentials', async
() => {
  const user = userEvent.setup();
  const mockOnLogin = jest.fn();

  jest
    .spyOn(global, 'fetch')
    .mockResolvedValue({
```

```
      ok: false,
      status: 401,
      json: async () => ({ error: 'Invalid credentials' }),
    });

  render(<Login onLogin={mockOnLogin} />);

  await user.type(screen.getByPlaceholderText(/username/i), 'wrong');
  await user.type(screen.getByPlaceholderText(/password/i), 'nope');
  await user.click(screen.getByRole('button', { name: /login/i }));

  await waitFor(() => expect(mockOnLogin).not.toHaveBeenCalled());
  // If your component renders an error message, assert it here:
  // expect(screen.getByText(/invalid credentials/i)).
toBeInTheDocument();
});
```

Mocking Authentication Context for Tests

In React applications, authentication state is often managed via context. To effectively test components that rely on authentication, you need to mock this context. This ensures that tests remain isolated and focused on the component behavior rather than on the authentication mechanism.

- **Create a Mock Authentication Provider**: Mock the provider that wraps components to simulate different authentication states.
- **Test Both Authenticated and Unauthenticated States**: Ensure that tests cover scenarios where the user is logged in and logged out.

An **AuthContext** that provides the current authentication state and a method to log in and out. This looks like:

```
// AuthContext.js
import React, { createContext, useContext, useMemo, useState } from
'react';

export const AuthContext = createContext(undefined);

export function AuthProvider({ children }) {
  const [isAuthenticated, setIsAuthenticated] = useState(false);

  const value = useMemo(
    () => ({
      isAuthenticated,
      login: () => setIsAuthenticated(true),
      logout: () => setIsAuthenticated(false),
```

```
    }),
    [isAuthenticated]
  );

  return <AuthContext.Provider value={value}>{children}</AuthContext.
Provider>;
}

export function useAuth() {
  const ctx = useContext(AuthContext);
  if (!ctx) {
    throw new Error('useAuth must be used within <AuthProvider>');
  }
  return ctx;
}
```

To test a component that relies on **AuthContext**, mock the context like this:

```
// Dashboard.test.js
import React from 'react';
import { render, screen } from '@testing-library/react';
import { AuthContext, useAuth } from './AuthContext';

// Simple component under test
function Dashboard() {
  const { isAuthenticated } = useAuth();
  return <h1>{isAuthenticated ? 'Welcome Back!' : 'Please Log In'}</h1>;
}

// Mock provider that supplies the full context shape
function MockAuthProvider({ isAuthenticated, children }) {
  const value = {
    isAuthenticated,
    login: jest.fn(),
    logout: jest.fn(),
  };
  return <AuthContext.Provider value={value}>{children}</AuthContext.
Provider>;
}

describe('Dashboard (auth-dependent rendering)', () => {
  test('shows welcome message when authenticated', () => {
    render(
      <MockAuthProvider isAuthenticated={true}>
        <Dashboard />
      </MockAuthProvider>
```

```
    );
    expect(
      screen.getByRole('heading', { name: /welcome back/i })
    ).toBeInTheDocument();
  });

  test('shows login prompt when not authenticated', () => {
    render(
      <MockAuthProvider isAuthenticated={false}>
        <Dashboard />
      </MockAuthProvider>
    );
    expect(
      screen.getByRole('heading', { name: /please log in/i })
    ).toBeInTheDocument();
  });
});
```

- **Flexibility**: By creating a mock provider, we can easily simulate different authentication states.
- **Isolated Testing**: This approach isolates the component's behavior from the actual authentication mechanism and makes tests more focused and reliable.

Testing Protected Routes and Components

Protected routes ensure that only authenticated users can access certain parts of your application. Testing these routes is crucial to ensure that unauthorized users are properly redirected, and authorized users can access the protected content.

- **Use `MemoryRouter`**: For testing routes, use React Router's **`MemoryRouter`**, which allows you to define and manipulate the history stack within your tests.
- **Test Redirection Logic**: Ensure that users are redirected to the login page or another appropriate page if they are not authenticated.

Suppose you have a protected route that only allows access to authenticated users. This might look like:

```
// ProtectedRoute.js (React Router v6)
import React from 'react';
import { Navigate, Outlet } from 'react-router-dom';
import { useAuth } from './AuthContext';

export default function ProtectedRoute({ redirectTo = '/login' }) {
```

```
  const { isAuthenticated } = useAuth();
  return isAuthenticated ? <Outlet /> : <Navigate to={redirectTo}
replace />;
}
```

Here is how you can write a test for the protected route using **`MemoryRouter`**:

```
// ProtectedRoute.test.js
import React from 'react';
import { render, screen } from '@testing-library/react';
import '@testing-library/jest-dom';
import { MemoryRouter, Routes, Route } from 'react-router-dom';
import ProtectedRoute from './ProtectedRoute';
import { AuthContext } from './AuthContext';

// Simple pages
function Dashboard() {
  return <h1>Dashboard</h1>;
}
function LoginPage() {
  return <h1>Login Page</h1>;
}

function renderWithAuth(isAuthenticated, initialEntries = ['/
dashboard']) {
  const authValue = { isAuthenticated, login: jest.fn(), logout: jest.
fn() };
  return render(
    <AuthContext.Provider value={authValue}>
      <MemoryRouter initialEntries={initialEntries}>
        <Routes>
          <Route path="/login" element={<LoginPage />} />
          {/* Gate any protected routes under this wrapper */}
          <Route element={<ProtectedRoute />}>
            <Route path="/dashboard" element={<Dashboard />} />
          </Route>
        </Routes>
      </MemoryRouter>
    </AuthContext.Provider>
  );
}

describe('ProtectedRoute (v6)', () => {
```

```
  test('redirects unauthenticated users to /login', () => {
    renderWithAuth(false);
    expect(
      screen.getByRole('heading', { name: /login page/i })
    ).toBeInTheDocument();
    expect(
      screen.queryByRole('heading', { name: /dashboard/i })
    ).not.toBeInTheDocument();
  });

  test('allows authenticated users to see the protected page', () => {
    renderWithAuth(true);
    expect(
      screen.getByRole('heading', { name: /dashboard/i })
    ).toBeInTheDocument();
    expect(
      screen.queryByRole('heading', { name: /login page/i })
    ).not.toBeInTheDocument();
  });
});
```

- **Comprehensive Coverage**: The tests cover both scenarios—when the user is authenticated and when they are not.
- **User Flow Simulation**: The tests ensure that users are redirected appropriately based on their authentication state.

Handling Redirects in Authentication Tests

Redirects are common in authentication flows, especially when dealing with protected routes. Testing these redirects ensures that users are navigated to the correct pages based on their authentication state.

- **Check for Specific Routes**: When testing redirects, you must check that the user is redirected to the exact route you expect.
- **Use `MemoryRouter`**: Again, the **`MemoryRouter`** is ideal for simulating navigation and redirects in a controlled testing environment.

Suppose your application redirects users to the dashboard after a successful login. It might look like this:

```
// App.jsx
import { Routes, Route, Navigate } from 'react-router-dom';
import { useAuth } from './AuthContext';
import AuthLogin from './AuthLogin';
```

```
import Dashboard from './Dashboard';

function ProtectedRoute({ children }) {
  const { isAuthenticated } = useAuth();
  return isAuthenticated ? children : <Navigate to="/login" replace />;
}

export default function App() {
  const { isAuthenticated } = useAuth();

  return (
    <Routes>
      <Route
        path="/login"
        element={isAuthenticated ? <Navigate to="/dashboard" replace />
: <AuthLogin />}
      />
      <Route
        path="/dashboard"
        element={
          <ProtectedRoute>
            <Dashboard />
          </ProtectedRoute>
        }
      />
    </Routes>
  );
}


// AuthLogin.jsx
import React, { useState } from 'react';
import { useAuth } from './AuthContext';

export default function AuthLogin() {
  const { login } = useAuth();
  const [username, setUsername] = useState('');
  const [password, setPassword] = useState('');

  async function handleSubmit(e) {
    e.preventDefault();
    // normally you'd call an API here; on success:
    login();
  }
```

```
  return (
    <form onSubmit={handleSubmit}>
      <input
        placeholder="Username"
        value={username}
        onChange={(e) => setUsername(e.target.value)}
      />
      <input
        placeholder="Password"
        type="password"
        value={password}
        onChange={(e) => setPassword(e.target.value)}
      />
      <button type="submit">Login</button>
    </form>
  );
}
```

Here is how you can test the redirect after a successful login:

```
// App.redirect.test.jsx
import React from 'react';
import { render, screen } from '@testing-library/react';
import userEvent from '@testing-library/user-event';
import { MemoryRouter } from 'react-router-dom';
import App from './App';
import { AuthContext } from './AuthContext';
import '@testing-library/jest-dom';

// A stateful provider so clicking "Login" flips auth and triggers
redirect
function StatefulAuthProvider({ children }) {
  const [isAuthenticated, setIsAuthenticated] = React.useState(false);
  const value = React.useMemo(
    () => ({
      isAuthenticated,
      login: () => setIsAuthenticated(true),
      logout: () => setIsAuthenticated(false),
    }),
    [isAuthenticated]
  );
  return <AuthContext.Provider value={value}>{children}</AuthContext.
Provider>;
```

```
}

test('redirects to dashboard after login', async () => {
  const user = userEvent.setup();

  render(
    <StatefulAuthProvider>
      <MemoryRouter initialEntries={['/login']}>
        <App />
      </MemoryRouter>
    </StatefulAuthProvider>
  );

  await user.type(screen.getByPlaceholderText(/username/i), 'testuser');
  await user.type(screen.getByPlaceholderText(/password/i),
'password123');
  await user.click(screen.getByRole('button', { name: /login/i }));

  // App naturally re-renders with isAuthenticated=true and navigates
  expect(
    await screen.findByRole('heading', { name: /dashboard/i })
  ).toBeInTheDocument();
});
```

By incorporating these practices and detailed examples into your testing strategy, you can ensure that your React application's authentication and routing mechanisms are reliable, secure, and user-friendly.

Challenges in Testing Dynamic Applications

Dynamic React UIs constantly change based on user input, async data, and state transitions. If your tests assert too early or against implementation details, they can quickly become flaky. In this section, you will see three patterns: search-as-you-type, state-driven messages, and conditional toggles.

Dealing with Dynamic Data (Search-as-you-type)

Dynamic React applications, which update in real-time based on user interactions, API responses, or state changes, require a focused testing approach to ensure consistency and reliability. Some of them are mentioned as follows:

- **Simulate Real-World Interactions**: Focus on simulating user interactions as they would occur in the real world. This includes typing in text inputs, clicking buttons, and triggering events like form submissions.
- **Use Asynchronous Testing Appropriately**: When dealing with dynamic applications, ensure that your tests handle asynchronous operations correctly. Use tools like **`waitFor`** from React Testing Library to wait for updates in the UI.
- **Test Edge Cases**: Consider edge cases, such as empty inputs or rapid user interactions to ensure that your application handles these scenarios gracefully.

This example illustrates a dynamic search component that fetches results from an API as the user types. It looks like:

```
// SearchComponent.jsx
import React, { useState } from 'react';

export default function SearchComponent({ fetchData }) {
  const [query, setQuery] = useState('');
  const [results, setResults] = useState([]);

  async function handleChange(e) {
    const q = e.target.value;
    setQuery(q);
    if (!q) return setResults([]);
    const data = await fetchData(q);
    setResults(data);
  }

  return (
    <div>
      <input type="text" value={query} onChange={handleChange} />
      <ul>
        {results.map((r) => (
          <li key={r.id}>{r.name}</li>
        ))}
      </ul>
    </div>
  );
}
```

Here is how to test **`SearchComponent`**:

```
// SearchComponent.int.test.jsx
import { render, screen } from '@testing-library/react';
```

```
import userEvent from '@testing-library/user-event';
import SearchComponent from './SearchComponent';

test('updates results from user input', async () => {
  const user = userEvent.setup();
  const fetchData = jest.fn().mockResolvedValue([
    { id: 1, name: 'Result 1' },
    { id: 2, name: 'Result 2' },
  ]);

  render(<SearchComponent fetchData={fetchData} />);
  await user.type(screen.getByRole('textbox'), 'query');

  expect(fetchData).toHaveBeenCalledWith('query');
  expect(await screen.findByText('Result 1')).toBeInTheDocument();
  expect(await screen.findByText('Result 2')).toBeInTheDocument();
});

test('clears results when input is cleared', async () => {
  const user = userEvent.setup();
  const fetchData = jest.fn().mockResolvedValue([{ id: 1, name: 'Result
1' }]);

  render(<SearchComponent fetchData={fetchData} />);

  const input = screen.getByRole('textbox');
  await user.type(input, 'query');

  expect(await screen.findByText('Result 1')).toBeInTheDocument();

  await user.clear(input);
  expect(screen.queryByText('Result 1')).not.toBeInTheDocument();
});
```

Testing State-Driven UI (Derived Messages)

React components often manage dynamic data through state changes, which can be triggered by user input, API responses, or other factors. Testing these components requires simulating state changes and verifying that the UI updates correctly. You can follow these strategies to test state-driven UI:

- **Test State Transitions**: Focus on testing how state transitions occur based on user actions. Ensure that state changes lead to the expected UI updates.
- **Isolate State Logic**: Wherever possible, isolate state logic in custom hooks or helper functions to make testing easier and more focused.

- **Use `beforeEach` for Consistent State**: Use the `beforeEach` hook in Jest to reset state or set up necessary preconditions before each test runs.

This example involves a form that updates its state based on user input, while enabling or disabling fields. It looks like:

```
// DynamicForm.jsx
import React, { useState } from 'react';

const DynamicForm = () => {
  const [formData, setFormData] = useState({ name: '', age: '' });
  const [isAdult, setIsAdult] = useState(false);

  const handleInputChange = (e) => {
    const { name, value } = e.target;
    setFormData((prev) => ({ ...prev, [name]: value }));

    if (name === 'age') {
      const n = Number(value);
      setIsAdult(!Number.isNaN(n) && n >= 18);
    }
  };

  return (
    <form>
      <label htmlFor="name">Name</label>
      <input
        id="name"
        name="name"
        value={formData.name}
        onChange={handleInputChange}
        placeholder="Name"
      />

      <label htmlFor="age">Age</label>
      <input
        id="age"
        name="age"
        inputMode="numeric"
        value={formData.age}
        onChange={handleInputChange}
        placeholder="Age"
      />

      {isAdult && (
        <p aria-live="polite">You are an adult</p>
```

```
    )}
    </form>
  );
};
export default DynamicForm;


// DynamicForm.test.jsx
import React from 'react';
import { render, screen } from '@testing-library/react';
import userEvent from '@testing-library/user-event';
import '@testing-library/jest-dom';
import DynamicForm from './DynamicForm';

describe('DynamicForm', () => {
  test('updates inputs and shows adult message at 20', async () => {
    const user = userEvent.setup();
    render(<DynamicForm />);

    const nameInput = screen.getByRole('textbox', { name: /name/i });
    const ageInput  = screen.getByRole('textbox', { name: /age/i });

    await user.clear(nameInput);
    await user.type(nameInput, 'John Doe');
    await user.clear(ageInput);
    await user.type(ageInput, '20');

    expect(nameInput).toHaveValue('John Doe');
    expect(ageInput).toHaveValue('20');
    expect(screen.getByText(/you are an adult/i)).toBeInTheDocument();
  });

  test('does not show adult message if age is below 18', async () => {
    const user = userEvent.setup();
    render(<DynamicForm />);

    const ageInput = screen.getByRole('textbox', { name: /age/i });
    await user.clear(ageInput);
    await user.type(ageInput, '16');

    expect(screen.queryByText(/you are an adult/i)).not.
toBeInTheDocument();
  });

  test('edge cases: exactly 18 shows message; non-numeric hides
message', async () => {
```

```
    const user = userEvent.setup();
    render(<DynamicForm />);

    const ageInput = screen.getByRole('textbox', { name: /age/i });

    // exactly 18 -> adult
    await user.clear(ageInput);
    await user.type(ageInput, '18');
    expect(screen.getByText(/you are an adult/i)).toBeInTheDocument();

    // non-numeric -> not adult
    await user.clear(ageInput);
    await user.type(ageInput, 'abc');
    expect(screen.queryByText(/you are an adult/i)).not.
toBeInTheDocument();
  });
});
```

Testing Conditional Rendering (Toggle UI)

Dynamic rendering involves displaying different parts of the UI based on the component's state or props. Testing these components ensures that the UI behaves correctly under various conditions. You can also follow these steps to further test conditional rendering in a robust way:

- Write tests that verify whether elements are rendered or hidden based on the component's state or props.
- Test how user interactions affect the rendered output. For example, clicking a button might toggle visibility or change displayed content.
- Ensure that tests cover all possible rendering scenarios, including edge cases where certain conditions might not be met.

This example demonstrates a component that toggles between two different views based on user interaction.

```
//ToggleComponent.jsx
import React, { useState } from 'react';

const ToggleComponent = () => {
 const [isToggled, setIsToggled] = useState(false);

 return (
   <div>
     <button onClick={() => setIsToggled(!isToggled)}>
       {isToggled ? 'Hide' : 'Show'} Details
```

```
      </button>
      {isToggled && <p>Here are some details...</p>}
    </div>
  );
};

export default ToggleComponent;

// ToggleComponent.test.jsx
import React from 'react';
import { render, screen } from '@testing-library/react';
import userEvent from '@testing-library/user-event'; // ⍰ user-event
instead of fireEvent
import '@testing-library/jest-dom'; // if not already in your test setup
import ToggleComponent from './ToggleComponent';

describe('ToggleComponent', () => {
  it('toggles visibility of details on button click', async () => {
    const user = userEvent.setup();
    render(<ToggleComponent />);

    const button = screen.getByRole('button', { name: /show details/i
});

    // Initial state: details hidden
    expect(screen.queryByText(/here are some details/i)).not.
toBeInTheDocument();

    // Click to show details
    await user.click(button);
    expect(screen.getByText(/here are some details/i)).
toBeInTheDocument();
    expect(button).toHaveTextContent(/hide details/i);

    // Click to hide details
    await user.click(button);
    expect(screen.queryByText(/here are some details/i)).not.
toBeInTheDocument();
    expect(button).toHaveTextContent(/show details/i);
  });
});
```

Mocking and Testing Dynamic API Responses

React components often rely on dynamic data fetched from APIs. Testing these components effectively requires mocking API responses to simulate different scenarios. You can use the following strategies to mock and text dynamic API responses:

- **Use Mocks for Consistency**: Mock API calls to ensure consistent test results, regardless of network conditions or API availability.
- **Simulate Different API Responses**: Test components against various API response scenarios like success, failure, and edge cases like empty or malformed data.
- **Focus on Error Handling**: Ensure tests verify that the component handles API errors gracefully, while providing appropriate feedback to the user.

This example shows how to mock API responses in Jest for a component that fetches data based on user input.

```
// DataFetchingComponent.jsx
import React, { useState, useEffect } from 'react';

const DataFetchingComponent = ({ fetchData }) => {
  const [data, setData] = useState(null);
  const [error, setError] = useState(null);    // NEW
  const [loading, setLoading] = useState(true);

  useEffect(() => {
    let cancelled = false;                      // prevents updates after
unmount
    (async () => {
      try {
        const result = await fetchData();
        if (!cancelled) {
          setData(result);
          setError(null);
        }
      } catch (e) {
        if (!cancelled) setError((e && e.message) || 'Failed to fetch');
      } finally {
        if (!cancelled) setLoading(false);
      }
    })();
    return () => { cancelled = true; };
  }, [fetchData]);

  if (loading) return <p>Loading...</p>;
  if (error)   return <p role="alert">Error: {error}</p>; // NEW

  return (
    <div>
```

```
      {data ? <p>{data.message}</p> : <p>No data</p>}
    </div>
  );
};

export default DataFetchingComponent;
```

Testing for **DataFetchingComponent** will look like:

```
// DataFetchingComponent.test.jsx
import React from 'react';
import { render, screen } from '@testing-library/react';
import DataFetchingComponent from './DataFetchingComponent';

afterEach(() => {
  jest.clearAllMocks();
  jest.restoreAllMocks();
});

describe('DataFetchingComponent', () => {
  it('displays data when fetched', async () => {
    const mockFetchData = jest.fn().mockResolvedValue({ message: 'Hello,
World!' });

    render(<DataFetchingComponent fetchData={mockFetchData} />);

    expect(screen.getByText('Loading...')).toBeInTheDocument();

    // simpler/robust: findBy*
    expect(await screen.findByText('Hello, World!')).toBeInTheDocument();
    expect(mockFetchData).toHaveBeenCalledTimes(1);
  });

  it('handles API failure gracefully', async () => {
    const mockFetchData = jest.fn().mockRejectedValue(new Error('Failed
to fetch data'));

    render(<DataFetchingComponent fetchData={mockFetchData} />);

    expect(screen.getByText('Loading...')).toBeInTheDocument();

    const alert = await screen.findByRole('alert');
    expect(alert).toHaveTextContent('Failed to fetch data');  // assert
actual error UI
  });

  it('shows "No data" when API returns null/empty', async () => {
    const mockFetchData = jest.fn().mockResolvedValue(null);

    render(<DataFetchingComponent fetchData={mockFetchData} />);
```

```
    expect(await screen.findByText('No data')).toBeInTheDocument();
  });
});
```

Addressing Performance Challenges in Dynamic Testing

Dynamic applications can face performance challenges, particularly while dealing with large datasets or complex state management. Performance testing ensures that the application remains responsive under various conditions. You can follow the given measures to address challenges:

- **Test with Realistic Data**: Use data sets that reflect real-world usage like large data sets to ensure application performs well under typical conditions.
- **Measure Performance**: Use tools like React's profiling tools or performance monitoring libraries to measure and optimize the rendering performance of components.
- **Optimize Rendering**: Ensure that components are optimized to prevent unnecessary re-renders, which can degrade performance.

Here is an example of a large list rendering component:

```
//LargeListComponent.jsx
import React from 'react';

const Row = React.memo(function Row({ item, onRender }) {
  onRender?.(item.id);
  return <li>{item.name}</li>;
});

export default function LargeListComponent({ items, onRowRender }) {
  return (
    <ul>
      {items.map((item) => (
        <Row key={item.id} item={item} onRender={onRowRender} />
      ))}
    </ul>
  );
}

// LargeListComponent.test.jsx
import { render } from '@testing-library/react';
import LargeList from './LargeListComponent';
```

```
test('only changed rows re-render', () => {
  const onRowRender = jest.fn();

  const items1 = [
    { id: 1, name: 'A' },
    { id: 2, name: 'B' },
    { id: 3, name: 'C' },
  ];

  const { rerender } = render(
    <LargeList items={items1} onRowRender={onRowRender} />
  );

  expect(onRowRender).toHaveBeenCalledTimes(3); // first paint
  onRowRender.mockClear();

  const items2 = [
    items1[0],                        // same reference
    { id: 2, name: 'B updated' },  // changed row
    items1[2],                        // same reference
  ];

  rerender(<LargeList items={items2} onRowRender={onRowRender} />);
  expect(onRowRender).toHaveBeenCalledTimes(1); // only row with id=2
re-rendered
});
```

Real-World Scaling with Virtualization

If you ever expect thousands of rows, switch the example to a virtualized list (for example, react-window) and test visible items and scroll behavior, and not total DOM size.

```
// VirtualList.jsx
import React from 'react';
import { FixedSizeList as List } from 'react-window';

export default function VirtualList({ items, height = 200, itemSize =
36, width = 300 }) {
  return (
    <List height={height} itemCount={items.length} itemSize={itemSize}
width={width} itemData={items}>
      {({ index, style, data }) => (
        <div style={style} role="listitem">{data[index].name}</div>
      )}
    </List>
```

```
  );
}

// VirtualList.test.jsx
import { render, screen } from '@testing-library/react';
import userEvent from '@testing-library/user-event';
import VirtualList from './VirtualList';

test('renders only visible rows and updates on scroll', async () => {
  const user = userEvent.setup();

  const items = Array.from({ length: 1000 }, (_, i) => ({
    id: i,
    name: `Item ${i}`,
  }));

  const { container } = render(
    <VirtualList items={items} height={120} itemSize={30} />
  );

  // Initially visible items
  expect(screen.getByText('Item 0')).toBeInTheDocument();
  expect(screen.queryByText('Item 999')).not.toBeInTheDocument();

  // react-window outer scroll element
  const scroller = container.firstChild;

  scroller.scrollTop = 999 * 30;
  await user.scroll(scroller, { deltaY: 999 * 30 });

  expect(await screen.findByText('Item 999')).toBeInTheDocument();
});
```

JSDOM does not perform real layout calculations, but react-window listens to **scrollTop** changes and scroll events. Therefore, updating **scrollTop** + firing a scroll event is enough to verify virtualization behavior. These tests assert only user-visible items after scrolling, not DOM size or timing. For real performance profiling, use React DevTools Profiler or browser performance tools outside Jest.

E2E Testing with User Interactions

End-to-end (E2E) testing simulates a user's journey through an application, while testing the entire stack from the UI down to the database. This is crucial for catching issues that may not be evident in unit or integration tests. You can deploy the following strategies for E2E testing:

- **Use Playwright or Cypress**: You can use them as both are powerful tools for E2E testing with robust APIs for simulating user interactions.
- **Keep Tests Focused**: Each E2E test should focus on a single user flow, which makes it easier to debug when something goes wrong.

Suppose we have a login form that redirects the user to a dashboard upon successful login. It might look like:

```
// LoginPage.jsx
import React, { useState } from 'react';

function Login() {
  const [username, setUsername] = useState('');
  const [password, setPassword] = useState('');

  const handleSubmit = async (e) => {
    e.preventDefault();
    const response = await fetch('/api/login', {
      method: 'POST',
      body: JSON.stringify({ username, password }),
    });
    if (response.ok) {
      window.location.href = '/dashboard';
    }
  };

  return (
    <form onSubmit={handleSubmit}>
      <input
        type="text"
        placeholder="Username"
        value={username}
        onChange={(e) => setUsername(e.target.value)}
      />
      <input
        type="password"
        placeholder="Password"
        value={password}
        onChange={(e) => setPassword(e.target.value)}
      />
      <button type="submit">Login</button>
    </form>
  );
}
```

```
export default Login;
```

Here is how we can write an E2E test for the login flow using Playwright:

```
const { test, expect } = require('@playwright/test');

 test('user can log in and see the dashboard', async ({ page }) => {
   // Navigate to the login page
   await page.goto('http://localhost:3000/login');
    // Fill out the login form
   await page.fill('input[placeholder="Username"]', 'testuser');
   await page.fill('input[placeholder="Password"]', 'password123');
    // Submit the form
   await page.click('button[type="submit"]');
    // Verify the user is redirected to the dashboard
   await expect(page).toHaveURL('http://localhost:3000/dashboard');
   await expect(page.locator('h1')).toHaveText('Welcome to the
Dashboard');
 });
```

By incorporating these practices and examples into your testing strategy, you will be able to create a comprehensive test suite that keeps React applications reliable, maintainable, and user-friendly.

Conclusion

You now know how to test real production React code through API-driven UIs, authentication flows, routing guards, redirects, dynamic rendering, search-as-you-type behavior, and performance-sensitive lists. Combined with E2E tests, these patterns give you a resilient test suite that prevents regressions and mirrors actual user behavior in CI.

Beyond preventing regressions, these tests act as release confidence checks for teams building dashboards, SaaS products, e-commerce flows, and any app that depends on routing, auth, and API-driven UI. They also make refactoring safer because you can change internals while still proving the user journeys remain intact. In the next chapter, we will strengthen this workflow by measuring Jest coverage and wiring tests into CI/CD so quality is enforced automatically on every pull request.

CHAPTER 9
Jest Coverage and CI/CD Integration

Introduction

In the previous chapter, you learned how to test real-world React applications by validating full user flows, authentication, routing, and dynamic behavior. While these tests build confidence in functionality, they do not automatically guarantee that all important code paths are exercised. This is where test coverage becomes essential—it exposes blind spots in your test suite, highlighting logic that is never executed and edge cases that may fail silently in production.

Jest provides built-in coverage tooling that helps teams quantify test effectiveness, enforce quality gates, and prevent regressions as the codebase evolves. When combined with CI/CD pipelines, coverage metrics become a continuous safety net, ensuring that new changes meet quality standards before they reach users. Used correctly, test coverage improves refactoring confidence, accelerates code reviews, and strengthens long-term system reliability without encouraging superficial or low-value tests.

Structure

This chapter covers the following topics:

- Configuring Jest for Code Coverage

- Running and Generating Coverage Reports
- Integrating Jest into CI/CD Pipelines
- End-to-End Testing with Jest

Configuring Jest for Code Coverage

Set up Jest to collect, measure, and report how much of your application code is tested. This will give you clear visibility into gaps and will help you enforce quality standards across your project.

Setting Up Jest Configuration

Configuring Jest for code coverage is the first step. You can enable coverage, choose where the reports are written, and optionally customize which files are included.

You can configure Jest either in a **jest.config.js** file or inside **package.json** under the "**jest**" field.

Enable Coverage Reporting: Add or update Jest configuration to enable coverage collection. This can be done in the **jest.config.js** file or directly in **package.json**., as shown here:

```
module.exports = {
 collectCoverage: true, // Enables coverage reporting
 coverageDirectory: 'coverage', // Specifies where the reports are saved
};
```

Define Output Directory: The **coverageDirectory** setting specifies where Jest stores the generated coverage reports. By default, it is named **coverage.**

Customize File Patterns (Optional): Further customize which files Jest considers for coverage using the **testMatch** or **testPathIgnorePatterns** settings.

The **Package.json** looks like:

```
"jest": {
 "collectCoverage": true,
 "coverageDirectory": "coverage"
}
```

Keep Jest configuration consistent across environments (local and CI) so that you do not get different coverage results depending on where you run tests.

Specifying Coverage Thresholds

Coverage thresholds let you enforce a **minimum level of testing**. If coverage drops below these thresholds, Jest can fail the test run, which is especially useful in CI pipelines.

Global Thresholds: Define thresholds for your entire project to maintain a consistent standard for all files, as shown here:

```
// jest.config.js
module.exports = {
  collectCoverage: true,
  coverageThreshold: {
    global: {
      branches: 80,
      functions: 90,
      lines: 85,
      statements: 85,
    },
  },
};
```

Jest's coverage thresholds are a powerful way to enforce a baseline level of testing across the codebase. Each key in the **`global`** configuration represents a specific aspect of the code's coverage. Let us break them down as follows:

Branches (80%)

- **What It Represents:** Branch coverage measures how many of the possible branches (for example, **`if/else`** or **`switch`** case conditions) in your code have been executed by your test suite.
- **Why It Matters:** Testing all branches ensures that every possible decision path in your code is validated, which reduces the likelihood of missed logic errors.

  ```
  function getStatus(isActive) {
   return isActive ? 'Active' : 'Inactive';
  }
  ```

- **Without branch coverage**: Testing only **`isActive = true`** neglects the **`false`** branch.
- **With branch coverage**: Tests would include cases for both **`isActive = true`** and **`isActive = false.`**

Functions (90%)

- **What It Represents:** Function coverage measures how many of the declared functions or methods in your code are invoked during testing.
- **Why It Matters:** High function coverage ensures that every function is validated for proper behavior under test conditions.

```
function add(a, b) {
 return a + b;
}

function subtract(a, b) {
 return a - b;
}
```

If your tests only cover **add** but not **subtract**, the function coverage will not be 100%.

Lines (85%)

- **What It Represents:** Line coverage measures the percentage of lines of code executed during testing.
- **Why It Matters:** High line coverage indicates that most of your codebase is executed at least once during testing. However, this does not guarantee logic validation (for example, all branches being tested).

```
function multiply(a, b) {
 const result = a * b;
 return result;
}
```

If your tests skip the line **const result = a * b;**, the line coverage will decrease.

Statements (85%)

- **What It Represents:** Statement coverage measures the percentage of executable statements that are executed during testing.
- **Why It Matters:** Like line coverage, statement coverage indicates whether the code has been run but is more granular, including even non-linear statements.

```
function processOrder(order) {
 console.log(order);
 return order.isPaid ? 'Complete' : 'Pending';
}
```

If tests do not call **processOrder**, both the console.log and the return are counted as uncovered statements.

File-Specific Thresholds: Apply stricter thresholds to critical files or components, as in the following code:

```
// jest.config.js
module.exports = {
  collectCoverage: true,
  coverageThreshold: {
    global: {
      branches: 80,
      functions: 90,
      lines: 85,
      statements: 85,
    },
    './src/components/': {
      branches: 90,
      lines: 90,
    },
  },
};
```

Enforcing Thresholds in CI: In **CI/CD** pipelines, ensure that builds fail if thresholds are not met. This encourages developers to address test gaps proactively. Start with realistic thresholds and gradually increase them as your tests improve. Do not jump from 0% to 90% overnight.

Including/Excluding Files for Coverage

You rarely want coverage for *every* file in the repo. For example, you generally would not care about coverage for configuration files, re-export barrels, or test files themselves.

Include Files for Coverage: Use the **collectCoverageFrom** option to specify which files should be included, as shown in this code:

```
module.exports = {
  collectCoverage: true,
  collectCoverageFrom: [
    'src/**/*.{js,jsx}', // Include all JS source files
  ],
};
```

Exclude Files from Coverage: Add patterns to exclude unnecessary files, as shown here:

```
// jest.config.js
```

```
module.exports = {
  collectCoverage: true,
  collectCoverageFrom: [
    'src/**/*.{js,jsx}',
    '!src/**/*.test.{js,jsx}', // Exclude test files
    '!src/setupTests.js',      // Exclude setup files
  ],
};
```

Check Patterns Using CLI: Run Jest with the **--collectCoverageFrom** option to verify the patterns, just like we have done here:

```
npx jest --collectCoverage --collectCoverageFrom="src/**/*.js"
```

Keep your include/exclude patterns simple and easy to maintain. Regularly review and update patterns as your project evolves.

Running and Generating Coverage Reports

Coverage reports are essential for analyzing how much of your code is tested. Jest makes it easy to execute tests with coverage enabled, generate reports, and interpret the metrics to improve your testing strategy.

Executing Tests with Coverage

Running tests with coverage ensures that Jest measures how much of your application code is executed by your test suite.

How to Execute:

To run Jest with coverage enabled, use the following command:

```
npm test -- --coverage
```

This generates the statement, branch, function, and line coverage. Suppose you have a file **mathUtils.js** here:

```
export function add(a, b) {
 return a + b;
}
export function subtract(a, b) {
 return a - b;
}
```

Running the tests with **--coverage** will show which functions or lines are covered by the test suite. Always run tests with coverage in a **CI/CD** pipeline to enforce consistent coverage metrics. Use **`--watchAll`** in local development to track coverage dynamically.

```
npm test -- --coverage --watchAll
```

Viewing Coverage Reports Locally

After executing tests, Jest generates a local report summarizing your coverage metrics. You can access this report in the terminal or view detailed results in HTML format.

How to View the Reports

Terminal Summary: The terminal provides a summary with metrics such as:

- Statements
- Branches
- Functions
- Lines

```
-----------------|----------|----------|----------|----------|---------
File             | % Stmts  | % Branch | % Funcs  | % Lines  | Uncovered
Line #s
-----------------|----------|----------|----------|----------|---------
All files       |   85.71 |   66.67 |   85.71 |   85.71 |
mathUtils.js     |   85.71 |   66.67 |   85.71|   85.71 | 4
-----------------|----------|----------|----------|----------|---------
```

HTML Reports: Jest generates an HTML coverage report in the directory specified by **`coverageDirectory`** (default is **`coverage`**). Open the **`index.html`** file in your browser to view a detailed, interactive report. Use the HTML report for identifying specific uncovered lines of code. Share reports with your team to highlight testing gaps.

Interpreting Coverage Metrics

Coverage metrics provide insight into which parts of your code are tested and which are not. Understanding these metrics is key to improving your test suite.

Coverage Metrics Explained:

Coverage metrics are not just numbers; they tell you where your tests are weak.

- **Statements** – Are you executing most of the code?
- **Branches** – Are all conditional paths tested?
- **Functions** – Are all functions exercised?

- **Lines** – Are most lines executed at least once?

Example of Metrics Analysis: For a file with uncovered lines like this:

```
-----------------|----------|----------|----------|----------|---------
File             |  % Stmts | % Branch |  % Funcs |  % Lines | Uncovered
Line #s
-----------------|----------|----------|----------|----------|---------
mathUtils.js     |    85.71 |    66.67 |    85.71 |    85.71 | 4
-----------------|----------|----------|----------|----------|---------
```

Observation: Branch coverage is low (66.67%).

- **Action**: Add tests for conditions in line 4 (Uncovered Line) to improve branch coverage.

Improving Coverage Based on Metrics

- Focus on areas with the lowest coverage first.
- Add tests for edge cases in uncovered lines or branches.
- Use Jest's interactive HTML report to drill down into uncovered areas.
- Maintain a balanced focus on all metrics, and do not focus on just one.

Integrating Jest into CI/CD Pipelines

Running Jest and collecting coverage locally helps individual developers catch issues early, but it does not guarantee consistent quality across a team or over time. In real-world projects, code is merged by multiple contributors, often under tight deadlines, making manual checks unreliable. Integrating Jest into CI/CD pipelines ensures that every change is automatically tested and validated against coverage thresholds before it reaches production. This turns testing from a best practice into an enforced quality gate that protects the codebase as it scales.

Automating Test Runs in CI Environments

Automating Jest test runs in CI environments allows your team to catch errors early and maintain a consistent codebase. It ensures that tests are executed automatically for every pull request or code merge.

Steps to Automate Jest in CI

- **Choose a CI Tool:** Common CI tools include GitHub Actions, GitLab CI, Jenkins, and CircleCI.
- **Set Up a CI Configuration File:** Create a configuration file to define your CI pipeline. For example, with GitHub Actions, you can use:

```yaml
#.github/workflows/ci.yml
name: CI Pipeline
on:
  push:
    branches:
      - main
  pull_request:
jobs:
  test:
    runs-on: ubuntu-latest
    steps:
      - uses: actions/checkout@v4
      - uses: actions/setup-node@v4
        with:
          node-version: '20'  # Use latest LTS
      - run: npm install
      - run: npm test -- --coverage
```

- **Run Jest Commands:** Ensure that Jest commands (**`npm test -- --coverage`**) are included in the pipeline to execute tests and generate coverage reports.
  - Trigger test runs for every pull request to enforce quality.
  - Use parallel jobs in CI to speed up test execution for large codebases.

Configuring Jest for Different Environments

Different environments often vary in configuration, feature flags, API endpoints, and runtime settings, which can influence how tests behave. Configuring Jest per environment ensures that tests run under realistic conditions and produce consistent, reproducible results across local development, staging, and CI pipelines. This prevents environment-specific failures, reduces false positives, and allows teams to catch issues that only appear under certain configurations. Proper environment-aware setup ultimately makes test results more trustworthy and easier to debug.

Environment-Specific Configuration:

- **Using Environment Variables:** Set environment-specific variables like the following to tailor Jest behavior:

  ```
  process.env.NODE_ENV = 'test';
  ```

- **Configure Separate Jest Files:** Create multiple Jest configuration files for different environments through:

  `jest.local.config.js` for local

  `jest.staging.config.js` for staging

- **Switch Configurations Dynamically:** Use scripts to load environment-specific configurations, as shown here:

```
"scripts": {
  "test:local": "jest --config=jest.local.config.js",
  "test:staging": "jest --config=jest.staging.config.js"
}
```

- **Mock External Dependencies:** In CI environments, mock external services (for example, APIs or databases) to ensure consistent test behavior, as shown here:

```
jest.mock('../api', () => ({
  fetchData: jest.fn(() => Promise.resolve({ data: 'mocked data'
})),
 }));
```

  - Use **`NODE_ENV`** to distinguish between development, test, and production environments.
  - Keep CI configurations lightweight to minimize execution time.

Reporting and Acting on Coverage in CI/CD

Automating coverage reporting in CI/CD helps ensure that all code changes meet defined coverage thresholds. This prevents untested code from being merged.

Steps to Enable Coverage Reporting:

- **Generate Coverage Reports:** Use the **`--coverage`** flag to generate reports via:

```
npm test -- --coverage
```

- **Upload Reports to Coverage Tools:** Integrate with tools such as **`Codecov`** or Coveralls for advanced coverage reporting and visualization. This can include the following steps:
  - Install a coverage uploader through:
    - **`npm install codecov --save-dev`**
  - Add the upload step to your CI configuration through:
    - **`run: npx codecov`**

- **Fail Builds on Low Coverage:** Use Jest's **`coverageThreshold`** to enforce minimum coverage standards. The CI pipelines will fail if thresholds are not met. You can use the following code:

```
coverageThreshold: {
 global: {
```

```
        branches: 80,
        functions: 90,
        lines: 85,
        statements: 85,
      },
    },
```

Acting on Coverage Reports:

- **Fail Build for Violations:** Ensure the CI pipeline halts when coverage drops below thresholds.
- **Highlight Issues:** Use detailed reports to pinpoint untested code areas and address them in subsequent updates.
- **Track Trends:** Use tools such as SonarQube to monitor coverage trends over time.
- Enable notifications for failed builds to alert developers about coverage violations.
- Regularly review coverage thresholds to ensure they align with project goals.

End-to-End Testing with Jest

E2E testing verifies full, real-world workflows like navigation, forms, redirects, API callbacks, and user journeys. While Jest is primarily designed for **unit and integration tests**, it *can* be used as a runner for E2E tests when combined with a browser automation tool like **Puppeteer** or **Playwright**.

Principles of End-to-End Testing

E2E testing focuses on the overall user experience by simulating real-world scenarios. Unlike unit tests, which test individual components, E2E tests validate the functionality of an entire application stack.

Key Principles:

- **User-Centric Testing:**
  - Focus on how users interact with your application.
  - Test workflows such as login, form submissions, and navigation.
- **Simulate Real Environments:** Test in environments that mirror production to ensure realistic results.
- **Test Critical Paths:** Prioritize key user journeys, such as registration, payments, or search functionality.

- **Minimize Flakiness:** Avoid tests that fail due to timing issues or inconsistent external dependencies.

Workflow: For an e-commerce app, an E2E test might simulate:

- Adding an item to the cart.
- Checking out and completing the payment.
- Verifying that the order confirmation page is displayed.

Setting Up Jest for End-to-End Tests

Jest does **not** include a browser environment. To execute real browser interactions, you must attach an automation library.

Most commonly:

- **Puppeteer** (Chrome automation)
- **Playwright** (multi-browser automation)
- **jest-puppeteer** (preset wrapper for easier config)

Below is the setup using **Jest + Puppeteer**, because this is the most classic, minimal option for Jest-driven E2E tests.

Steps to Set Up Jest for E2E

Install Necessary Packages: Use Jest, a browser automation library, and the Jest-Puppeteer preset:

```
npm install --save-dev jest puppeteer jest-puppeteer
```

Configure Jest for E2E: Create a `jest.e2e.config.js` file like this one:

```
module.exports = {
  preset: 'jest-puppeteer',
  testMatch: ['**/*.e2e.test.js'],
  verbose: true
};
```

- **preset**: '**`jest-puppeteer`**' → sets up browser before/after tests
- **`testMatch`** → only E2E test files

Set Up Puppeteer for Browser Automation: Install and configure Puppeteer in `jest-puppeteer.config.js`, as shown here:

```
module.exports = {
  launch: {
    headless: true,
```

```
    slowMo: 0
  },
  browserContext: 'default'
};
```

This ensures that:

- A headless Chrome browser starts before tests.
- The same browser context is maintained across test steps.

Add this to package.json, as shown here:

```
"scripts": {
  "test:e2e": "jest --config=jest.e2e.config.js"
}
```

Writing and Running End-to-End Tests with Jest

E2E tests validate entire workflows, while ensuring your application behaves as expected across all components.

Suppose you want to test the login flow of an application, which looks like this:

```
// login.e2e.test.js
describe('Login Flow', () => {
  let page;

  beforeAll(async () => {
    page = await browser.newPage();
  });

  afterAll(async () => {
    await page.close();
  });

  test('user can log in successfully', async () => {
    await page.goto('http://localhost:3000/login');

    await page.type('#username', 'testuser');
    await page.type('#password', 'password123');
    await page.click('#login-button');

    await page.waitForSelector('#dashboard');

    const title = await page.$eval('#dashboard-title', el =>
el.textContent);
    expect(title).toBe('Welcome, Test User!');
```

```
  });
});
```

The preceding code covers:

- Navigation
- Typing
- Clicking
- Waiting for DOM Changes
- Extracting UI Text
- Validating User Journey

Execute the test with the following command:

```
npm run test:e2e
```

Analyzing End-to-End Test Coverage

End-to-end (E2E) test coverage focuses on code paths exercised through real user interactions in a browser, making it fundamentally different from Node-based unit or integration coverage. Because E2E tests run against compiled client-side bundles, they require instrumented code to accurately track execution. This type of coverage is especially valuable for validating critical user journeys such as onboarding, checkout, authentication, and navigation flows. While it does not replace unit coverage, browser-level coverage helps teams identify gaps where real users interact with the app but tests never reach certain logic. Used together, E2E and unit coverage provide a more complete picture of application quality and risk.

Here are some important corrections you should consider:

- Jest cannot automatically gather real browser coverage.
- Puppeteer alone does not generate Jest coverage.
- Coverage for E2E requires bundling the app with Istanbul instrumentation.

To enable E2E coverage with Puppeteer: Add Istanbul instrumentation to your build step.

Use webpack, Vite, or Babel with the Istanbul plugin, as shown here:

```
npm install --save-dev babel-plugin-istanbul
```

Add to Babel config the following:

```
plugins: ['istanbul']
```

Now, your app will deliver the instrumented code to the browser.

Update your E2E Jest config as shown here:

```
module.exports = {
  preset: 'jest-puppeteer',
  collectCoverage: true,
  coverageDirectory: 'coverage/e2e',
  collectCoverageFrom: ['src/**/*.{js,jsx}', '!src/**/*.test.{js,jsx}']
};
```

Run with coverage as follows:

```
npm run test:e2e -- --coverage
```

This shows the browser-executed lines that were touched during E2E interactions.

The report appears under the link:

```
coverage/e2e/index.html
```

Note: *The E2E coverage collected this way is approximate and depends on how your bundler instruments the code. Treat it as a supporting signal, not a single source of truth. Modern tools like Playwright provide more accurate browser coverage reporting out of the box.*

Conclusion

While Jest can technically run end-to-end tests when paired with Puppeteer, it is not designed for large-scale or production-grade E2E automation. Jest lacks auto-waiting, trace viewer, screenshots, videos, and stable browser control. Therefore, using Jest for unit and integration tests is a better choice. For E2E, the recommended modern tools are Playwright or Cypress due to their reliability, debugging features, and production-ready browser automation. The next chapter is on practical exercises.

CHAPTER 10
Practical Exercises and Challenges

Introduction

This chapter is designed to transform theory into practice. By tackling quizzes, hands-on coding tasks, and real-world scenarios, you will reinforce what you have learned throughout the book. These exercises simulate actual development environments where testing is essential for maintaining application reliability and scalability. To help you assess and improve your solutions, we have provided complete, well-documented answers on GitHub.

Structure

This chapter covers the following topics:

- Quizzes and Knowledge Reinforcement
- Scenario-Based Exercises

Quizzes and Knowledge Reinforcement

This section helps reinforce key concepts from the chapter by testing your understanding and encouraging active recall, ensuring the ideas translate into long-term knowledge rather than passive reading.

Core RTL Concepts

1. What does **`getByText()`** do in RTL?
    a. Queries an element by its text content
    b. Finds an element by ID
    c. Simulates a click
    d. Gets data from API

    Answer: a

    Explanation: **`getByText`** locates DOM elements based on visible text and throws an error if the element is not found.

2. **True/False**: The **`render()`** method in RTL mounts a React component for testing.

    Answer: True

    Explanation: **`render()`** creates a virtual DOM using **`jsdom`**, which allows the component to be tested in isolation.

3. Which tool is best for testing React components?
    a. Axios
    b. React Testing Library
    c. Redux
    d. ESLint

    Answer: b

    Explanation: RTL is specifically built to test React components through user interactions and behavior.

4. Which matcher checks element existence?
    a. `toExist()`
    b. `toBePresent()`
    c. `toBeInTheDocument()`
    d. `toHaveLength()`

    Answer: c

    Explanation: The **`toBeInTheDocument()`** matcher (from **`@testing-library/jest-dom`**) checks whether an element exists in the DOM.

5. What is the first step in writing a test?
   a. Call an API.
   b. Render the component.
   c. Write styles.
   d. Setup the database.

   Answer: b

   Explanation: You must render the component before performing queries or assertions.

6. Which function simulates user interactions in RTL?
   a. `simulateClick()`
   b. `fireEvent`
   c. `trigger()`
   d. `reactClick()`

   Answer: b

   Explanation: **`fireEvent`** triggers DOM events (like click, change, and so on) to simulate user actions.

7. **True/False**: You should test 3rd-party libraries to ensure their functionality.

   Answer: False

   Explanation: External libraries are already tested; you should only verify how your code integrates with them.

8. Which assertion checks button text?
   a. `expect(button).toContain("text")`
   b. `expect(button).toHaveTextContent("Submit")`
   c. `expect(button).text = "Submit"`
   d. `expectText(button) === "Submit"`

   Answer: b

   Explanation: **`toHaveTextContent()`** verifies whether the rendered text inside the button matches the expected string.

9. What should every test do?
   a. Render JSX.
   b. Console log the result.
   c. Assert the expected outcome.
   d. Mock API calls.

Answer: c

Explanation: A test is incomplete without an assertion; it must verify the outcome of code execution.

10. **True/False**: Tests should break with every minor UI change.

    Answer: False

    Explanation: Tests should focus on **behavior and intent**, not fragile UI structure.

11. What is the primary purpose of unit testing?

    a. To test the entire application

    b. To test individual units/components in isolation

    c. To replace integration tests

    d. To check UI alignment

    Answer: b

    Explanation: Unit tests validate small, independent pieces of functionality.

12. Which of the following can Jest mock?

    a. Modules

    b. Functions

    c. Timers

    d. All of the above

Answer: d

Explanation: Jest can mock functions, timers, and even modules to isolate code behavior.

13. **True/False**: getByText throws an error if the element is not found.

    Answer: True

    Explanation: getByText throws immediately when no matching element exists; use `queryByText` for optional elements.

14. What is the default testing environment used by Jest?

    a. Node

    b. jsdom

    c. Browser

    d. Puppeteer

    Answer: b

Explanation: Jest uses jsdom as the default environment, which provides a browser-like DOM for tests. For pure backend or Node-only code, you can explicitly set **`testEnvironment`** to **`'node'`**.

Inputs, Forms, and Events

1. Which event simulates typing in an input?
   a. `typeEvent()`
   b. `fireEvent.change()`
   c. `setValue()`
   d. `click()`

   Answer: b

   Explanation: **`fireEvent.change()`** simulates a user updating an input field value.

2. What does `userEvent.type(input, "Hello")` do?
   a. Clears the input
   b. Triggers a change
   c. Types text character by character
   d. Submits the form

   Answer: c

   Explanation: **`userEvent.type`** mimics real typing behavior by dispatching multiple keyboard events sequentially.

3. **True/False**: **`fireEvent.click()`** simulates a real browser click.

   Answer: False

   Explanation: **`fireEvent`** only dispatches the event; **`userEvent.click`** more accurately simulates an actual browser click.

4. What query finds a button with the text "Save"?
   a. `getByRole("button", { name: "Save" })`
   b. `getButton("Save")`
   c. `findButton("Save")`
   d. `getByText("button", "Save")`

   Answer: a

   Explanation: Role-based queries like **`getByRole`** ensure accessibility alignment.

5. How do you clear an input in a test?
   a. `input.clear()`
   b. `fireEvent.change(input, { target: { value: "" } })`
   c. `input.value = ""`
   d. `clear(input)`

   Answer: b

   Explanation: Changing the value through **`fireEvent.change`** simulates the real DOM behavior.

6. Which is a good practice while testing forms?
   a. Use actual API.
   b. Bypass validation.
   c. Simulate user input and submit
   d. Skip field testing

   Answer: c

   Explanation: Tests should simulate **real user actions** such as typing and form submission.

7. **True/False**: Inputs need to be queried by placeholders when labels are missing.

   Answer: False

   Explanation: Prefer queries by **label** or **role** for accessibility; placeholders are a fallback, not a rule.

8. What does `screen.getByRole()` do?
   a. Finds elements by class
   b. Gets all headings
   c. Queries elements by their semantic role
   d. Checks element height

   Answer: c

   Explanation: getByRole searches for elements using ARIA roles (like "**`button`**", "**`textbox`**", "**`heading`**").

9. Why use **`act()`** in tests?
   a. To mount components
   b. To mock timers

c. To handle async updates
d. To create routes

Answer: c

Explanation: **`act()`** ensures all effects and state updates have been applied before making assertions.

10. Best method to test checkboxes?

a. `fireEvent.toggle()`
b. `userEvent.click(checkbox)`
c. `checkbox.toggle()`
d. `checkbox.checked = true`

Answer: b

Explanation: userEvent.click is the most realistic way to toggle a checkbox as a user would.

Structure, Queries, and Assertions

1. Which query throws an error if nothing is found?

a. `queryByText()`
b. `findByText()`
c. `getByText()`
d. `optionalByText()`

Answer: c

Explanation: **`getBy*`** queries throw immediately when no element matches.

2. **True/False**: **`queryByText()`** returns null if nothing is found.

Answer: True

Explanation: Unlike **`getByText`**, **`queryByText`** safely returns **`null`** for missing elements.

3. Which query waits for the element to appear?

a. `getByText()`
b. `findByText()`
c. `querySelector()`
d. `getElement()`

Answer: b

Explanation: **`findBy*`** queries are asynchronous and wait for DOM updates.

4. How do you test conditionally rendered elements?
   a. Always render it.
   b. Use **`queryBy...`** and assert **`null`**.
   c. Hide them with CSS.
   d. Skip testing.

   Answer: b

   Explanation: Use **`queryBy`*** for elements that might or might not render and assert accordingly.

5. **True/False**: Test names should be descriptive and specific.

   Answer: True

   Explanation: Clear names communicate the purpose and expected behavior of each test.

6. Which matcher checks for a class name?
   a. `toHaveClass("btn")`
   b. `hasClass("btn")`
   c. `expectClass("btn")`
   d. `toHaveAttribute("btn")`

   Answer: a

   Explanation: **`toHaveClass`** checks for one or more class names applied to an element.

7. Which query checks if an element is disabled?
   a. `expect(el).toBeDisabled()`
   b. `expect(el).disabled = true`
   c. `el.disabled === true`
   d. `el.toBeInactive()`

   Answer: a

   Explanation: **`toBeDisabled()`** verifies whether the element cannot be interacted with.

8. What does **`toBeVisible()`** assert?
   a. Element has display: block.
   b. Element is in DOM and visible.
   c. Element has no opacity.
   d. Element has a role.

Answer: b

Explanation: The command checks visibility based on style, attributes, and layout.

9. **True/False**: You can use **`jest.fn()`** to mock a handler.

   Answer: True

   Explanation: **`jest.fn()`** creates a spy function to track calls and arguments.

10. Which matcher checks for an attribute?
    a. `toHaveAttribute("src", "logo.png")`
    b. `expectAttr("src", "logo.png")`
    c. `hasAttr("src")`
    d. `toContainAttribute()`

    Answer: a

    Explanation: **`toHaveAttribute`** asserts that an element has the specified attribute and value.

Testing Workflow and Good Practices

1. Best place to put test files?
   a. Inside `src/__tests__`
   b. In `public/`
   c. Root folder
   d. With CSS files

   Answer: a

   Explanation: A **`__tests__`** folder inside src keeps test files organized and keeps them out of production bundles as long as they aren't imported.

2. Which filename extension is correct for Jest tests?
   a. `.spec.html`
   b. `.test.js`
   c. `.unit.react`
   d. `.jsx.test`

   Answer: b

   Explanation: Jest recognizes **`.test.js`** and **`.spec.js`** as standard test file extensions.

3. **True/False:** Tests should be small and focused.

   Answer: True

   Explanation: Smaller tests are easier to debug, maintain, and clearly convey intent.

4. How do you run only one test?

   a. `.only (test.only(...))`

   b. Comment others.

   c. Rename test.

   d. Add a console.log.

   Answer: a

   Explanation: Using **`.only`** runs that specific test or suite in isolation.

5. How can you skip a test temporarily?

   a. Remove it.

   b. Use `test.skip(...)`.

   c. Add `//`.

   d. Disable Jest.

   Answer: b

   Explanation: **`test.skip`** prevents the test from executing while keeping it in the codebase.

6. **True/False:** Tests should be deterministic (same result every time).

   Answer: True

   Explanation: Deterministic tests ensure consistent and reliable results across runs.

7. Why mock API calls in unit tests?

   a. Faster, isolated testing

   b. To test backend

   c. To avoid timeouts

   d. So it runs offline

   Answer: a

   Explanation: Mocking APIs makes tests faster and isolates frontend logic from backend dependencies.

8. What is a test suite?
    a. A single test
    b. A group of related tests
    c. An ESLint rule
    d. A Jest plugin

    Answer: b

    Explanation: Test suites (usually via `describe()`) group related tests logically.

9. Which lifecycle hook runs before each test?
    a. `beforeAll()`
    b. `beforeEach()`
    c. `useEffect()`
    d. `setup()`

    Answer: b

    Explanation: `beforeEach()` runs setup code before every individual test in a suite.

10. **True/False:** Tests should cover both positive and negative scenarios.

    Answer: True

    Explanation: Comprehensive coverage ensures both success and failure paths are validated.

Component Behavior and User Interactions

1. Which query is best when testing elements that may not always be in the DOM?
    a. `getByText()`
    b. `queryByText()`
    c. `findByText()`
    d. `getElementById()`

    Answer: b

    Explanation: `queryBy*` safely returns null if the element doesn't exist, avoiding errors.

2. **True/False**: `findBy*` queries are asynchronous and return a promise.

    Answer: True

    Explanation: `findBy*` waits for elements to appear before resolving.

3. What is the purpose of `waitFor()` in the React Testing Library?
   a. Delay test execution.
   b. Wait for `async` DOM changes.
   c. Debounce a function.
   d. Replace `setTimeout`.

   Answer: b

   Explanation: `waitFor()` retries assertions until the DOM stabilizes, ideal for `async` updates.

4. Which of the following is NOT a good reason to mock API calls?
   a. Make tests faster.
   b. Reduce flakiness.
   c. Test backend endpoints.
   d. Enable isolation.

   Answer: c

   Explanation: Backend endpoints should be tested separately in integration or API tests.

5. **True/False**: `fireEvent.input()` is preferred over `userEvent.type()` for simulating realistic input.

   Answer: False

   Explanation: `userEvent.type` simulates actual typing behavior, including key events.

6. How do you test the conditional rendering of a component based on props?
   a. Use a snapshot.
   b. Render with different props.
   c. Use global mocks.
   d. Avoid testing it.

   Answer: b

   Explanation: Render the component with various props and assert the correct elements appear or disappear.

7. Which matcher verifies `style/class` changes?
   a. `toBeStyled()`
   b. `toHaveStyle()`

   c. `expectStyle()`
   d. `styleEquals()`

   Answer: b

   Explanation: **`toHaveStyle`** checks inline style changes or dynamic updates.

8. **How can you simulate typing multiple characters in a form field?**
   a. `fireEvent.type()`
   b. `userEvent.type()`
   c. `simulateTyping()`
   d. `writeText()`

   Answer: b

   Explanation: **`userEvent.type`** sends key events one by one, mimicking real typing.

9. **True/False**: Tests should verify side effects (for example, API call after button click).

   Answer: True

   Explanation: Verifying side effects ensures the component behaves correctly after user interaction.

10. What does **`screen.debug()`** do?
    a. Runs Jest in debug mode.
    b. Logs the virtual DOM to the console.
    c. Breaks the test.
    d. Displays component props.

    Answer: b

    Explanation: **`screen.debug()`** prints the current DOM tree, useful for troubleshooting queries.

Hooks, State, and Props

1. How can you test state changes?
   a. Inspect variables directly.
   b. Simulate actions and check the resulting UI.
   c. Use console logs.
   d. Mock `useState`.

Answer: b

Explanation: State should be verified through its visible UI outcome, not internal values.

2. **True/False**: You can spy on `useEffect()` using Jest.

   Answer: False

   Explanation: You should not spy on React internals—test their resulting behavior instead.

3. What is a good approach to test components using `useContext()`?

   a. Render without context.

   b. Use a mock context provider.

   c. Spy on context.

   d. Use `localStorage`.

   Answer: b

   Explanation: Mock the provider to control values and test different states.

4. How do you mock props passed from a parent component?

   a. Wrap with a mock parent.

   b. Pass props directly to render.

   c. Use global state.

   d. Set state internally.

   Answer: b

   Explanation: You can simply pass test props when rendering the component.

5. **True/False**: A component can be tested without exporting it.

   Answer: True

   Explanation: It can be tested indirectly via another exported component that renders it.

6. Which hook is commonly tested indirectly through rendered UI?

   a. `useMemo()`

   b. `useEffect()`

   c. `useRef()`

   d. `useId()`

Answer: b

Explanation: Effects produce observable outcomes like DOM updates or API calls.

7. Which method mocks **`useNavigate()`** from **`react-router-dom`**?
   a. `jest.fn()`
   b. `jest.mock('react-router-dom')`
   c. `mockNavigate()`
   d. `spyNavigate()`

   Answer: b

   Explanation: You can mock react-router-dom to stub navigation functions.

8. What is the preferred way to test custom hooks?
   a. Use in a test component.
   b. Directly call them.
   c. Use setTimeout.
   d. Only snapshot.

   Answer: a

   Explanation: Create a test component that uses the hook, then test behavior through that component.

9. How do you assert on props received by a child component mock?
   a. Spy on render call.
   b. Read internal variables.
   c. Use a snapshot.
   d. Guess from output.

   Answer: a

   Explanation: You can inspect **`mock.calls`** of a mocked child to assert the props passed.

10. Which context utility is used for the authenticated user state?
    a. `AuthContext`
    b. `useLogin()`
    c. `Redux`
    d. `StateProvider`

    Answer: a

Explanation: AuthContext is a common pattern to share authentication state globally.

API, Mocks, and Async Testing

1. What library can mock API at the network layer?

    a. React Query

    b. Axios

    c. MSW (Mock Service Worker)

    d. Redux Toolkit

    Answer: c

    Explanation: MSW intercepts network requests, simulating real server responses.

2. **True/False:** You can use `jest.fn()` to track function calls and arguments.

    Answer: True

    Explanation: `jest.fn()` records each call and argument for assertion.

3. What is the role of `jest.clearAllMocks()`?

    a. Delete test data.

    b. Reset mocks between tests.

    c. Cancel network requests.

    d. Flush async calls.

    Answer: b

    Explanation: It clears the call history for all mocks between tests.

4. How do you mock fetch in Jest?

    a. `global.fetch = jest.fn()`

    b. `window.mockFetch()`

    c. `mock('fetch')`

    d. `fetch.override()`

    Answer: a

    Explanation: You can override the global fetch with a mock function.

5. Which matcher checks how many times a function was called?

    a. `toHaveBeenCalled()`

    b. `toHaveBeenCalledTimes(n)`

   c. `callCount()`
   d. `calledTimes()`

   Answer: b

   Explanation: Asserts the number of times the mock function was invoked.

6. **True/False:** API error handling should be tested like success states.

   Answer: True

   Explanation: Error handling ensures the UI behaves correctly during failures.

7. What function pauses tests for **`async`** logic?
   a. `setTimeout()`
   b. `waitFor()`
   c. `pause()`
   d. `asyncSleep()`

   Answer: b

   Explanation: waitFor waits until conditions in async tests are satisfied.

8. Why use fake timers in tests?
   a. Test time-based logic.
   b. Animate UI.
   c. Debug logs.
   d. Slow down execution.

   Answer: a

   Explanation: Fake timers allow control over **`setTimeout`** and **`setInterval`** for deterministic testing.

9. What is the output of **`mockFn.mock.calls`**?
   a. Execution time
   b. Array of call arguments
   c. Return values
   d. Component instances

   Answer: b

   Explanation: Each entry in `mock.calls` is an array of arguments passed per call.

10. How do you simulate a delayed response in a mock?

    a. Use await new `Promise()` inside mock.

    b. Use `timeout` prop.

    c. Use `setTimeout` directly.

    d. Use `fireEvent.delay()`.

    Answer: a

    Explanation: Wrapping in a promise simulates async delay in a mock implementation.

Testing Practices, Debugging, and Tools

1. **True/False**: Snapshot tests are useful but should not be overused.

   Answer: True

   Explanation: Snapshots detect unintentional UI changes, but behavioral tests are more reliable.

2. Which of the following is a flaky test?

   a. Always passes

   b. Depends on async timing

   c. Uses `jest.fn()`

   d. Checks props

   Answer: b

   Explanation: Tests relying on unpredictable timing often fail randomly.

3. **How do you find accessibility issues in tests?**

   a. Manual inspection

   b. Use axe-core integration

   c. Snapshot comparison

   d. Inspect with devtools

   Answer: b

   Explanation: jest-axe or axe-core automatically identifies a11y violations.

4. What tool helps test how screen readers interpret your UI?

   a. Cypress

   b. Axe

c. Jest

d. Mocha

Answer: b

Explanation: The Axe toolkit audits accessibility based on WCAG standards.

5. What is the benefit of using **`data-testid`**?
   a. Improves styling
   b. Assists with testing-specific selection
   c. Optimizes bundle size
   d. Improves accessibility

   Answer: b

   Explanation: It provides stable selectors for testing without affecting production behavior.

6. What is code coverage in testing?
   a. App size
   b. Lines of code tested
   c. Lines of code per file
   d. Time to run the test

   Answer: b

   Explanation: These are coverage measures where parts of the code are executed by tests.

7. Which command runs only changed tests in Jest?
   a. `jest`
   b. `jest --watch`
   c. `npm run test`
   d. `jest --only`

   Answer: b

   Explanation: Watch mode reruns only tests related to changed files.

8. **True/False:** Component snapshots should be updated manually every release.

   Answer: False

   Explanation: Update snapshots only when intended UI changes occur.

9. How do you ensure test files are excluded from production builds?
    a. Put in tests.
    b. Use **`.test.js`** or **`.spec.js`** extension.
    c. Add **`.hidden`**.
    d. Use a different repo.

    Answer: b

    Explanation: Building tools ignores test file extensions automatically.

10. Which Jest CLI option shows test coverage?
    a. `--report`
    b. `--coverage`
    c. `--stats`
    d. `--summary`

    Answer: b

    Explanation: `--coverage` generates code coverage reports in Jest.

Async Patterns, Time, and Error States

1. What is the best way to test a component with polling logic?
    a. Use `setInterval()`.
    b. Mock time and simulate interval ticks.
    c. Spy on data changes.
    d. Use snapshots repeatedly.

    Answer: b

    Explanation: Fake timers let you advance time and simulate repeated polls deterministically.

2. **True/False:** Jest's fake timers work seamlessly with promises out of the box.

    Answer: False

    Explanation: Promises use microtasks; fake timers only affect **`macrotasks`** like setTimeout.

3. How do you test an API retry mechanism in a component?
    a. Expect the same mock to be called again.
    b. Use `jest.retry()`.

   c. Wrap it in `waitFor()`.
   d. Count async retries.

   Answer: a

   Explanation: Verify that the same mock API function is invoked multiple times.

4. Which method ensures pending timers are flushed instantly?
   a. `advanceTimersByTime()`
   b. `runAllTimers()`
   c. `flushTimers()`
   d. `forceRunTimers()`

   Answer: b

   Explanation: Executes all queued timers without waiting.

5. **True/False:** Testing loading → success → error flows is unnecessary if success is tested.

   Answer: False

   Explanation: Each state transition must be validated to ensure robust UI behavior.

6. In what scenario should you test for fallback UI?
   a. Lazy-loaded components
   b. Static routes
   c. Non-conditional render
   d. Snapshot-only rendering

   Answer: a

   Explanation: Fallbacks appear during Suspense/lazy loading and need testing.

7. Which assertion checks element re-renders correctly?
   a. Use `rerender()` with new props.
   b. `useEffect()` spy.
   c. Re-mount component.
   d. `forceUpdate()`.

   Answer: a

   Explanation: **`rerender()`** allows verifying how the UI changes with updated props.

8. **What is the best tool for mocking API network failure scenarios?**
   a. `userEvent`
   b. `axios.cancel()`
   c. `msw`
   d. `jest.fn().fail()`

   Answer: c

   Explanation: MSW can simulate success, timeout, and error responses at the network level.

9. Which hook commonly causes tests to fail if not wrapped in **`act()`**?
   a. `useMemo()`
   b. `useEffect()`
   c. `useCallback()`
   d. `useId()`

   Answer: b

   Explanation: Effects trigger state updates that need to be wrapped in **`act()`** to flush DOM updates.

10. Which matcher ensures no unexpected elements are present?
    a. `toBeNull()`
    a. `not.toBeInTheDocument()`
    a. `toBeUndefined()`
    a. `toNotExist()`

    Answer: b

    Explanation: **`not.toBeInTheDocument()`** verifies element absence after conditional rendering.

Advanced Component Design Testing

1. How do you test error boundaries in React?
   a. Mock error and render child.
   b. Use `componentDidCatch()`.
   c. Snapshot the error message.
   d. Throw in the test directly.

   Answer: a

Explanation: The right approach is to mock an error thrown by a child component and assert that the **Error Boundary** renders its fallback UI correctly.

2. Which strategy tests render performance impact?
   a. Use React DevTools.
   b. Wrap component in Profiler and assert counts.
   c. Use `performance.now()`.
   d. Monitor DOM nodes.

   Answer: b

   Explanation: React's Profiler API can wrap components to measure render times and frequency for performance testing.

3. **True/False:** Code coverage of 100% always means your code is fully tested.

   Answer: False

   Explanation: 100% coverage only means that every line was executed and not that all edge cases or logic paths were validated.

4. What is the best way to assert a memoized component does not re-render?
   a. Use `jest.fn()` on render logic.
   b. Use `memoCount()`.
   c. Take two snapshots.
   d. Time it with console logs.

   Answer: a

   Explanation: Wrapping a child render or effect in a `jest.fn()` allows you to track render counts and confirm the memoization is effective.

5. What type of test verifies coordination between multiple components?
   a. Unit
   b. Snapshot
   c. Integration
   d. Static test

   Answer: c

   Explanation: Integration tests verify that components work together correctly, not just in isolation.

6. Which query fails immediately if no match is found?
   a. `getByText()`
   b. `queryByText()`
   c. `findByText()`
   d. `selectByText()`

   Answer: a

   Explanation: **`getBy*`** queries throw an error if an element is not found, while **`queryBy*`** returns null.

7. How do you test infinite scroll components?
   a. Use `scrollIntoView()`.
   b. Simulate scroll events with `fireEvent`.
   c. Resize window.
   d. Use mock pages.

   Answer: b

   Explanation: You can use **`fireEvent.scroll()`** on the scroll container to simulate user scrolling behavior and trigger loading logic.

8. What utility simulates scroll events in RTL?
   a. `userEvent.scroll()`
   b. `fireEvent.scroll()`
   c. `window.scroll()`
   d. `scrollWindow()`

   Answer: b

   Explanation: `fireEvent.scroll()` is used to dispatch a scroll event in the DOM for testing scroll-based functionality.

9. **True/False:** Performance profiling is typically out of scope for unit testing.

   Answer: True

   Explanation: Unit tests focus on correctness; performance is usually handled through profiling tools or integration tests.

10. Which test best simulates real user behavior?
    a. RTL + fireEvent
    b. RTL + userEvent
    c. Snapshot test
    d. Manual testing

Answer: b

Explanation: userEvent provides more realistic interactions than fireEvent, simulating real typing, clicking, and navigation behaviors.

Accessibility, Portals, and Context

1. How do you test a component rendered in a React Portal?
   a. `getByPortal()`
   b. Query the base DOM.
   c. Use shadow DOM.
   d. Mock the portal API.

   Answer: b

   Explanation: Portals render into another DOM node, but you can still query them via the global document as long as they exist within the same DOM.

2. **True/False:** You can test ARIA roles with **`getByRole()`**.

   Answer: True

   Explanation: **`getByRole()`** is the preferred query for accessible testing since it aligns with how assistive technologies read the UI.

3. What is a sign of a good accessible UI test?
   a. Uses **`getByRole()`**
   b. Only checks snapshots
   c. Ignores focus
   d. Verifies HTML structure

   Answer: a

   Explanation: Accessibility-first tests use role-based queries, ensuring elements are discoverable by screen readers.

4. Which library is commonly used to add accessibility checking to Jest unit tests?
   a. `jest-axe`
   b. `rtl-access`
   c. `ariatest`
   d. `AXE-dev`

   Answer: a

Explanation: `jest-axe` runs WCAG compliance rules against your rendered output in Jest tests to flag accessibility issues automatically.

5. How do you simulate focus trap behavior?
   a. Use tab simulation and `document.activeElement`.
   b. Click repeatedly.
   c. Use mouseover.
   d. Perform a hover-test.

   Answer: a

   Explanation: By simulating Tab key presses and checking `document.activeElement`, you can ensure the focus stays within the intended area.

6. What is the best way to test a component that renders based on user roles from context?
   a. Mock the context provider.
   b. Use state.
   c. Spy on context.
   d. Skip role-based logic.

   Answer: a

   Explanation: Mocking the context provider allows you to test how different user roles affect conditional rendering.

7. **True/False:** Portals can be tested using normal DOM queries if rendered correctly.

   Answer: True

   Explanation: React Portals are rendered into the same DOM tree, making them testable with standard RTL queries.

8. How do you assert screen reader accessibility without a screen reader?
   a. Run axe-core or jest-axe.
   b. Enable TTS.
   c. Use role guess.
   d. Manual tabbing.

   Answer: a

   Explanation: axe-core or jest-axe can analyze your rendered output for accessibility compliance programmatically.

9. Which helper name is commonly used for a custom render that wraps components with a context/provider?
   a. `renderWithContext()`
   b. `wrapRender()`
   c. `useTestProvider()`
   d. `ContextRender()`

   Answer: a

   Explanation: **`renderWithContext`** (custom helper) wraps render with a provider like Redux or Context for easy setup.

10. What is the best way to test keypress accessibility?
    a. `userEvent.keyboard()`
    b. `fireEvent.key()`
    c. `triggerKey()`
    d. `typeKey()`

    Answer: a

    Explanation: **`userEvent.keyboard()`** simulates real keyboard input including modifier keys, ensuring accessible keyboard navigation.

Patterns, Strategies, and Best Practices

1. What is the term for components that fetch their own data on mount?
   a. SSR
   b. Self-contained
   c. Lazy
   d. Static

   Answer: b

   Explanation: Self-contained components manage their own data fetching and state internally when mounted.

2. Which testing pattern avoids brittle snapshots and focuses on behavior?
   a. Snapshot-first
   b. Behavior-driven
   c. Unit-only
   d. Static-only

   Answer: b

Explanation: Behavior-driven testing (BDT) ensures that tests validate user outcomes rather than internal implementation.

3. **True/False:** Tests should focus on the implementation details of the component.

   Answer: False

   Explanation: Good tests focus on **what users see and do**, not how the logic is implemented internally.

4. Which of the following is NOT a best practice?

   a. Test only public behavior.

   b. Avoid testing internal logic directly.

   c. Write tests based on UI changes.

   d. Perform group-related tests.

   Answer: c

   Explanation: Tests tied to visual or DOM changes tend to break easily; focus on stable, user-driven behaviors.

5. How can you make your tests resilient to UI refactors?

   a. Use role-based queries.

   b. Use class selectors.

   c. Use hardcode indexes.

   d. Use snapshots.

   Answer: a

   Explanation: Role-based queries follow accessibility standards, staying stable even after refactors.

6. What does TDD stand for?

   a. Type-Driven Development

   b. Test-Driven Development

   c. Test-Design Drafting

   d. Time-Delayed Deployment

   Answer: b

   Explanation: In TDD, you write tests first, see them fail, then write code to make them pass.

7. Which of these helps test concurrent rendering (React 18+)?
    a. `act()`
    b. `startTransition()`
    c. `renderSync()`
    d. `flushSync()`

    Answer: b

    Explanation: startTransition simulates concurrent rendering behavior introduced in React 18.

8. **True/False:** You should write tests before the component is complete in TDD.

    Answer: True

    Explanation: TDD encourages writing failing tests first to guide the component's design and logic.

9. What do integration tests cover that unit tests do not?
    a. Function internals
    b. Interaction between components
    c. Styling
    d. Imports

    Answer: b

    Explanation: Integration tests ensure multiple components or modules interact correctly as a whole.

10. What is the key benefit of co-locating tests with components?
    a. Smaller file size
    b. Easier to find and maintain
    c. Shared snapshot files
    d. Faster test runs

    Answer: b

    Explanation: Co-locating tests keeps related code together, simplifying maintenance and improving discoverability.

Scenario-Based Exercises

Exercise 1: Button Click Counter

Scenario: You are building a simple component with a + button that increases the number on each click.

Objectives:

- Render a count starting from 0.
- Clicking the button increases the count.
- Show "`No clicks yet`" when the count is 0.

Test Ideas:

- Verify initial render (should show 0 or "`No clicks yet`").
- Simulate a click and verify increment.
- Test multiple clicks.
- Ensure text changes once count > 0.

Exercise 2: Newsletter Signup Form

Scenario: A basic form with an email input and a "`Subscribe`" button.

Objectives:

- Input field for email.
- The submit button should be disabled until the input is valid.
- Show "`Thank you!`" on successful submission.

Test Ideas:

- Verify button disabled by default.
- Simulate typing a valid email to enable it.
- Submit the form and assert a success message.

Exercise 3: Toggle Dark Mode

Scenario: A toggle button that switches between light and dark mode.

Objectives:

- Default to light mode.
- Toggle applies a class to the body.
- UI updates the label/text accordingly.

Test Ideas:

- Initial mode is light.
- Toggle applies the correct class.
- Toggle text reflects state.

Exercise 4: Show/Hide Password Field

Scenario: A password input with a checkbox to show/hide the password.

Objectives:

- Input type changes between password and text.
- Default is hidden.

Test Ideas:

- Assert input type is a password by default.
- Simulate checking box; type changes to text.
- Unchecking goes back to the password.

Exercise 5: Loading Spinner

Scenario: A spinner shows while loading, then shows content.

Objectives:

- Show spinner immediately on mount.
- Hide the spinner and render content after a delay.

Test Ideas:

- Assert spinner is in the document on load.
- Use `waitFor` to assert content is shown.
- Assert spinner is removed after loading.

Exercise 6: Simple Dropdown Menu

Scenario: A select dropdown with three options.

Objectives:

- Select an option and display the selected value.
- The default is "`Please select`".

Test Ideas:

- Render with placeholder.
- Simulate selection and verify the change.

- Test resetting to default.

Exercise 7: Basic Tabs Component

Scenario: A UI with three tabs: Home, About, and Contact.

Objectives:

- Default to "`Home`".
- Click on the tab to change the content.

Test Ideas:

- Render with the Home tab active.
- Click "`About`" and verify the content.
- Click "`Contact`" and verify the content.

Exercise 8: Notification Badge

Scenario: A bell icon shows a notification badge when there are unread messages.

Objectives:

- Badge shows a number of notifications.
- Clicking the bell marks them as read and hides the badge.

Test Ideas:

- Render with badge (mock unread count).
- Simulate click and assert badge disappears.
- Optional: mock API call.

Exercise 9: Read More/Read Less Toggle

Scenario: Long content is truncated. "`Read more`" expands it.

Objectives:

- Initially show truncated content.
- Clicking "`Read more`" expands it.
- Toggle text switches to "`Read less`".

Test Ideas:

- Assert content is truncated on render.
- Click "`Read more`" to expand the full content.
- Click "`Read less`" re-truncates.

Exercise 10: Static Contact Card

Scenario: A reusable `<ContactCard />` that displays name, email, and phone.

Objectives:

- Render props correctly.
- Format phone number.

Test Ideas:

- Render with mock props and assert each value.
- Validate phone formatting logic.
- Snapshot test to prevent accidental UI changes.

Exercise 11: Form Validation with Error Handling

Scenario: You have a form with inputs for email and password. The submit button should be disabled unless all validations pass.

Objectives:

- Display inline validation errors.
- Disable submit until the form is valid.
- Call the `onSubmit` handler with the correct values.

Test Cases:

- Submit with empty fields → show validation errors.
- Fill valid inputs → enable submit.
- Mock `onSubmit` → assert correct data sent.

Exercise 12: Toast Notification Component

Scenario: A toast component displays success or error messages and disappears after 3 seconds.

Objectives:

- Render toast with message and type.
- Auto-dismiss after timeout.
- Dismiss on click.

Test Cases:

- Assert toast appears on the trigger.
- Use fake timers to verify auto-dismiss.
- Simulate manual close.

Exercise 13: Accordion Component

Scenario: You have built an accordion with multiple panels that expand/collapse on click.

Objectives:

- Only one panel should open at a time.
- Clicking an open panel closes it.

Test Cases:

- Click to expand one panel.
- Open one, then open another → first should collapse.
- Click the expanded panel again → should collapse.

Exercise 14: Modal with Form and Escape Handling

Scenario: A modal has a short form with cancel and escape-key close support.

Objectives:

- Modal opens on button click.
- Modal closes on cancel or escape key.
- Submit triggers handler and closes modal.

Test Cases:

- Simulate open/close via click and ESC.
- Validate form interaction.
- Submit the form and check the side effects.

Exercise 15: Tabs Component with Dynamic Data

Scenario: A tab interface loads content dynamically per tab (for example, Products, Reviews, FAQ).

Objectives:

- Default to the first tab.
- Each tab fetches and displays unique content.
- Handle loading states per tab.

Test Cases:

- Simulate tab switching and verify correct content.
- Assert loading state.
- Use mock fetch or msw.

Exercise 16: Component Consuming useContext (Theme/Language)

Scenario: A component displays a welcome message based on language from `LanguageContext`.

Objectives:

- Render with different context values.
- Check language switch updates text.

Test Cases:

- Wrap with a custom provider.
- Assert text in English and Spanish.
- Simulate context change (if toggle exists).

Exercise 17: API Data Table with Search Filter

Scenario: A table shows fetched user data. It includes a filter input.

Objectives:

- Display loading initially.
- Show data after API returns.
- Filter results based on user input.

Test Cases:

- Test initial loading and final render.
- Type into filter input and assert filtered output.
- Test empty state when no results match.

Exercise 18: Pagination Component

Scenario: A pagination component renders Previous, Next, and current page indicators.

Objectives:

- Start on page 1.
- Clicking `next/prev` updates page.
- Disable Previous on the first page.

Test Cases:

- Assert page changes on navigation.
- Validate button disables logic.
- Optionally, assert a callback with the page number.

Exercise 19: Debounced Search Box

Scenario: The user types a search term and the results update after a 500ms debounce.

Objectives:

- Debounce API or search call.
- Avoid calling on every keystroke.

Test Cases:

- Use fake timers to simulate debounce.
- Assert number of calls to API.
- Check result update post-debounce.

Exercise 20: Role-Based Access Rendering

Scenario: A component shows certain buttons only to admin users.

Objectives:

- Render differently based on role prop.
- Admins see "`Delete`", users do not.

Test Cases:

- Render as admin → assert button present.
- Render as user → assert button absent.
- Render as guest → assert fallback text.

Exercise 21: Error Boundary Component

Scenario: You have implemented a global Error Boundary that catches errors from child components and renders a fallback UI.

Objectives:

- Throw an error in a child.
- Verify fallback UI renders.
- Check error log behavior (for example, a `console.error` or `Sentry`).

Test Ideas:

- Mock a component that throws.
- Assert fallback message is shown.
- Spy on the logging function to assert it is called.

Exercise 22: Optimized List with Virtualization (for example, `react-window`)

Scenario: The app uses a virtualized list to render thousands of items without performance issues.

Objectives:

- Ensure only visible rows render.
- Scroll triggers new item renders.
- Item interaction (for example, click) works.

Test Ideas:

- Query visible item range.
- Simulate scroll and check new items.

Assert item click triggers correct handler.

Exercise 23: Lazy Loaded Component with Suspense

Scenario: A feature uses `React.lazy()` to defer loading, wrapped in a Suspense fallback.

Objectives:

- Render fallback UI while loading.
- Lazy component shows after load.

Test Ideas:

- Assert fallback renders initially.
- Use `waitFor()` to verify a lazy component appears.
- Mock delayed import.

Exercise 24: Concurrent UI State Updates (React 18)

Scenario: Your component updates state using `startTransition()` for a non-blocking UX.

Objectives:

- Primary state updates immediately.
- Transition state updates after a delay.

Test Ideas:

- Simulate click to trigger `startTransition`.
- Assert synchronous update appears first.
- Await and assert transition update next.

Exercise 25: External API Integration with Retry and Timeout

Scenario: A component calls an external API and implements a 3-attempt retry strategy with 1s delay each.

Objectives:

- Call retries up to 3 times on failure.
- Show fallback after 3 failures.
- Display data if one retry succeeds.

Test Ideas:

- Use `jest.useFakeTimers()`.
- Assert retry count.
- Test both recovery and failure paths.

Exercise 26: Feature Flag-Based UI Toggle

Scenario: Certain features are conditionally rendered based on environment or remote flags.

Objectives:

- Test feature on/off states.
- Ensure fallback is shown if the flag is false.

Test Ideas:

- Render with flag=true → show feature component.
- Render with flag=false → show default.
- Optionally, test behavior switches dynamically.

Exercise 27: Custom Hook with Global Side Effect

Scenario: A hook `useDocumentTitle(title)` sets the page title.

Objectives:

- Call hook with different titles.
- Ensure `document.title` changes.

Test Ideas:

- Render test component with a hook.
- Assert title updates.
- Change prop and rerender → verify new title.

Exercise 28: Multistep Wizard with Context and Validation

Scenario: A multi-page wizard uses context to track data and only allows advancing if the current step is valid.

Objectives:

- Manage state via context.
- Render conditional fields based on earlier inputs.

Test Ideas:

- Fill out step 1 and go to step 2.
- Check context values persist.
- Test edge case validations (for example, date logic).

Exercise 29: Component Rendering Inside a Portal with Accessibility Traps

Scenario: A modal renders inside a portal and handles ARIA roles and focus traps correctly.

Objectives:

- Focus is trapped in a modal.
- ESC closes modal.
- ARIA roles are correct.

Test Ideas:

- Simulate the tab key and assert focus remains in the modal.
- Press ESC → modal closes.
- Assert ARIA roles/labels.

Exercise 30: Dashboard with Dynamic Widgets (Drag-and-Drop)

Scenario: A dashboard lets users rearrange widgets via drag-and-drop (using `react-beautiful-dnd` or similar).

Objectives:

- Verify drag and drop behavior.
- Ensure widget order updates in the state.

Test Ideas:

- Mock drag-and-drop interaction.
- Assert updated DOM order.
- Confirm new order persisted (mock save call).

Conclusion

This chapter was not just about checking boxes, it was about **putting everything you have learned into practice**. Through a structured progression of quizzes, real-life scenarios, and hands-on challenges, you have deepened your understanding of testing in React with Jest and the React Testing Library.

You have tackled knowledge-based quizzes to reinforce key testing concepts, beginner to advanced challenges that mirror real-world development tasks, contextual testing strategies for forms, UI logic, async behavior, and more, and best practices for mocking, accessibility, and state-driven testing.

Remember, **writing tests is not just about coverage; it is about confidence, maintainability, and creating a better developer experience.**

The skills you have developed here will directly improve how you ship features, refactor components, and catch bugs before they reach production.

CHAPTER 11

Future-proof Testing with RTL

Introduction

Testing in React has evolved dramatically, as it has shifted from verifying component internals to mimicking real user behavior. With every new React release, testing strategies have matured. This chapter traces the evolution from the early days with Enzyme to the modern, user-centric approach of React Testing Library (RTL) and explains how RTL continues to stay aligned with React 19 and beyond.

As React introduces features like *Concurrent Rendering*, *Suspense for Data Fetching*, *Actions*, the new `use()` API, and *Server Components*, our testing mindset must evolve as well. RTL enables this shift by focusing on behavior and accessibility rather than internal component mechanics, which ensures that your tests remain stable across future React versions.

Structure

This chapter covers the following topics:

- History of Testing Libraries
- Choosing React Testing Library over Enzyme
- Adapting to React Ecosystem Changes

History of Testing Libraries

In this section, we will have a look at React's testing evolution, beginning from Enzyme's implementation-focused approach and going towards React Testing Library's user-centric, behavior-driven philosophy. React testing libraries evolved alongside React itself. Enzyme was introduced by Airbnb in the early days of React to make it easier to test component internals through shallow rendering and direct access to component instances. As React applications grew more complex and user-focused, React Testing Library—created by Kent C. Dodds—emerged to promote behavior-driven testing based on how users interact with the UI. This shift marked a move away from implementation details toward accessibility, resilience, and long-term maintainability.

Early Testing Approaches

Introduction to Initial Testing Practices

- In the early React days (React 0.14–15), testing practices were fairly primitive and often relied on tools that were not specifically designed for React.
- Developers used Jasmine, Mocha, and Chai alongside DOM manipulation libraries like jsdom.
- Tests focused primarily on:
    - Verifying internal state (`component.state`)
    - Testing prop changes manually
    - Performing shallow render checks for static outputs

Challenges Faced in Early Development

- Tight coupling to implementation details made tests fragile and hard to maintain.
- Lacked proper support for asynchronous behavior such as timeouts or network calls.
- Tools struggled to test React-specific constructs like portals, refs, or later hooks.
- Minimal focus on accessibility or user behavior simulation—most tests checked if the DOM looked "*about right*."

The result was tests that looked correct on paper but did not reflect how real users interacted with the app.

Evolution of Testing Libraries

As React's architecture evolved, new test frameworks emerged to address these issues:

- **Enzyme**: Created by Airbnb; brought in shallow, mount, and utilities to introspect the React component tree
- **Jest**: Developed by Facebook; became the de facto test runner with snapshot support and out-of-the-box performance
- **React Testing Library (RTL)**: Introduced in 2018; emphasized testing behavior over structure, while aligning with how users interact with applications

Shifting Paradigms in Software Testing

- The community started to shift from:
  - Focus moved away from inspecting internals → Toward verifying actual user-visible behavior.
  - Shallow rendering became obsolete → Full DOM rendering became the norm.
- RTL pushed the ecosystem toward testing visible output instead of internal structures. This shift emphasized:
  - Accessibility-based queries
  - Realistic event simulation using **`userEvent`**
  - Semantic queries (**`getByRole`**, **`getByLabelText`**) instead of test IDs

Key Milestones in Testing Libraries

Era	Dominant Library	Focus	Limitations Introduced
React 15–16	Enzyme	Implementation details (props, state, lifecycle)	Stopped evolving once React moved to hooks and concurrent rendering because no new official adapters were created
React 17–18	RTL	User-centric, accessibility-based	Requires async awareness
React 19	RTL (modern)	Async-focused, supports rendering triggered by Actions, and resilient under concurrent updates	Needs updated async testing patterns

Table 11.1: *Key Milestones in Testing Libraries*

Enzyme once ruled the ecosystem, but as React 18+ introduced Hooks, Suspense, and Concurrent Rendering, it fell behind.

React Testing Library continues to evolve by embracing async rendering patterns that continue to work even with React 19's Actions and `use()`, which keeps tests future-proof.

How React's Evolution Changed Testing

As React evolved, each release reshaped how components render and how tests must adapt:

- **Hooks (16.8)**: Introduced functional, effect-driven logic
- **Concurrent Mode (18)**: Enabled interruptible and batched rendering
- **Suspense for Data Fetching (19)**: Added async boundaries and delayed UI states
- **React Server Components (18+)**: Split client and server responsibilities
- **React 19**: Introduced Actions, the new `use()` API, optimistic UI, metadata tags, and ref as prop, which require async-aware, user-centric testing patterns

Testing libraries had to evolve alongside these features. React Testing Library continues to lead by:

- Auto-handling `act()` for updates, but React 19 Actions still requires async-aware patterns like `await userEvent.*` and `findBy*` queries
- RTL *does not natively understand React 19's Actions or* `use();` *instead, it relies on async-aware patterns* (`findBy`, `waitFor`, `userEvent`) that work regardless of React's underlying rendering model.
- Encouraging tests that focus on user behavior instead of internal implementation

Choosing React Testing Library over Enzyme

In this section, we compare two major libraries that have shaped how React developers test their applications: **Enzyme**, once the industry standard, and **React Testing Library (RTL)**, the modern choice aligned with React's future direction. As React evolves toward concurrency and async-driven rendering, our testing approach must evolve too.

Introduction to Enzyme and React Testing Library

Overview of Testing Libraries in the React Ecosystem

- Enzyme was created by Airbnb to make it easier to test React components by inspecting component internals (props, state, lifecycle).
- React Testing Library, created by Kent C. Dodds, focuses on testing UI the way users interact with it rather than how components are implemented.

Library	Created By	Testing Style	First Released
Enzyme	Airbnb	Implementation-focused	2015
RTL	Kent C. Dodds	Behavior-focused	2018

Table 11.2: *Enzyme and React Testing Library*

Core Features and Use Cases

Enzyme:

- Supports shallow, mount, and render modes
- Allows introspection of component internals (**`.state()`**, **`.setProps()`**, **`.instance()`**)
- Ideal for testing class-based components and life-cycle methods

React Testing Library:

- Encourages rendering components as the user sees them (via the DOM)
- Provides queries like **`getByRole`**, **`findByText`**, **`getByLabelText`**, supporting accessibility-first practices
- Ideal for testing hooks, functional components, async behavior, and real user flows

Advantages of React Testing Library

User-Centric Testing Philosophy

- RTL encourages tests that **interact with your app like a real user** through the following features:
    - Clicking buttons
    - Filling out forms
    - Waiting for elements to appear

- This ensures tests remain valid even if implementation details change, which aligns with **React's declarative nature**.

Simplified API and Improved Readability

- RTL uses query methods (such as `getByRole` and `findByText`) that align closely with how users and assistive technologies interact with the UI. Because these queries are based on semantic HTML and ARIA roles, they are intuitive to use and easy to reason about—each selector clearly expresses what element is being targeted and why. This approach produces tests that read like user behavior descriptions, resulting in cleaner, more maintainable test code that also doubles as living documentation of the interface.
- Results in **cleaner, more maintainable test code** that also serves as documentation.

Here is an RTL example:

```
await user.click(screen.getByRole('button', { name: /submit/i }))
expect(screen.getByText(/successfully logged in/i)).toBeInTheDocument()
```

Encouraging Best Practices in Testing

- Discourages reliance on **test IDs** unless necessary
- Promotes **semantic HTML** and accessibility, which in turn improves the app
- Prevents over-mocking and over-isolation by focusing on user outcomes and not on component machinery

Considerations in Choosing

Specific Use Cases for Enzyme: While Enzyme is generally not recommended for modern React, there are still cases where you might find it such as:

- **Legacy React apps** using class components and Enzyme-based tests
- Complex internal logic where state manipulation or lifecycle inspection is needed
- Projects stuck on older React versions where RTL's newer patterns might not apply

However, even these use cases are becoming rarer as more teams migrate to modern React patterns (hooks, suspense, etc.).

Criteria for Choosing the Right Testing Library

Here is a simple checklist to help teams choose the right testing library:

Criteria	Enzyme	RTL
Supports hooks	Limited	Full
Tests behavior like users	No	Yes
Compatible with Concurrent React	Not fully	Yes
Emphasizes implementation details	Yes	No
Future-proof for React 18+	Falling behind	Actively maintained
Ideal for new projects	Not recommended	Recommended

Table 11.3: *Choosing the Right Testing Library*

React Testing Library is not just a library, but a **philosophy shift** from **testing internals** to **testing behavior** and from **unit-like precision** to **user-centric clarity.**

Adapting to React Ecosystem Changes

React is a fast-evolving library as each major release introduces new patterns, paradigms, and features that challenge how developers build and test components. In this section, we will explore how the React ecosystem has changed, what that means for testing, and how React Testing Library (RTL) helps future-proof your tests.

Overview of React Ecosystem Changes

React's journey from 2013 to 2025 has continuously redefined how components render, update, and communicate. This is shown in the following features through a comparison of different React versions:

React Version	Key Features	Testing Impact
16.8	Hooks	Lifecycle tests replaced with effect-based async testing
17	Smooth upgrades	Focus on gradual adoption, event delegation
18	Concurrent Rendering, `startTransition`, Suspense for Data Fetching	Tests must account for async rendering and transitions
19	Actions API, `use()`, `useActionState`, `useFormStatus`, `useOptimistic`, ref as prop, built-in metadata, enhanced streaming SSR	Tests must handle async UI states triggered by Actions and `use()`, and rely on observable DOM output rather than internal transitions.

Table 11.4: *React Ecosystem Changes*

Impact on Testing Practices

React 19 fundamentally changes testing assumptions like:

- **Hooks and Actions Replace Lifecycles:** Tests must simulate async UI flows instead of inspecting lifecycle hooks.
- **Concurrent Mode = Non-Deterministic Rendering:** React can pause or resume updates; tests should rely on visible UI, not render count.
- **Suspense and `Use()` Introduce Natural "`Pauses`":** Do not use **`getBy*`** for UI that relies on Suspense or **`use();`** use **`findBy*`** (**`async`**) because rendering is not immediate.
- **Automatic Batching May Reorder Updates:** Always wrap interactions inside *act()* or use **`userEvent`** which already wraps it.
- **Actions API (React 19):** It enables declarative async behavior within components (like forms or transitions). Tests should assert pending, optimistic, and error states based on visible DOM.
- **`ref`**: ref as prop simplifies ref passing between components. Metadata tags update **`document.head`** automatically; test them by asserting **`document.title`** or the relevant meta tag.

The takeaway is simple: tests tied to internal mechanics will keep breaking. Tests based on what the user actually sees remain stable. This shift has a direct impact on how tests are written, maintained, and trusted in modern React applications. By focusing on visible UI output instead of internal mechanics, tests become resilient to refactors, concurrent rendering behavior, and framework-level changes introduced in React 19. This approach is especially effective in real-world applications such as form-heavy workflows, dashboards, streaming UIs, and data-driven interfaces where rendering is asynchronous and state transitions are non-linear. Ultimately, user-focused tests reduce flakiness, improve confidence during upgrades, and ensure that testing validates real behavior rather than fragile implementation details.

React 19 and New Testing Patterns

React 19 Feature	Description	How to Test
Actions API	Handles async form submissions & transitions with pending/error states	Use `userEvent.click + await findByText(/pending/i)`
use() hook	Suspends while awaiting async values	Use `waitFor` or `findBy*` to verify rendered output
useActionState / useFormStatus	Track form progress & success	Assert on UI states (loading spinner, disabled button)

React 19 Feature	Description	How to Test
useOptimistic	Displays temporary optimistic UI before server response	Verify that optimistic content appears before resolution
ref as prop	Simplifies forwarding refs to DOM nodes	Test behavior (focus, scroll) instead of implementation
Metadata tags	Allows `<title>`, `<meta>` inside components	Assert via `expect(document.title).toBe("...")`
Enhanced SSR and streaming	React streams components incrementally	Use integration tests or E2E setups with Jest+Playwright

Table 11.5: *React 19 and New Testing Patterns*

Here is an example of testing a React 19 Action with pending + success state:

```
test('handles React 19 Action with pending + success states', async () => {
  const user = userEvent.setup();
  render(<MyForm />);
  await user.click(screen.getByRole('button', { name: /submit/i }));
  expect(screen.getByText(/submitting/i)).toBeInTheDocument();
  await waitFor(() =>
    expect(screen.getByText(/submission complete/i)).toBeInTheDocument()
  );
});
```

Adapting Testing Strategies

React Testing Library already embraces these new patterns:

- *Mostly wraps UI updates in* **`act();`** *users need to await* **`userEvent`** *and* **`async`** *queries*
- **Async-aware utilities** like **`findBy`**, **`waitFor`**, and **`userEvent`**
- **A focus on user-visible behavior** while ignoring intermediate renders

Recommendations

- Use **`userEvent`** (not **`fireEvent`**) for form interactions, especially with Actions.
- Use *await* **`waitFor(...)`** when asserting async UI changes triggered by **`use()`** or Suspense.
- Assert **UI states**, not intermediate function calls.
- Avoid tests that depend on timing or internal hook values.
- For metadata or title testing, try the following code:

```
expect(document.title).toBe('Profile - MyApp')
```

- For optimistic updates, try this:
```
await user.click(screen.getByText(/save/i))
expect(screen.getByText(/saving.../i)).toBeInTheDocument()
await waitFor(() => expect(screen.getByText(/saved!/i)).
toBeInTheDocument())
```

Best Practices for Continuous Adaptation

Staying Informed on React Changes:

- Follow **React RFCs**: https://github.com/reactjs/rfcs.
- Subscribe to release blogs from React and Testing Library.
- Monitor major updates on GitHub discussions and changelogs

Updating Testing Approaches for Compatibility

- Regularly upgrade `theReact` Testing Library to benefit from updates that support React's latest APIs.
- Replace brittle `act()` wrappers and manual timeouts with RTL's `async` utilities.
- If your project still uses Enzyme or test IDs excessively, **plan for migration** toward more resilient test styles.

Rule of thumb: *If your React code changes and your tests break because of how it changed rather than what it does, you must think again about the test.*

Conclusion

React now spans client components, server components, streamed UI, and progressively revealed content, introducing new testing challenges around async behavior and concurrency. With React 19 features such as Actions, `use(),` and optimistic UI, applications increasingly rely on partial renders, delayed data, and temporary UI states that change over time. In real-world applications—such as dashboards, checkout flows, collaborative tools, and content-heavy platforms—testing must shift from inspecting internal execution to validating what users actually see at each stage of the interaction.

React Testing Library naturally supports this shift by encouraging assertions on visible output, accessibility roles, and user interactions rather than lifecycle timing or render counts. By focusing on user-perceived behavior, your test suite remains resilient across async-first, concurrent, and server-aware React architectures, ensuring long-term stability as React continues to evolve beyond React 19.

CHAPTER 12

Mastering Mock Service Worker in Jest: Patterns, Best Practices, and Pitfalls

Introduction

As modern React applications grow more dynamic and API-driven, testing them effectively requires more than just simple unit tests. We need tools that allow us to simulate real-world interactions between the frontend and backend, handle unpredictable network behavior, and confidently cover edge cases—all without sacrificing test speed or reliability.

Mock Service Worker (MSW) has become a game-changer in this space, as it offers a flexible, network-level approach to API mocking that works beautifully alongside **Jest**, which is the most widely used testing framework in the React ecosystem. This chapter is your practical guide to mastering MSW in a Jest environment. Here, you will go beyond the basics to explore **advanced mocking patterns, error simulations, authentication flows, performance optimizations, and common pitfalls to avoid**.

By the end of this chapter, you will have the tools and insights to write more resilient, realistic, and maintainable tests, which will allow you to ship them even in complex, API-heavy applications.

Structure

This chapter covers the following topics:

- Mock Service Worker

Mock Service Worker

Mock Service Worker is a JavaScript library that intercepts HTTP requests such as `fetch` or `XMLHttpRequest` and returns mocked responses without hitting a real backend. Unlike many traditional mocking tools that patch the request functions directly, MSW works at the **network layer** via:

- A service worker in the browser
- A request interceptor in Node.js (used by Jest tests)

This allows it to produce **realistic, production-like interactions** between the frontend and mocked services, thereby making it an excellent tool for testing, development, and demos.

Purpose and Key Features

MSW's core purpose is to **mock backend services in a way that's indistinguishable from real backend behavior**.

Here is why it is loved by developers:

- **Reliable Testing:** Write frontend tests without depending on backend readiness or network stability.
- **Smooth Local Development:** Build UI features even if backend APIs are incomplete or evolving.
- **Support for REST and GraphQL:** Mock traditional REST endpoints or modern GraphQL operations with equal ease.
- **Real Request Interception:** See API requests appear in browser DevTools as if they were real network calls.
- **Seamless Node.js Support:** Mock APIs in test environments to make sure that unit and integration tests are fast, reliable, and isolated.
- **Advanced Mocking Capabilities:** Simulate errors, delays, timeouts, or specific response conditions.

In short, MSW helps teams **decouple frontend and backend work**, thus empowering them to move faster and with more confidence.

Syntax Updates in Version 2

With version 2, MSW introduced the following improvements:

- **Composable Handlers:** You can now create modular handlers and combine them into flexible server setups, which will allow you to reuse handler logic across projects or test suites.
- **Improved `setupServer` and `setupWorker` APIs:** The APIs for initializing MSW in Node.js and browsers have been refined, thereby providing better control over setup, teardown, and configuration.
- **Advanced Response Composition:** You can now compose multiple response transformers (**`ctx.status()`**, **`ctx.json()`**, **`ctx.delay()`**) more intuitively, so that your mocks are easier to read and maintain.
- **Better Error Handling and Logging:** v2 improved diagnostics, warnings, and error messages, which makes it easier to spot misconfigurations or unhandled requests.

These updates make MSW a top choice for modern frontend teams handling complex API mocking needs.

Syntax Examples for Common Use Cases

Let us walk through practical examples of how MSW v2 is typically used:

Mocking a GET Request

```
import { rest } from 'msw';

export const handlers = [
 rest.get('/api/user', (req, res, ctx) => {
   return res(
     ctx.status(200),
     ctx.json({ id: 1, username: 'johndoe' })
   );
 }),
];
```

Mocking a POST Request with Conditional Logic

```
rest.post('/api/login', (req, res, ctx) => {
 const { username, password } = req.body;
 if (username === 'admin' && password === 'secret') {
   return res(ctx.json({ token: 'abc123' }));
 }
 return res(ctx.status(401), ctx.json({ message: 'Unauthorized' }));
});
```

Simulating Slow Network Responses

```
rest.get('/api/products', (req, res, ctx) => {
 return res(
   ctx.delay(1000),
   ctx.json([{ id: 1, name: 'Laptop' }, { id: 2, name: 'Phone' }])
 );
});
```

Combining Multiple Handlers

```
import { setupServer } from 'msw/node';
import { handlers } from './handlers';

const server = setupServer(...handlers);
```

Handling Requests and Responses

Defining Routes and Responses

In MSW, **routes** are defined using rest or **`graphql`** methods that are mentioned as follows:

- **`rest.get()`**, **`rest.post()`**, **`rest.put()`**, and so on, for REST APIs
- **`graphql.query()`** or **`graphql.mutation()`** for GraphQL

For each route, you provide:

- **`req`**: The incoming request object
- **`res`**: The response resolver
- **`ctx`**: A context object with helpers like **`ctx.json()`**, **`ctx.status()`**, and **`ctx.delay()`**

Example:

```
rest.get('/api/user', (req, res, ctx) => {
 return res(
   ctx.status(200),
   ctx.json({ name: 'Jane Doe' }),
   ctx.delay(500)
 );
});
```

Dynamic Response Generation with MSW

In real-world applications, backend responses often change based on request inputs such as query parameters, route variables, headers, or request bodies. MSW allows you to model this behavior directly inside your tests, making mocked

APIs behave much closer to real production services. The following examples demonstrate how MSW can generate dynamic responses based on different parts of an incoming request.

- **Query Parameters:** Useful for simulating search, filtering, pagination, and autocomplete APIs where responses depend on user input.

```
rest.get('/api/search', (req, res, ctx) => {
 const query = req.url.searchParams.get('q');
 return res(ctx.json({ results: [`You searched for: ${query}`] }));
});
```

- **Path Parameters:** Commonly used when fetching user-specific or resource-specific data, such as profiles or detail pages.

```
rest.get('/api/user/:userId', (req, res, ctx) => {
 const { userId } = req.params;
 return res(ctx.json({ userId, name: `User ${userId}` }));
});
```

- **Headers:** Essential for testing authorization, feature flags, or conditional access logic based on request metadata.

```
rest.get('/api/data', (req, res, ctx) => {
 const token = req.headers.get('Authorization');
 if (!token) {
   return res(ctx.status(401), ctx.json({ error: 'Unauthorized' }));
 }
 return res(ctx.json({ message: 'Access granted' }));
});
```

- **Request Body:** Useful for form submissions, mutations, and APIs that validate or transform posted data.

```
rest.post('/api/submit', (req, res, ctx) => {
 const { formData } = req.body;
 return res(ctx.json({ received: formData }));
});
```

These capabilities allow you to **simulate realistic behaviors** like authorization checks, user-spl-world API complexities.

Mocking Pagination APIs: Pagination is a common API pattern where the server returns data in smaller chunks (pages) instead of sending everything at once. Mocking pagination with MSW helps you verify that your UI correctly requests the right page, renders incremental results, and handles real-world states such as "**`loading next page`**," "**`no results`**," or "**`end of list`**." This is widely used in dashboards, search screens, activity feeds, admin tables, and any interface that displays large datasets efficiently.

```
rest.get('/api/items', (req, res, ctx) => {
 const page = Number(req.url.searchParams.get('page')) || 1;
 const pageSize = 10;
 const start = (page - 1) * pageSize;
 const end = start + pageSize;
 const items = allItems.slice(start, end);
 return res(ctx.json(items));
});
```

Mocking Infinite Scroll: Infinite scroll APIs typically return a subset of data along with metadata indicating whether more content is available. By simulating **hasMore** or **nextPage** values, MSW allows you to test how components react when additional data should be fetched, when loading indicators appear, and when the list correctly stops requesting new data. This ensures scrolling behavior, state accumulation, and edge conditions—such as reaching the end of a feed—are handled reliably before reaching production.

```
import { rest } from 'msw';
const allItems = Array.from({ length: 50 }, (_, i) => ({
 id: i + 1,
 name: `Item ${i + 1}`,
}));

export const handlers = [
  rest.get('/api/items', (req, res, ctx) => {
   const page = Number(req.url.searchParams.get('page')) || 1;
   const pageSize = 10;
   const start = (page - 1) * pageSize;
   const end = start + pageSize;
   const pagedItems = allItems.slice(start, end);
   const hasMore = end < allItems.length;

   return res(
     ctx.status(200),
     ctx.json({
       items: pagedItems,
       hasMore,  // ? indicates if more data is available
       nextPage: hasMore ? page + 1 : null, // ? gives next page number
if exists
     })
   );
 }),
];
```

Mocking Polling APIs (WebSocket-Like Behavior): Polling APIs simulate real-time updates by repeatedly fetching data at regular intervals, often used when WebSockets are unavailable or unnecessary. Mocking polling behavior with MSW allows you to test how components react to delayed responses, changing data, and intermittent updates such as notifications or status changes. This pattern is commonly used in alert systems, dashboards, background sync processes, and monitoring interfaces, where timely UI updates are critical for user awareness.

```
rest.get('/api/notifications', (req, res, ctx) => {
  return res(
    ctx.delay(2000),
    ctx.json({ newNotifications: Math.random() > 0.5 })
  );
});
```

Mocking Complex GraphQL Queries: GraphQL APIs often involve deeply nested queries, conditional fields, and variable-driven responses that change based on client input. Mocking complex GraphQL queries with MSW allows you to test how components handle structured data, partial responses, and evolving schemas without relying on a live GraphQL server. This is especially useful for applications with flexible data requirements such as content platforms, analytics dashboards, and enterprise systems where query shape and response complexity can vary significantly.

```
import { graphql } from 'msw';
graphql.query('GetUser', (req, res, ctx) => {
  return res(ctx.data({ user: { id: '1', name: 'Jane Doe' } }));
});
```

These patterns help test components that handle data loading, pagination, or real-time updates, while ensuring that they behave correctly across a wide range of conditions.

Simulating Error States and Edge Cases

In production, failures are not exceptions—they are normal: networks drop, servers return unexpected payloads, users retry actions, and APIs throttle requests. If your tests only validate success responses, you are effectively testing the easiest 10% of your application. Simulating error states and edge cases ensures your UI shows the right feedback, preserves data safely, and recovers gracefully without leaving users stuck. The following scenarios represent the most common failure patterns you should model in tests to make your application genuinely reliable.

Simulate 404, 500 Errors

```
rest.get('/api/user', (req, res, ctx) => res(ctx.status(404)));
```

Add Artificial Delays

```
rest.get('/api/data', (req, res, ctx) => res(ctx.delay(1500), ctx.
json({})));
```

Introduce Random Failures

```
rest.get('/api/random', (req, res, ctx) => {
 if (Math.random() < 0.3) return res(ctx.status(500));
 return res(ctx.json({ success: true }));
});
```

Combine Errors + Delays

```
rest.get('/api/slow-error', (req, res, ctx) => res(ctx.delay(2000),
ctx.status(503)));
```

These techniques ensure that your app is ready for unpredictable real-world conditions like flaky networks and failing services.

Best Practices for MSW in a Jest Environment

A solid MSW setup makes your test suite stable, fast, and maintainable. You can follow these best practices to strengthen it further:

Set Up the Server Globally: Make sure to start MSW before importing components under test, otherwise requests may bypass the mock.

```
import { setupServer } from 'msw/node';
beforeAll(() => server.listen());
afterEach(() => server.resetHandlers());
afterAll(() => server.close());
```

Reset Handlers after Each Test: It prevents test pollution, as shown in the code below:

```
afterEach(() => server.resetHandlers());
```

Override Handlers Per Test

```
server.use(
 rest.get('/api/user', (req, res, ctx) => res(ctx.status(500)))
);
server.use(
  rest.post('/api/login', (req, res, ctx) =>
    res(ctx.status(500), ctx.json({ message: 'Login failed' }))
  )
);
```

Keep Handlers Modular: Organize handlers in separate files and import them wherever needed.

Test Behavior, Not Implementation: Avoid brittle tests that check internal details; focus on visible outcomes.

Testing Authentication and Authorization Flows

Authentication and authorization determine who a user is and what they are allowed to do within an application. These mechanisms protect sensitive data, enforce permission boundaries, and ensure users see only what they are entitled to access. In real-world applications—such as dashboards, admin panels, and financial systems—testing these flows verifies that protected routes, role-based UI, and restricted actions behave correctly under different user states. Proper testing prevents security regressions while ensuring a smooth and predictable user experience.

Mock Login Endpoints: Mocking login endpoints allows you to simulate authentication scenarios without relying on a real backend or identity provider. This makes it possible to test successful logins, invalid credentials, expired sessions, and error responses in a controlled and repeatable way. It is especially useful for validating login forms, error messaging, redirects, and post-login state changes while keeping tests fast, deterministic, and independent of external services.

```
rest.post('/api/login', (req, res, ctx) => {
 const { username } = req.body;
 return res(ctx.json({ token: 'abc123', user: { username } }));
});
```

Simulate Protected Routes: Protected routes restrict access to certain pages based on a user's authentication or authorization state. Simulating these routes in tests ensures that unauthenticated users are redirected appropriately and that authorized users can access protected content without friction. This is critical for applications with role-based access, private dashboards, admin panels, or sensitive workflows where navigation and security must work together correctly.

```
rest.get('/api/profile', (req, res, ctx) => {
 const auth = req.headers.get('Authorization');
 if (auth !== 'Bearer abc123') return res(ctx.status(401));
 return res(ctx.json({ username: 'Jane' }));
});
```

Test UI Flows

- Check redirect to login on 401.
- Verify user info shows when they are authenticated.
- Ensure logout clears user data.

These patterns ensure that your app handles both **happy paths** and **restricted access flows** properly.

Performance Considerations and Optimizations

- **Mock Only What Matters:** Do not overmock—stick to APIs the component under test depends on.
- **Share Common Handlers:** Put frequently used handlers in a shared handlers.js file.
- **Avoid Test Bloat:** Skip MSW when unit testing isolated logic that does not need network calls.
- **Keep Tests Deterministic:** Use randomness only in stress tests, not in your main CI suite.
- **Leverage Parallelism:** Jest runs test files in parallel. MSW works reliably as long as each test file resets handlers in `afterEach()`.

Common Pitfalls and How to Avoid Them

- **Forgetting to Reset Handlers:** If you do not reset MSW handlers between tests, overrides from one test can leak into the next one, causing flaky failures and misleading results. This makes tests order-dependent and hard to debug.
- **Over-Mocking:** Only mock APIs you control; do not stub every detail.
- **Testing Implementation Details:** Focus on what the user sees or interacts with, rather than internal functions.
- **Skipping Error Tests:** Always test success, error, and loading states.
- **Ignoring Real-World Performance:** Use `ctx.delay()` to uncover bottlenecks or UI jank.
- **Not Cleaning Up:** Always stop the server in `afterAll()` to avoid memory leaks or port conflicts.

Conclusion

Mastering MSW in a Jest environment will transform your tests from basic to bulletproof. By combining **advanced mocking patterns, robust error handling, best practices, auth testing, performance tuning, and awareness of common pitfalls**, you will be ready to ship apps with confidence regardless of how complex the backend is. Great tests do not just validate logic; they guarantee stable user experience across real network conditions.

CHAPTER 13

Conclusion and Next Steps

Introduction

Testing modern React applications is not just a best practice, but a necessity. Throughout this book, we have walked through the lifecycle of a testing-first mindset, starting from foundational concepts to real-world testing challenges. Whether you are a beginner who just learned to test user interactions with **`userEvent`**, or an experienced developer refining end-to-end flows and CI/CD integration, you have now built a well-rounded understanding of how to approach testing effectively.

Structure

This chapter covers the following topics:

- Summarizing Key Learnings
- Applying Testing in Real-World Projects
- Final Thoughts

Summarizing Key Learnings

Let us take a moment to revisit the essential knowledge you have gained so far:

Testing Fundamentals

- **Why Test:** To gain confidence in learned abilities
- **Types of Tests:** Unit, integration, end-to-end (E2E)
- **Tools Used:** Jest, React Testing Library (RTL), MSW

Advanced Techniques

- **Mocking APIs:** Seamless control over network calls in both unit and E2E tests
- **Handling Asynchronous Code**: Proper use of `waitFor`, `findBy`, and `async` handlers
- **Testing Hooks and Custom Logic:** Extracting testable logic and using `renderHook`

Best Practices and Alternatives

- **Testing User Behavior, Not Implementation:** RTL encourages tests that reflect actual user actions.
- **Avoiding Over-Mocking:** Strike a balance between isolation and realism.
- **Using Data-Testid Wisely:** Prefer semantic queries when possible.
- **Avoiding Flaky Tests:** Stabilize setup/teardown, controlled mocks, and error boundary testing.

Applying Testing in Real-World Projects

Transitioning from a tutorial mindset to production-ready testing requires practice, experimentation, and reflection.

Here is how you can apply what you have learned:

- Integrate testing early into the development cycle; treat tests as part of your feature delivery.
- Start with critical paths: login, navigation, API flows.
- Create a checklist: loading states, error states, empty states, role-based views.
- Measure and improve code coverage, but remember, 100% coverage does not mean 100% quality.

Hands-On Practice Suggestions

You have encountered challenges and exercises throughout this book. You can continue to learn and evolve by:

Cloning the GitHub repo that includes all exemplar components and tests mentioned in this book.

Running the Tests Locally:

You can use the following code to run your tests:

```
git clone https://github.com/your-repo/react-testing-guide
cd react-testing-guide
npm install
npm test
```

Try Enhancing Through These Steps:

- Convert tests to use `userEvent` where you have used `fireEvent`.
- Add more edge cases (empty inputs, API failures, network delays).
- Build your own component and write tests from scratch.

Self-Assessment and Continued Exploration

Test yourself:

- Can you test a form with complex validation rules?
- Can you mock different network states with MSW?
- Can you run tests in CI and block merge if critical tests fail?

Explore further:

- Learn about Contract Testing (for example, with Pact).
- Study Visual Regression Testing (for example, with Percy).
- Explore Test-Driven Development (TDD) in React.

Final Thoughts

Testing is not a checkbox; it is a continuous conversation between code and confidence. You now have the toolkit to lead that conversation in your team, codebase, and career.

Remember: *untested code becomes legacy code the moment it is written.*

How to Think About Testing Different Scenarios

- Functional Testing
  - Render without crashing
  - Default UI setup
  - Props variations
- Visual and Accessibility Testing
  - Labels, ARIA roles
  - Tabbing, focus trap testing
- Interaction Testing
  - Typing, clicking, submitting forms
  - Visual response to interactions
- API Call Testing
  - Show loading indicator
  - Show success or error messages
- Local State Testing
  - Form value updates
  - Modal opening/closing
- Global State Testing
  - Dispatch actions
  - Selectors/Atoms affecting UI
- Error Boundary Testing
  - Fallback UI displayed
  - Errors logged
- Edge Case Testing
  - Empty fields
  - Very large data inputs
- Timer/Interval Testing
  - Delayed API retries
  - Auto-dismiss notifications

- External System Testing
    - Save/Load from `localStorage` or `sessionStorage`
    - Mock external libraries cleanly and predictably
- Navigation Testing
    - Simulate clicking links
    - Assert URL path or router behavior
- Accessibility and Focus Testing
    - Keyboard-only interaction
    - Proper tab order and focus
- Snapshot Testing (Use Sparingly)
    - Snapshots of UI with limited changes

Common Mistakes to Avoid

- Over-mocking everything
- Testing implementation details
- Ignoring async behavior
- Using `setTimeout` unnecessarily
- Overusing snapshot testing
- Not resetting mocks/states
- Ignoring accessibility
- Testing private state

Mastering Testing Mindset

- Focus on user-facing behaviors
- Prefer realistic interactions over artificial setups
- Mock where necessary but test reality as much as possible
- Build a test suite that gives confidence to ship
- Remember that quick feedback builds resilient tests that benefit from clear intent.

Index

P

R

S

T

U